THREE JAPANESE PLAYS
from the
Traditional Theatre

THREE
JAPANESE PLAYS

from the Traditional Theatre

Edited with Introductions by
EARLE ERNST

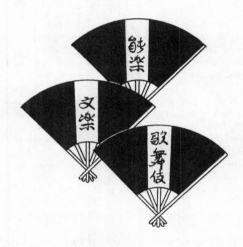

GREENWOOD PRESS, PUBLISHERS
WESTPORT, CONNECTICUT

Library of Congress Cataloging in Publication Data

Ernst, Earle, ed.
    Three Japanese plays from the traditional theatre.

    Reprint of the ed. published by Oxford University
Press, London.
    Bibliography: p.
    CONTENTS: The nō: The maple viewing.--The doll
theatre: The house of Sugawara.--The kabuki: Benten
the thief.
    1. Japanese drama--Translations into English.
    2. English drama--Translations from Japanese.
    I. Title.
[PL782.E5E7 1976]   895.6'2'008   75-31473
ISBN 0-8371-8532-7

Originally published in 1959 by Oxford University Press, London

Reprinted with the permission of Oxford University Press

Reprinted in 1976 by Greenwood Press,
a division of Williamhouse-Regency Inc.

Library of Congress Catalog Card Number 75-31473

ISBN 0-8371-8532-7

Printed in the United States of America

To my
mother and father

PREFACE

THESE plays, previously not available in English, are examples of the three traditional forms of Japanese drama: the Nō, the Doll Theatre, and the Kabuki. There are many English translations of Nō plays, but very few of these provide enough stage directions (since few appear in the Japanese scripts) to give the reader an adequate notion of the performance. Meredith Weatherby, by incorporating into his version of *The Maple Viewing* stage directions based upon performances of the play, has given a detailed account of the production. The other texts, representative of types of drama less well known to Westerners than the Nō, also describe what happens on the stage.

Trying to shape foreign plays into English so that they will be serviceable works for the theatre rather than exercises in philology is a perilous undertaking. The cultural differences between one nation and another are likely to find their purest expression in the theatre, for the theatre must always address itself to the here and now and to this particular audience. Since the performance moves inexorably in time and does not permit the luxury of footnotes, each moment must be dramatically comprehensible, or it is irretrievably, and damagingly, lost. For these reasons we prefer the Giraudoux of Christopher Fry and the Anouilh of Lillian Hellman to the painstaking work of a literal translator, for such playwrights can judge the degree of adjustment which must be made for the English-speaking audience as well as the immediate effectiveness of a line spoken in the theatre.

If such difficulties are encountered when plays are rendered from French into English, they are greatly multiplied when English versions of Japanese plays, particularly those from the purely native theatre, are attempted. The French- and the English-speaking playwrights share at least a common culture, but the Japanese play grows out of what is to most of us a remote society, its philosophy, its religion, its customs not immediately accessible to the Westerner. The Japanese play even moves in a realm of time different from that of the contemporary Western theatre, where time tends to be the living theatrical entity which Ibsen and Chekhov made of it and where the playwright is usually obliged to restrict his work to the two and a half hours' traffic of his stage. But neither of these considerations obtains in Japan, where the forward movement of the performance is little affected by temporal complexities and where the audience comes to spend a good part of the day in the theatre.

In these circumstances it may be thought presumptuous to believe that traditional Japanese plays can be brought to life in the English-speaking theatre. That the plays must suffer a disfiguring change is evident, and it can be argued, fairly convincingly, that this necessary transposition so falsifies them that they give only a dim and distorted impression of their originals. Yet when *The House of Sugawara* and *Benten the Thief* were first presented in English, American audiences were caught up by them, laughed or wept, at precisely the points at which Japanese are similarly affected. Since most audiences, everywhere in the world, go to the theatre with the sole intent of being so moved, the English versions of the plays are perhaps justified.

It should be made clear that these versions will not serve as cribs for the student of the Japanese text. Meredith Weatherby says of *The Maple Viewing*, 'Fluency, intelligibility, and ease of oral presentation have been given more weight in the present English text than sheer literalness, but without, it is hoped, any violation of the overall meaning and effect of the drama.' The texts of *The House of Sugawara* and *Benten the Thief* were arrived at by first making a precise, literal translation of the Japanese text and then refashioning this into a working script for performance in the theatre. The process involved, in general, deletion of repetitious passages and of patently untranslatable words and figures of speech; condensation of lines, many of which have literary and euphonic qualities in Japanese which add to their length and cannot be rendered sensibly in English; and occasionally very free improvisation upon the Japanese themes. (As a case in point, the final chorus of *The House of Sugawara* is only very loosely related to the Japanese text.) During rehearsals many lines were recast to give them greater effectiveness when spoken, and the performances suggested further changes. Since the resultant texts are far removed from the original literal translations, they have not been described as translations but as English versions. The intent throughout was to make the plays viable in English.

The plays were not originally intended for Japanese readers, but for Japanese audiences. Whatever purposes the present versions may be put to, their appropriate habitat is the theatre. Although it is impossible for a Western actor, amateur or professional, to re-create accurately the physical patterns of movement of the Japanese actor in these plays, some stylization of movement and gesture is necessary if the production is to convey anything of the feeling of the Japanese theatre. The prospective director who has not seen Japanese performances might proceed in one of two ways. By reading the material available in English and by studying photographs and Japanese prints, he might conceive a production which suggested, rather than attempted to imitate, the Japanese theatre. Or, more freely, he might devise a purely arbitrary stylization which had little or no relation to the actualities of the Japanese stage. The problem, in either case, is to avoid creating that effect of mere quaintness which, for instance, often characterizes productions of Chinese and pseudo-Chinese plays. If an audience is to be left with such an impression, it would seem better, in the interests of artistic integrity and international understanding, not to try to stage the plays.

At present it is somewhat difficult to produce, for most Western audiences, an effect of heightened reality within a highly stylized form of theatre. But as our stage works its way out of the cul-de-sac of realism and looks for wider avenues of expression, the techniques of the Japanese theatre (which have already influenced Reinhardt, Meyerhold, and Brecht, among others) may be helpful in suggesting how the Western theatre can get on with its somewhat neglected but requisite business of being larger than life.

EARLE ERNST

University of Hawaii
  October 1958

CONTENTS

ACKNOWLEDGEMENTS

I AM indebted to the Rockefeller Foundation and to Charles B. Fahs, Director of the Division of Humanities, for the grant of funds to the University of Hawaii which made possible the preparation of the English versions of *The House of Sugawara* and *Benten the Thief* and, subsequently, the first production of these plays in English.

The help given me by Dorothy George, Florence Maney, and Stanley Yamamoto was far greater than that which may reasonably be expected of good friends.

EDITOR'S NOTE

THE pronunciation of Japanese consonants does not differ greatly, except in the case of *f* (which sounds like a compromise between *f* and *h*) and *r* (which is subject to lallation), from that of their English equivalents. Vowels are pronounced much as they are in Italian and are never unstressed. There is no accent in Japanese words other than that slightly induced by a long vowel. All syllables end in a vowel, except those ending in *n* or followed by a doubled consonant.

In Japanese usage, which is followed in this book, the 'family' name comes first, the given name second.

Stage-right is used to mean that area to the right of the actor as he stands at the centre of the stage facing the audience; *stage-left* is the area to his left.

THE NŌ

SINCE the Nō theatre has preserved, relatively unchanged, the methods of production, the style of acting, the music, and the plays which it evolved towards the end of the fourteenth century, it ᴸ probably the only highly civilized theatre in the world today which gives a contemporary audience a fairly accurate re-creation of its earliest productions. The Nō performance today is somewhat less free and more stylized than it was originally, but its audience is in much the same position as a contemporary British audience would be if it were able to see plays of the Chester cycle performed with much the same language, costumes, and movement used in 1400.

The various elements out of which the Nō was synthesized have an even earlier origin. Among these was *sangaku* (the word can possibly be translated as 'informal music'), a combination of music, dancing, and sometimes jugglery, probably imported into Japan in the early eighth century from Korea and China. The effort has been made to trace its origin ultimately, and laboriously, to India. Among the native materials which contributed to the Nō, the two principal ones seem to have been *dengaku* ('rustic music'), a folk-dance ritual associated with rice planting and harvesting, and *kagura*, a religious dance performed at shrines of the native religion, Shintō. By the middle of the fourteenth century the word *sangaku* had been corrupted to *sarugaku* ('monkey music'), and we hear of performances of *sarugaku-nō* and *dengaku-nō*, the use of the word *nō*, which means 'accomplishment' or 'ability', implying that the performers were professionals rather than amateurs. Towards the end of the fourteenth century, *sarugaku* began to absorb *dengaku*, as well as other native mimetic and musical materials, and troupes of professional actors were generally known as performers of *sarugaku* Nō. The more important of such troupes were usually attached to Shintō shrines and Buddhist temples, the actors frequently priests of low rank, but even these troupes were not above touring the provinces, giving benefit performances before the most ordinary audiences. In fact, the troupes seem to have

been about equally engaged in money-making and in propa-
gandizing for their temples and shrines.

The present Nō theatre, if the beginnings of this art can be
ascribed a date, derives from the innovations and refinements
wrought by a father and son, Kannami (1333–84) and Zeami [1]
(1363–1443), upon the *sarugaku* Nō. Kannami, leader of one of
the four principal troupes which performed for festivals at the
Kasuga Shrine at Nara, was a thorough showman, capable of
playing before audiences of farmers or of nobles and adjusting
his performance to the tastes of both. It was doubtless the desire to please his audiences that led him to add new elements to
the extant *sarugaku* and thus give it much the form which the Nō
has today. He accomplished this revolution by placing greater
emphasis upon the rhythm of the musical accompaniment, and
he made considerable changes in plot and acting by borrowing
elements from a dance called *kusemai*, in which the dancer
mimed as well as chanted the history of a priest or of a temple.
Kannami's innovations would probably have been less influential had he not had the good luck, at a shrine in Kyoto in 1374,
to have in his audience Yoshimitsu (1358–1408), the temporal
ruler of Japan. Yoshimitsu, delighted with the performance,
particularly with that of Kannami's twelve-year-old son,
Zeami, established the troupe in his palace. Thereafter, until
the death of Yoshimitsu, these players enjoyed the position of
being the foremost *sarugaku* actors in the country, and their
methods of production and style of acting, admired and imit-
ated by less fortunate troupes, came to be widely influential.
When Kannami died, Zeami became the leader of the troupe.
Unhappily, neither of Yoshimitsu's sons and successors liked
Zeami, apparently resenting his intimacy with their father.
After suffering the indignity of neglect, Zeami was exiled in
1434 to the distant island of Sado by Yoshinori, Yoshimitsu's
youngest son.

Despite Kannami's desire and ability to please audiences of
the lowest social level, he was not without a strong artistic sense
—had he lacked this he could not have attracted the attention

---

[1] *Zeami* is a phonetic spelling of the name which sometimes appears as
Seami in English texts. Most Japanese scholars prefer the phonetic spelling
in English.

of that remarkable aesthete Yoshimitsu. But Kannami learned his craft in what was almost a commercial theatre, and he enjoyed the benefits of Yoshimitsu's patronage and highly refined artistic taste for only ten years before his death. Zeami, on the contrary, grew to maturity in an atmosphere of the most rarefied and delicate aesthetic sensibility. He wrote plays, and of the contemporary 241 pieces, about 100 are attributed to him. But he also wrote, over a period of some thirty years, a remarkable series of sixteen essays about *sarugaku* Nō. (The term was not abbreviated to *Nō* until after his death.) The first of the essays, written between 1400 and 1402, is in the nature of a memoir of his father's ideas about the theatre. These are extraordinary theatre documents not only in that they are one of the oldest complete statements of an actor concerning his art and his theories of acting that have come down to us, but also in that they were not equalled in their sophisticated and subtle discussion of acting until the contemporary works of Stanislavsky. (Bharata's *Nātsya-sāstra* of the third century A.D. deals less with the acting of the Indian theatre than with production and dramatic theory.) When Zeami writes of 'intuitive perception', and 'becoming the part', or discusses the elaborate and lengthy process of becoming a great actor, his words have a striking modernity, though obviously the kind of acting he was describing was quite unlike that exhibited in the West today.

Zeami's aesthetic of acting and of production was posited on Zen, a form of Buddhism which conceives contemplation, *zen*, as the means of attaining freedom from the phenomenal world and achieving a mystical contemplation of the infinite. It would be foolhardy to attempt an explanation of Zen, since by its very nature it cannot be expressed in words, can be understood only by intuition, and can be transmitted only from 'heart to heart'. The immediate effect of Zen upon the Japanese arts is fortunately somewhat less abstruse, and its influence is graphically demonstrated in the work of the painters of the fourteenth and fifteenth centuries. At the risk of falsifying the aesthetic of Zen by simplification, it may be said that it bears analogies with Platonic forms and archetypes. The Zen artists sought to capture the essential forms which underlay the multiplicity of external appearances. Generally eschewing the use of colour, they painted in monochrome, for, among other reasons, they found colour inimical to form, obscuring sharp outlines and creating a 'liveliness' which suggested rather than eliminated the phenomenal world. They wished, on the contrary, to arrive at a statement of the quietude possible when the agitations on the surface of actuality have reached an equilibrium and the essential form of objects emerges in an aura of timelessness. The description of a picture as 'quiet' was the highest critical praise. The Zen artists did not paint abstractly; they did not ignore, break up, or fragment natural forms. Their process was rather one of constant reduction, in which objects were depicted with delicate selectivity and an austere economy of line. From these general ideas came the artistic concepts of selectivity, reduction to essential forms (consequently, a non-realistic treatment of time and space), and the creation of a tranquil, generally static, mood. Arthur Waley translates the instructions of Buddhapriya, a missionary from India to China in the seventh century, to one who wishes to practise Zen, and these instructions suggest also the methods of restriction and elimination of the Zen artist:

If for example he were meditating in this room, he must first banish from his mind every part of the world except the city of Ch'ang-an. Next every building in the city except this monastery. Next, every room in the monastery except this cell, every object but himself, every part of himself except the end of his nose. Finally the end of his nose hangs in space like a drop of dew and on this nose-end he concentrates his mind.[1]

Not all the notions of the Zen artists were transferred bodily to the Nō performance. The Nō, for example, did not proscribe the use of colour. But, like the graphic arts, it made an artistic virtue of restriction and reduction. The Nō stage is a bare platform, usually devoid of scenic indications. Properties are used sparingly and only when they can be given a more than literal meaning. The actor, wearing a theatricalized version of fourteenth-century court dress, moves in the slow, stylized pattern of sculpture come to a tentative life, his face either masked or expressionless. The number of characters is sharply restricted.

[1] Arthur Waley, *Zen Buddhism and its Relation to Art* (London, 1922), p. 12.

There are only two important roles in most Nō plays: the *shite*, the principal character, and the *waki*, the secondary one. Each of these may have followers (*tsure*), but such characters are usually not in themselves individuals, but vocal and physical extensions of the principal characters. Dramatically, the Nō play tends to be a two-character play, and structurally it comes close to being a one-character play. The *waki* and the *shite* are not protagonist and antagonist, for there is seldom any conflict between them. And even when conflict exists, the sense of conflict is diminished by substituting at this point a dance by the *shite*. The importance of the *shite* is further increased by his being given the best lines, the most poetic passages. Nevertheless, the *shite* does not emerge as a three-dimensional, complex character, for he is subject to the same artistic reduction as the other elements of the Nō theatre. The plays themselves in their subject matter, in their characters, are a similar distillation of human experience to its essence, as this essence is reflected in Buddhist philosophy. Perhaps it is misleading to speak of the *shite* and the *waki* as characters, for they have little in common with the three-dimensional persons who inhabit the Western theatre and whose complexity is capable of revealing new facets of personality to successive generations. The allegorical characters of the late medieval French and English morality plays are probably the closest Western approximation to the figures of the Nō, but even these must have displayed in performance considerably more vitality and humanness than the tenuous, tentative beings evoked on the Nō stage. The quality of these delicately sketched creations derives, of course, from the aesthetic and, in a certain sense, the religious quality of the Nō plays.

Thus the Nō performance in its style of production and its conception of drama seems remote from and even antithetical to the theatre of the West. Yet all dramatic art, anywhere in the world, tends towards selectivity and the elimination of the non-essential. Even the realistic theatre of the West has found it necessary to limit the materials which it places upon the stage, to restrict the length of the play, to control the depiction of character. The physical fact of producing a play upon a stage sets its own limitations upon the quantity and quality of the materials which can be displayed. But while the Western theatre has tended to regard a bare platform, a lack of scenery, the inhibition of movement and of characterization as restrictions upon expressiveness, the Nō conceived these as positive artistic values. Even Shakespeare expressed impatience with his unworthy scaffold and wooden O, and asked his audience to co-operate in piecing out their imperfections. It could perhaps be demonstrated that the theatre of the West has inevitably moved towards piecing out its imperfections by an increasing literality and that the film represents the greatest achievement, to date, of this effort; only occasionally in the history of the Western theatre has there been a conscious attempt to arrest this process by strictly limiting the materials and the subject matter employed by the theatre artist. The paradox of the Western movement in the theatre is that the more the appetite for realism was satisfied, the more restricted—in subject matter, in characters, in movement in time and space—the theatre became.

By choosing an artistic path leading in the opposite direction, the Nō theatre rejected all attempts at literal representation. And so the Nō stage remains a stage, never losing its spatial identity, never hiding its beautifully polished surface of Japanese cypress, which gently reflects the sculptural figure of the actor. It has never occurred to the performers to speak disparagingly of it as unworthy, for it provides all that a good actor could ask of a stage: the opportunity for making impressive entrances and exits, the ability to be seen in the round by the audience, close rapport with musicians and chorus, and freedom from involvement with scenery and scenic effects.

The actor makes his entrance from the mirror room, where he has stood before a full-length mirror in order to enter into the character by studying its reflected figure. The curtain between the mirror room and the stage is lifted from the bottom on two bamboo poles by backstage assistants, and the actor moves on to the 'bridge', an area railed on either side, about 6½ feet wide, varying in length from 33 to 52 feet. The bridge, like the stage proper to which it leads, is roofed, even though the entire structure is today usually placed within a larger building. The Nō stage was originally set in the open, the important members of the audience viewing the performance from an adjacent build-

ing, while those less favoured sat or stood in the open air near
the stage. The rear wall of the stage proper also recalls the out-
door Nō stage, for on it is painted a stylized pine-tree, a re-
minder, it is said, of the pine-trees behind the stage at the
Kasuga shrine in Nara. The out-of-doors persists in a strip of
white pebbles, about three feet wide, in front of the stage and
the bridge, and in the three small pine-trees equidistantly
placed in this area before the bridge.

Almost in slow motion, for there are no rapid movements in
the Nō, the actor moves towards the stage proper, his walk of a
kind peculiar to the Nō. His feet, shod in cotton cloth, are not
lifted from the floor, but are slid along it, the toes raised at each
step. When he reaches the stage proper, an area some 18 feet
square, he pauses beside the pillar placed where the bridge
joins the stage, to the right of the musicians seated in the upstage
area. The pillar is called 'the pillar of the principal character',
the area to the side of it the name-saying-seat, although frequently the character who tells, standing in this place, who he is,
where he has come from, and where he is going, is not the principal character, the *shite*, but the subordinate one, the *waki*.
The actor's next movement is normally towards the front of the
stage, and since the principal character can see but poorly
through the narrow slits of his mask, he guides himself by looking at the downstage pillar, which has therefore been named
'the pillar on which the eye is fixed' or 'the facing pillar'. On
the opposite side of the stage from this is the *waki*'s pillar, so
named because in many plays the subordinate character takes
a position in its vicinity when the principal character makes his
entrance. Along the stage-left side of the stage proper is an
area about 4 feet wide on which are seated the six or eight members of the chorus, who have made their entrance through a low
door, the Hurry Door, in the upstage-left corner of the stage.
This door is also used by lesser characters, for only the principal
character and the subordinate one, together with the attendants who may accompany them, make their entrances upon the
bridge.

Only rarely are scenic indications put upon the stage, and in
most instances these are not constructions which resemble literal
objects. A boat is reduced to a kind of diagrammatic outline of

its form. A tomb may be suggested by four upright poles topped with greenery. A well is indicated by the outlines of a cube. Such pieces, called 'fictional things', do not actually occupy space in the manner of objects in the realistic theatre, but rather surround a given space with a sketch, or rather an *aperçu*, of the literal object. Here as elsewhere, stripped of its external attributes, the natural object appears in its basic, essential form, indicated only by outlines, and expressing, indirectly, the unsubstantiality and evanescence of reality.

Some of the sparingly-used properties have a similar sketch-like quality. The most frequently used, characteristic one is the folding fan, which, closed, partially closed, or open, serves as any object suggested by its form or by its manipulation. Thus the fan may be a sword, a lantern, a tray, or it can be made completely non-literal by the actor and convey such ideas as the falling of rain or of snow. Other properties tend to resemble literal objects, although they appear in somewhat idealized form. A rake is theatricalized by its handle being wrapped in white paper, its enlarged prongs painted gold; a bundle of firewood becomes a small, neat construction of twigs decorated on both ends with flowers. None of these properties, however, even such real-looking ones as baskets, drums, or Buddhist rosaries, is used in a completely realistic fashion. They are simply extensions of the character who uses them rather than objects in their own right. A twig of bamboo carried by a bereaved mother is the visible sign of her insanity. A demon is recognized both by his wig and mask and by a kind of baton he holds which has no meaning in itself. Only rarely does a property exist in its own right apart from the character. In the play *Aoi-no-Ue*, the Princess Aoi, made ill by a spiteful demon, is created not by an actor but by a kimono laid on the stage floor. In *Utō* the hat of the dead bird-hunter, when placed at the front of the stage, is the sign of the birds he hunted.

In some instances it is difficult to decide whether something worn by the actor should be regarded as part of his costume or as a property, for it exhibits the uses of both. The elaborate head-dresses of deities, demons, and other supernatural beings are often surmounted by relatively literal objects: a fox goddess wears a metallic fox, the dragon god a dragon. This headgear is not simply an indicatory device like the crown of the Western stage king, but, like the properties in general, becomes a kind of externalization of the character. The same is true of the feather 'apron' worn by a hunter, the hemp one worn by the fisherman, the red wig of the lion, or the tufted pallium of the travelling priest. The Western theatre provides examples of costumes used to show social position as well as the inner nature of the character; but only in certain stylized forms, such as the *commedia dell'arte* and the English renaissance court theatre, have the materials worn by the actor been not merely dress from which can be deduced the nature of the character but a specific and yet non-literal statement of that character, sharing the same aesthetic purpose as the properties the actor carries.

The limitation of properties, the scarcity of scenic elements, and the consequently almost bare stage of the Nō theatre suggest similarities with the 'platform' stages of the West, particularly that of the Shakespearian theatre. It is true that the spatial identification of the Shakespearian forestage could be established by the words of the actor as is that of the Nō stage. It is also true that the Shakespearian forestage, like the Nō stage, could be divided into spatially disparate areas, widely separated in actual space, so that, for instance, the tents of Richard III and of Richmond could be set side by side. But in other respects these stages were quite differently conceived. The Shakespearian forestage was surrounded by an ambiance of actuality set up by the inner stages in which furniture was placed, by the doors on to the forestage and the windows above them which could be given literal identification, and by the façade of the scene house, which must have strongly suggested the world of actuality. The force of these relatively explicit areas flowed, as it were, into the forestage and made it part of a theatrically, and aesthetically, realistic whole. Then, too, the relation of the forestage to the other acting levels seems to have been one in which the vertical dimension corresponded closely to that of actual space: Romeo descends 'the cords' to the forestage, and Antony is heaved aloft to Cleopatra. In the Nō theatre, on the contrary, no such sense of actual space is created. Unlike the three-dimensional doors to the Shakespearian forestage, the curtained entrance to the bridge cannot be translated into solid architecture.[1] It is simply a conventional entrance, not realistically related to the bridge or to the offstage area. The upstage area of the Nō stage, far from being conceived realistically, is occupied not by the actor but by the musicians and the stage assistants. No realistic use is made of levels, and no platforms are placed upon the stage except in the few plays in which low platforms are used for decorative effect. Although the Shakespearian forestage could be divided into disparate areas, this practice was not usual; the Nō stage shows such a division more often than not. At the beginning of the typical Nō play the subordinate actor, after stopping at the 'name-saying-seat' and telling who he is and where he has come from, moves a few steps to the centre of the stage and announces his arrival at a spot at some distance from that which he previously occupied. In the principal dance which concludes the Nō play, realistic considerations of space are entirely suspended in a fashion apparently unknown in the Shakespearian theatre. Furthermore, the space of the Nō stage is always used by the actor in a conventionalized, stylized pattern, and the actor is loath to use all the space, restricting himself in movement as he does in gesture and attitude. But there is every indication that the Shakespearian actor moved freely about the forestage, a much larger area than that available to the Nō actor, and that he tried, as does the contemporary Western actor, to 'take stage'. In brief, space on the Nō stage tends to be treated non-realistically and theatrically, with the same restraint as is shown in the other elements of the performance.

Despite this freedom from realistic spatial considerations, place is of tremendous importance to the Nō theatre. This fact is attested to both by the scripts of the extant Nō plays and by Zeami's statement that: 'It is sometimes possible to win plaudits with an original piece which has no direct source by placing it in a setting of a noted place or historical spot.' [2] Zeami was aware that his countrymen, like the contemporary Japanese,

[1] Some Nō scripts suggest a realistic conception of the entrance, such as the door of an inn; but a curtain cannot become a door, even a Japanese one, and this three-dimensional effect is not conveyed in performance.

[2] Richard N. McKinnon, *Zeami on the Nō: A Study of 15th Century Japanese Dramatic Criticism*, unpublished doctoral dissertation (Harvard University, 1951), p. 7.

had a consuming interest, much greater than that of Westerners, in the places where notable happenings had occurred. In
the majority of the Nō plays the subordinate character, who
enters first, is and has been travelling, and the beginning of the
play conveys a sense of free, casual movement. The *waki* is
often simply 'suddenly minded' to go to a certain place, and
the audience is given a panoramic, almost cinematic view of
the places through which he has passed. He comes upon the
principal character, a person unknown to him, by what seems
a chance encounter at his destination, frequently a temple or
shrine. It is only when the meeting occurs that the play really
begins, so that, in fact, place crystallizes the drama.

The Japanese classification of the plays results in five principal groups: there are god plays, man plays, woman plays,
plays of mental derangement, plays about demons. And each
of these groups is further divided and subdivided. The traditional Nō performance consisted of the presentation of a play
from each of the groups, in the above order, with comic interludes (*kyōgen*) played between them, but today the usual programme consists of two plays and a comic interlude. Looked at
apart from the esoteric and somewhat inconsistent Japanese
classification (among the 'woman plays', for instance, are some
in which a man plays the principal role), the Nō plays are actually of two types: those which are set entirely in the 'real' world,
and those which involve the appearance of an apparition or
supernatural being. The plots of the former are concerned
largely with the meetings of long-separated parents and children, or brothers and sisters, brought about, usually, by a priest
or at times a deity. The majority of the plays belong to the
latter group, and are the ones most frequently performed.
Plays of this sort are almost invariably divided into two parts.
In the first part the *waki*, often a monk or priest, meets the *shite*
at a place of special significance. They speak of what happened
there in the past, and the *shite*, appearing first to be an ordinary,
even innocuous, person, displays a rather unusual knowledge of
the event. The *shite* then exits. During a short interlude (con-
fusingly called *kyōgen*, although there is usually nothing comic
about it), he changes costume and mask and reappears for the
second part in what might be said to be his basic identity. The

Japanese describe him in his first appearance as the 'before'-*shite* and in his second as the 'after'-*shite*. There is often a complete contrast between the two, so that they are entirely different roles. The *shite* may first be a beautiful girl, then a serpent; an old village woman, then a demoness; a boy, then the spirit of a warrior.

After his second appearance the *shite*, with the help of the chorus, gives an account, as it were, of his essential being, climaxed by his principal dance. A hunter dances his killing of birds in life and the punishment he now suffers in hell for this sin. The woman who in life had an illicit passion for a priest reveals her true demonic nature wearing the mask of a demon and a costume of stylized pattern representing the scales of a snake. The great warrior relives his last battle. All such characters are chained to their earthly passions, which continue to bind them to the world of actuality and prevent their attainment of Nirvana. It is the priest or monk, though sometimes a deity is invoked, who can pray for the repose of the spirit. Because he possesses knowledge of the inevitable likeness between all living things, the priest receives requests for deliverance and enlightenment not only from the spirits of human beings but also from the snow, a butterfly, or the wisteria. These shades and apparitions are unsubstantial evocations of a single emotion which haunts the tortured spirit.

The area of dramatic activity of the Nō play shows the same distance and remoteness from the world of actuality as the physical techniques with which it is performed. In this respect the Nō script also shows the influence of Zen, for Zen concerns itself basically with escape from the exigencies of time and place, and the Nō play moves in a shadowy realm at the edge of life and death. Even the language of the Nō play and the untranslatable literary devices it employs reveal a similar ambiguity of movement in time and space. It is difficult to think of Western plays which take place in a comparable region. Yeats experimented in the form of the Nō, and Maeterlinck in such plays as *The Intruder* and in his essays suggested a like theatre. The Western theatre has concerned itself almost wholly with the here and now, and its fearsome ghosts and apparitions are not figures of central interest; they appear only to influence action

in the world of actuality. (Zeami insisted that the apparitions
be not terrifying, but beautiful, and he conceived these two
qualities to be mutually exclusive.) Western drama shows
human activity in the complex, ambiguous movement of the
character, rarely in the reduction of the life of man to a single
fulcrum, poised at the point where the now and the hereafter
touch and where the problem of the tortured spirit has a single
solution. Western tragedy establishes a focal point in actual
time, and its hero is caught up in life's fitful fever. The *shite*
demonstrates the necessity for escape from this world, the desir-
ability of being done with that part of living which still clings to
him. When Oedipus is at last received by the gods, when Macbeth's head is brought on the stage by Macduff, the drama is
finished. In the context of the Nō it has just begun. If the entire past of the Nō play is reconstructed, it frequently reveals all
the conflict, struggle, pain, and bloodshed of the most agitated
and lurid melodrama. But none of this appears in the theatre.
The actual events are faded and distant; only the essence of the
experience of living remains. As he appears on the bridge, the
shite seems drawn into being from a remote world of history,
legends, and phantoms. He sometimes comes to fuller 'realiza-
tion' in the second part of the play (though at times this part is
the dream of the *waki*), but at the end his transient vision fades.
He is not an individual, but the shade of remembered emotion.
If the spirit of Oedipus were to come again to Colonus and tell
of his great moment of horror, or if the ghost of Macbeth were
to recount his sufferings in hell and to relive in stylized dance
the murder of Duncan, the nature of the piece would be close to
the Nō and to the sphere of theatrical activity which Maeterlinck describes as 'the truly tragic in life [which] begins only at
the moment when what are called adventures, sorrows, and
dangers have passed'.

In performance the Nō theatre creates the effect, emanating
from the central figure of the actor, of a quasi-animate, quasi-
inanimate surface that one associates with the graphic arts but
seldom with the theatre, a surface which, like the role of the
shite, both man and spirit, involves both life and death. The
inanimate, even deathlike mask worn by the *shite* is brought to
a subtle, momentary life by the actor, while the faces of the

unmasked actors are so rigidly expressionless that they assume
the quality of masks. The voice does not reproduce the sounds
of colloquial speech but moves lyrically in a region between
speech and chant, functioning as a musical instrument rather
than as part of the actor's personality. An actor playing a
female role does not change his voice in range or pitch, but suggests femininity, as a violinist might, through the quality of his
tone. The unison, Gregorian-like chanting of the chorus, a
group of men seated on stage left, is an equally impersonal and
formal voice. The gesture is grave, restrained, avoiding any
suggestion of warm-blooded life. Zeami warned the prospective playwright not to write scenes in which reunited parents
and children display their tearful emotions, for an audience
would find such scenes disgusting in their literalness. The
actor's gesture shows a like consideration for the sensibilities of
the audience. The actor moves slowly, more slowly than he did
in Zeami's time, and his most important moments of expression
are conveyed by a static attitude which, like sculpture, suggests
'motionless activity'. Even his movement, like that of a figure
in slow-motion film, reveals more of the human body in motion
than can be observed in actuality. His movement is, of course,
dance, but it is dance expressed in traditional stylization, so
tranquil, restrained, and unlifelike that it gives time for the
imagination of the audience to play about its suggestive images.
The Nō therefore shows greater affinities with the graphic arts
than does any contemporary Western form of theatre. All art
must exist outside time and must overcome the tyranny of
space, and like the graphic arts the Nō has conquered time and
space and used them for its own aesthetic ends. It is the sort of
theatre which Maeterlinck envisioned as 'a theatre of peace,
and of beauty without tears'.

The influence of the Nō upon the subsequent forms of the
traditional theatre can hardly be over-estimated. The doll
theatre and the Kabuki echo its language and subject matter,
and, in varying degrees, pattern their methods of production
upon it. The Nō practice of using only male performers is carried on in the other theatres. The costuming of the Nō, which
enlarges the actor to heroic proportions and at the same time
dictates his slow, stately movement, becomes even more weighty

and lavish in the Kabuki. Music and dance are integral to the Nō, and the other theatres create an aura of rhythmic movement and sound. The persistence of the artistic concepts of the Nō is perhaps most obvious in the use made of narration. From proto-dramatic forms the Nō inherited the tradition of the story-teller, and in all three theatres narration can serve as important a function as the chorus in the early tragedies of Aeschylus. Only in the Kabuki does it become, at times, as dramatically extraneous as the chorus of Euripides. The Western distinction between the narrative and the dramatic is not made, for, particularly in the Nō and the doll theatre, the drama has its genesis in the chorus or the narrator-singer, while the images of the actor or the doll furnish visual extensions of the narration. In the Nō the dramatic emphasis passes fluidly from the actor to the narration as the chorus describes scenes, explains what is passing in the mind of the character, or declaims the actor's lines as he dances. In the doll theatre the narration is even more prominent, for, apart from its visual aspects, the entire performance rises out of the astonishing vocal virtuosity of the narrator-singer.

The importance given the narration and, by inference, the text of the play may suggest that the traditional theatre is literary rather than theatrical. This is not the case. Most Japanese scholars regard the texts, even those of the Nō, as scenarios whose artistic validity can be proved only in performance. Although the word is necessary to the Japanese theatre, its claims are not advanced over those of the other elements of the production, nor is it possible for the Japanese to conceive of a play, such as a Western closet drama, which may have literary merit but is unactable. The artificial war between literature and theatre has never been waged in Japan, and probably a good deal of the vitality and richness of the traditional theatre can be attributed to its being conceived as a total, indivisible art.

The Maple Viewing: The text used was that of the Kanze school, which was founded by Kannami for the training of the principal actor. (Four other schools survive today—Komparu, Hōshō, Kongō, and Kita.) The stage directions and costume descriptions are based upon those given by Sanari Kentarō in *Yōkyoku Taikan* and upon a number of actual performances.

THE MAPLE VIEWING
(Momijigari)

A Nō Play attributed to

KANZE KOJIRŌ NOBUMITSU
(1434–1516)

English version by Meredith Weatherby

PART ONE

The time is autumn, in the eleventh century; the place is Mount Togakushi in Shinano Province.

After the musicians are seated, the stage attendants (dressed in Japanese formal costume) bring in a low platform, approximately 3 feet by 6 feet, its sides decorated with a bold, geometric pattern and its top covered with straw matting or red felt. They place the platform at the rear of the stage proper, just in front of the musicians, and on its stage-left half they place a framework covered with dark-coloured cloth and surmounted by an arrangement of moss and red maple leaves, representing an autumn mountain; the framework is large enough to accommodate the actor who will subsequently disappear into it.

Following an introductory passage of music the curtain is swept back and the GENTLEWOMAN *(the* shite) *walks slowly on to the bridge, followed by three (occasionally five)* LADIES IN WAITING *(the* tsure). *They all are gorgeously costumed (red neckbands showing at the throat, under-robes printed with designs in gold and silver, trailing outer-robes of red, patterned brocade) and wear simple wigs, parted in the middle and tied with decorated headbands. The* GENTLEWOMAN *wears the mask associated with ladies of rank, while the masks of the others are less expressive.*

Continuing down the bridge and to the centre of the stage proper, they form a square, first facing outward and then turning to face inward as they chant the opening lines in unison. They have been followed by a SERVING-WOMAN *(kyōgen)—unmasked, plainly dressed in an embroidered kimono and wearing a white headcloth which hangs down on either side of her face—who seats herself on the floor at the Kyōgen's Seat, an area to stage-right of the musicians.*

GENTLEWOMAN and LADIES IN WAITING.
> The drizzling rains of autumn . . .
> The scarlet maple leaves . . .
>
> The drizzling rains of autumn . . .
> The scarlet maple leaves . . .
>
> Oh, impatient then,
> Let us hasten deep into the mountains,
> Excursion bent,
> To view the scarlet leaves.

(Having thus stated the purpose that brings her on to the scene, the GENTLEWOMAN *faces front to introduce herself, while the* CHORUS *repeats the refrain.)*

CHORUS. The drizzling rains of autumn . . .
> The scarlet maple leaves . . .

19

Oh, impatient then,
Let us hasten deep into the mountains,
Excursion bent,
To view the scarlet leaves.

GENTLEWOMAN. I am a person who lives in this vicinity. (*She turns back to face her* LADIES IN WAITING.)

GENTLEWOMAN and LADIES IN WAITING.

Yes,
Long have I dwelt in this transitory world,
And yet now
There is none to be concerned for me.
How lonely then my crumbling house,
Banked white with clouds
And rankly overgrown with vines!
And there,
Where no living person ever comes to call,
It was the autumn that came calling
All too soon,
And in the garden
The white chrysanthemums faded
Until they too
Resembled my life of sadness.

GENTLEWOMAN (*turning front*).

At last the twilight
Was too lonely to be borne:
Gazing on the rainy skies,
I felt a yearning
To be out amid the autumn leaves.
And, lo . . .

(*She turns back to face her* LADIES IN WAITING.)

GENTLEWOMAN and LADIES IN WAITING.

. . . lo!
Even the colour of the blades of grass
Along the paths I follow
Has deepened with each day's passing.
And the maples,
Have not their lower branches too
Been stained by the night's soft dew?
Have not their lower branches too
Been stained by the night's soft dew?
Only since yesterday
The fields of morning
Have turned these darkening hues,

And through deep, dark crimson
We have made our way here,
Deep into the mountain fastness.

And here,
Even as the poet says,
The wind in very truth
Has built its dams of scarlet leaves,
Turning this rivulet
Into a length of rare brocade,
Which our wading feet
Would rend in twain.
So let us rest here,
Beneath these trees,
And gaze our fill
Upon the autumn foliage.

(*During the last sentence they move towards the* waki's *pillar, where the* GENTLEWOMAN *turns towards the facing pillar, and the* LADIES IN WAITING *line up beyond her in front of the* CHORUS. *They take seats simultaneously, the* GENTLEWOMAN *on a hatbox-like stool which a stage attendant brings, and the* LADIES IN WAITING *on the floor. The* SERVING-WOMAN *now rises and moves to the name-saying-seat, where she sits.*)

SERVING-WOMAN (*using ordinary speech*). My, my, but the autumn leaves are beautiful! I'll hang a curtain about my ladies, set up the folding screens, and offer the nine felicitous sips of wine.

(*The* SERVING-WOMAN *moves to the far end of the line of* LADIES *and takes a seat near the flute pillar, thereby indicating that the preparations are made and the maple-viewing party is under way. During the ensuing scene all the* LADIES *sit immobile; they are understood to be passing the rice wine, hidden within their curtained enclosure.*

The curtain is swept back and KOREMOCHI (*the* waki) *marches on to the bridge. He wears an under-robe, a hip-length outer-robe tied with a belt, and white divided skirts. Using neither mask nor wig, he wears a tall black cap, its peak bent backward, tied with strings under the chin, and he carries a bow and an arrow. Following him are a number (usually four) of* GENTLEMEN ATTENDANTS (*the* waki-tsure), *wearing short robes over divided skirts of the same pattern. They also are unmasked, and one carries his lord's sword, while the others carry bamboo staffs.* KOREMOCHI *and the* GENTLEMEN ATTENDANTS *stand in a line on the bridge and are understood to be on a deer hunt.*)

KOREMOCHI. Delightful!
The time of frosts has come;
The trees take on their myriad hues,
As though they were brocade
And the drizzling, twilight rains
Were dyes of many colours.
In the dusk of evening,
Wet through by these same autumn rains,
A lone deer went crying for its mate,
Its plaintive voice
Guiding us here
Into this hunting ground . . .
Oh,
Truly a delightful spot!

GENTLEMEN ATTENDANTS.
Calling to each other
That the dawn has come,
The deer return now,
Making their way from the plains
Deep into the mountains.
Their scent comes borne upon the wind,
Fretting the hooves of our horses.

(KOREMOCHI *raises his bow in one hand.*)

GENTLEMEN ATTENDANTS.
The warriors,
Brave and ardent . . .
Bamboo arrows taking wing
From bows of finest catalpa wood . . .
Ardent warriors . . .
Winging arrows . . .
Bending bows . . .
See them making their way across the plains,
Through the dew-drenched pampas grass.

(KOREMOCHI, *still standing and posturing on the bridge, has turned several times to look back towards the curtain. Now for the first time he begins to turn towards the stage.*)

GENTLEMEN ATTENDANTS.
See them climbing the steep paths
Towards their distant goal,
A deer-blind far up a mountain valley;
Hear the deer-calls
Come rolling down towards them.
Oh,

May the wind take care
To blow in this direction . . .
Oh,
May the wind take care!
(KOREMOCHI *is now facing the stage. Riding through the mountains, he has approached within sight of the maple-viewing party. He stands a moment looking directly towards the group on the stage.*)

KOREMOCHI (*calling to his men*).
    Ho! someone.

GENTLEMAN ATTENDANT (*the sword-bearer, who stands next to his lord*).
    I await your commands.

KOREMOCHI (*turning to face the man*).
    Look you yonder,
    There in the mountain cove—
    Human shapes!
    Go then and ask what persons they may be.

GENTLEMAN ATTENDANT.
    I hear and obey.
(*He passes down the bridge and stops at the name-saying-seat, facing the seated ladies. Using ordinary speech.*)

GENTLEMAN ATTENDANT. Ho! Will not someone invite me in?

SERVING-WOMAN (*rising and coming to centre stage, where she faces the man*).
And who is it that seeks to enter here?

GENTLEMAN ATTENDANT. It is I. Who is the honourable personage within?

SERVING-WOMAN. But first, who is the honourable personage that sends to ask?

GENTLEMAN ATTENDANT. It is Koremochi of the Taira from whom I come.

SERVING-WOMAN. Be he Koremochi or whoever, say to him only that it is a certain person of gentle breeding, come here for a maple-viewing party.
(*The* SERVING-WOMAN *resumes her seat near the* CHORUS *and later makes an unobtrusive exit through the hurry door. The* GENTLEMAN ATTENDANT *moves back and kneels before* KOREMOCHI.)

GENTLEMAN ATTENDANT.
    I went to ask,
    And seemingly
    It was a gentlewoman of high estate,
    Making merry within the enclosure
    Of curtains and folding screens.
    So I inquired most courteously.

And even so
I was not so much as told her name,
But only that she was
An honourable personage.

KOREMOCHI. A strange thing indeed.
How undreamed of,
That such a person
Should be here in this wilderness!
And, no matter what her name,
Still it is a gentlewoman
Who has stopped along our path
To view the scarlet leaves.
Unseemly would it be then,
To pass her thus,
Mounted on our horses,
To cloud with dust her merry-making.

CHORUS. And with these words,
Dismounting from his horse,
Removing too his footgear . . .

(KOREMOCHI *hands his bow and arrow to one of the men.*)

CHORUS. Dismounting from his horse,
Removing too his footgear,
He moves far off the path,
This Koremochi,
And makes to follow the faint, steep trail
That leaps the crags about this mountain cove. . . .
Oh, matchless courtesy!
Oh, courtliness unmatched!

(KOREMOCHI *moves on to the main stage and stands at the* shite's
pillar. The GENTLEMEN ATTENDANTS *exit by the hurry door.*)

GENTLEWOMAN (*speaking as though to herself, but doubtless with the inten-
tion of being overheard*).
Truly a person of humble station,
Worthy of no account,
I came here deep into the mountains
And thinking none would know,
Laid all reserve aside,
Made merry,
And gazed alone upon the autumn foliage.
But has the colour
Of these same scarlet leaves
Been discovered in my cheeks?
Oh, what to do?

KOREMOCHI (*unmoving*).
> As white and nameless
> As an unused bow is she,
> Hiding bashfully from view
> As might an arrow in its target.
> And I know only
> That she is a lady of high estate,
> A gentlewoman hiding.

GENTLEWOMAN (*turning slowly on her stool to face him*).
> Hiding?
> But the poet says,
> 'It is not I but you who hides from love',
> And just so is it you
> Who deigns not tell his name.
> Oh,
> I pray you then,
> Do pause if but a moment:
> Surely such a chance encounter by the roadside
> Has a meaning.

KOREMOCHI. An undreamed of thing—
> That she should deign to summon
> Even such a one as I.
>   (*Describing his action*)
> And so saying,
> He tries to pass her by,
> Pretending not to notice.
>   (*Taking a few steps to stage centre*)
> Thereupon . . .

GENTLEWOMAN.
> Oh,
> Heartless one!
> Does not the proverb have it thus:
> 'To take shelter from a passing shower . . .

KOREMOCHI (*speaking for the* GENTLEWOMAN).
> '. . . under the same tree; . . .

GENTLEWOMAN.
> '. . . to stop . . .

CHORUS (*speaking for the* GENTLEWOMAN, *who rises and moves slowly towards stage centre*).
> '. . . and drink of the same stream;
> To be husband and wife for a day—
> All these are meetings fated
> Since lives lived long ago.'

Does not the proverb have it so?
And is it not a similar fate
That has brought us to this roadside meeting?
Oh, pause,
I beg of you;
Take shelter here beneath this tree;
Do not forsake me thus.

(*The* GENTLEWOMAN *reaches* KOREMOCHI *and, during the following speech, places her hand momentarily on his sleeve.*)

CHORUS (*describing the scene*).

At once she lays her hand,
Bashfully,
Detainingly,
Upon his sleeve.
His footsteps falter. . . .
No,
Neither insensate stone
Nor unfeeling tree is he.
And so,
With softening heart,
Back he turns to her.

CHORUS (*speaking for the* GENTLEWOMAN, *who takes a few steps to the rear*).

Here,
Far up on a mountain trail,
And a draught of wine
As pure as dew upon chrysanthemums—
What possible harm could it be?

(*The* GENTLEWOMAN *sits in the centre of the stage, while* KOREMOCHI *goes and sits at the* waki's *pillar, these movements indicating that he has now entered the curtained enclosure and that the revelry has begun.*)

CHORUS (*for* KOREMOCHI).

Was there not the sage of old
Who, esteeming friendship
Even above his solemn vows of hermitage,
Crossed over the Tiger Stream?
How much less possible
Is it then for such as I
To refuse a cup of wine
So filled with human kindness.

GENTLEWOMAN. Like the ancient poet,
'In the woods
We build a fire of scarlet maple leaves
And mull our wine.'

CHORUS (*for* KOREMOCHI).
> A beautiful scene!
> She spreads a sleeve
> Upon the moss-grown rock,
> As though for a loverless sleep.
> Her cheeks flushing a darkest crimson—
> Surely a reflection of the scarlet leaves
> That flutter down to clothe her—
> She seems . . .

KOREMOCHI. . . . too . . .
> Beautiful
> To be a creature of this earth.

CHORUS (*for* KOREMOCHI).
> My heart is clamouring within me.

(KOREMOCHI *opens his fan and with it makes a spirited gesture.*)

CHORUS. Even without the temptings of such earthly beauty,
> Still there is the thing called wine
> To corrupt man's heart
> Even as a bamboo
> May force its way between the rocks.
> At the very moment of thinking
> I would not so much as sip the dew
> That falls from that bamboo,
> There the wine cup was before me—
> And lo!
> How inconstant is man's will.

(*The* GENTLEWOMAN *rises and, going to* KOREMOCHI, *makes a gesture of pouring wine from her fan into his. During the following speech she begins a flirtatious dance, first turning slowly in the centre of the stage and then gradually moving in ever-widening, gliding circles. In the meantime* KOREMOCHI *is sitting in the informal cross-legged fashion and is understood to be becoming more and more confused with wine.*)

CHORUS.
> Now,
> Many are the Buddha's commandments,
> But even as you break the command against wine
> So will you surely break two more—
> That against falsehood,
> That against adultery—
> And in an instant
> Three commandments have been broken. . . .

Oh,
In all the world has there ever been
A more disgusting drunkenness than this of mine—
My mind a storm,
The flower of my heart nought
But a bauble hanging in a lady's hair.
If any should happen to see me thus,
Even though they looked as casually
As at the wild cherries blooming on Storm Mountain—
How would I look to them now?

GENTLEWOMAN (*continuing her gliding dance*).
                    Yes,
                    Truly,
                    Consider well . . .

CHORUS (*for the* GENTLEWOMAN, *still dancing*).
          . . . and surely this our meeting
          Was ordained from some deep love
          We felt for one another
          In lives long past.
          Why else, then,
          In this most unexpected meeting of the roadside,
          Would I have shown this great emotion,
          Entreating you to stop,
          Reproaching your coldness
          With words as slight
          As the dew upon a blade of grass,
          And pledged you my troth forever?
          Why else,
          I ask you,
          Would I have been so impudent,
          So bold?
          But oh,
          What a vain hope was mine,
          For a man's heart is indeed inconstant,
          As vacillating
          As the drifting white clouds.
          I know not what to do.

CHORUS (*describing the scene, while the* GENTLEWOMAN'*s dance shows signs
    of increasing drunkenness*).
                    Time is passing . . .
                    Passing.
                    Out of the drifting clouds
                    There sounds the voice of a storm.

(*The* GENTLEWOMAN *looks upward for a moment.*)

CHORUS. Or is it perhaps
                The sound of vine leaves
                Scattering before the gale?
                And night is near—
                Night as black
                As that beloved of the Ugly Goddess.

(*The* GENTLEWOMAN *advances towards the front of the stage and stands still, opening her fan in preparation for a formal dance.*)

CHORUS. The moon rises,
                Filling the moon-round wine cup,
                Which passes more and more often.
                She points her dancing hand—
                And lo!
                Her trailing sleeves,
                Twirling as gracefully as the snow.

(*The* GENTLEWOMAN *begins her formal dance to add to the revelry. The dance starts very slowly, but gradually mounts in intensity, together with the music, and becomes quite active, demon-like, once she is certain* KOREMOCHI *is asleep.*)

GENTLEWOMAN. 'Oh,
                The painful beauty of red leaves
                Scattered upon green moss. . . .

CHORUS (*for the* GENTLEWOMAN).
                'Oh,
                The painful beauty of red leaves
                Scattered upon green moss.
                And then,
                To add still more,
                There comes a cold wind,
                Blowing rain through the twilit sky.'

(*Seeing that* KOREMOCHI *has at last fallen into a drunken sleep, the* GENTLEWOMAN *summons her* LADIES IN WAITING *with a gesture of the fan. They stand, as the dance becomes more and more rapid.*)

CHORUS. And so he slumbers here,
                Deep in the mountain cove,
                Beset by night and frightful storm,
                Dreaming of the rising of the moon.
                Even the sleeve on which he rests his head
                In lonely sleep
                Is wet as though with heavy dew.

(*The* GENTLEWOMAN *turns and gazes towards the fictional mountain.*)

CHORUS. Oh,

> Waken not from dreaming.
> Oh,
> Waken not from dreaming.

(*The* GENTLEWOMAN *circles around the stage to the right, mounts the platform, and disappears into the mountain. The* LADIES IN WAITING *exit slowly by the bridge, leaving the sleeping* KOREMOCHI *upon the stage.*)

INTERLUDE

The curtain is swept back to reveal a figure readily recognizable to the Nō audience as a minor Shintō deity, a stock character, in this case subsequently identified as the deified spirit of the semi-historical 'first prime minister' of Japan, Takenouchi no Sukune, enshrined at the shrine of Hachiman, God of War and patron of warriors, at Iwashimizu, near Kyoto. He wears a deeply carved and rather ascetic golden mask with a fringe of chin-whiskers extending from ear to ear, a peaked cap of patterned brocade, a patterned under-robe, short outer-robe of a sombre colour, divided skirts, and leggings. He carries a large sword in his right hand.

Passing down the bridge to the name-saying-seat, he stops, faces front, and remains motionless during the first part of his speech.

(*As the long speech he gives is in large part only a prose résumé of the action thus far, the following version has been substantially cut.*)

DEITY. It is an urgent matter that brings me forth. Koremochi, the great Taira general, has been sent by imperial command to extirpate the demons dwelling on Mount Togakushi and harassing the countryside. Brave beyond compare, he was not daunted in the least by the prospect and enjoyed himself greatly along the way, viewing the autumn foliage, hunting deer. But the demons, learning of his approach, turned themselves into lovely maidens and, thus disguised, lured Koremochi towards his death, weakening his will with their beauty and dimming his mind with the wine they urged upon him. Thus has it come about that the great Koremochi, scourge of the Emperor's enemies, now lies in drunken stupor; and at this very moment are the demons preparing to take his life.

But lo! Hachiman himself, patron of all brave warriors, has graciously taken note of what betides and has entrusted me with a divine message for Koremochi. Even now I am bound for Mount Togakushi. (*Turning towards the* waki's *pillar.*) Yea, possessing powers of divinity, I have now arrived at Mount Togakushi. . . . (*Turning and looking towards the sleeping man.*) O Koremochi, hear

me now! Those you thought were beautiful maidens are in very
fact the demons who dwell upon this mountain. By them you are
bewitched, your very life at forfeit. And this is the divine message
so graciously bestowed by Hachiman: 'I send you this noble
sword in order that you may easily vanquish the demons and
return quickly home.' Even thus says the great Hachiman. . . .
Such drunken stupor! Quick, quick! Awake, awake!
(*The* DEITY *places the sword on the stage before* KOREMOCHI, *stamps his
foot resoundingly to waken the sleeper, and exits by the bridge.*)

PART TWO

KOREMOCHI (*waking slowly and raising his head*).
>Oh,
>Base creature am I!
>And yet,
>Even as I dozed,
>My heart deranged with wine,
>That fountainhead of all worldly passion,
>There was vouchsafed me in my dreaming
>A miraculous revelation . . .

CHORUS (*for* KOREMOCHI).
>. . . and I was awakened.
>Oh, the lightning's fire
>Plays wildly about my pillow!
>Heaven and earth reverberate!
>The wind swoops down!
>And here I am,
>Lost in the trackless mountain wastes . . .
>Hopeless . . .
>Forlorn.

(*In the meanwhile, the erstwhile* GENTLEWOMAN, *hidden in the scenic
mountain, has been changing her costume with the help of the stage
attendants. Now she suddenly springs forth in her true shape of a*
DEMONESS. (*Rarely the* LADIES IN WAITING *also reappear at this
point as other demonesses, but more commonly the single character is
understood to represent the entire group.*) *Her costume—deep-blue
neckband, patterned under-robe, and a short, belted outer-robe and
divided skirts of boldly patterned brocade—is extremely full, giving a
feeling of great bulk. She carries a* T-*shaped wand, and her head and
face are hidden with a large shawl of sheer silk which she holds over*

her head on outstretched arms. Suddenly she casts the shawl behind her and stands erect, revealing the mask of a ferocious demon—lean face, jutting jaws, open mouth painted red, large golden eyeballs, and long golden fangs—surmounted by a bright-red wig which hangs low in the back and over both shoulders. Assuming a threatening stance, she stands on the platform and faces KOREMOCHI, *who has half-risen to his feet.)*

CHORUS *(describing the scene).*

>Oh, fearsome!
>Beautiful women but just a moment past—
>Oh, fearsome!
>Beautiful women but just a moment past—
>And now
>Stand they revealed in shapes of monsters,
>Now spitting flames as they perch on the crags,
>Now letting fall blazes from the empty air,
>As though writhing
>In the burning
>Of that ancient palace
>Whose flames scorched Heaven for fourscore days,
>As though perching on the storied screen
>Within those fabled halls.
>Taller even than the tallest giants are they,
>With horns like flaming trees
>And eyes as flashing
>As though they were the very sun and moon.
>Oh,
>How could any mortal man
>Dare face such ones as these?

(Brandishing her wand and glaring at KOREMOCHI, *the* DEMONESS *leaps from the platform to dance a violent dance expressing the fearsomeness of all demons, while* KOREMOCHI *stands motionless in an attitude of calm defence. When the dance is done, the* DEMONESS *remounts the platform.)*

KOREMOCHI. Still stands he

>Staunch and undismayed,
>This Koremochi.

(During the following staccato chant, the two dancers mime the words in stylized fashion. KOREMOCHI *draws his sword. The* DEMONESS *stamps her foot and leaps towards him from the platform. They make gestures of grappling and violent combat. She flees back to the platform. He pulls her down again and touches her breast with his sword.)*

CHORUS. Still stands he
        Staunch and undismayed,
        This Koremochi.
        In his heart he prays:
        'All hail, O greatest Hachiman!'
        And with the words
        Unsheathes his sword,
        Waiting,
        Waiting for the charge.

        Down swoops the demoness then upon him,
        Destruction bent.

        He dodges and grapples with her,
        And the heavenly sword
        Cuts deep into the demon flesh.
        And still she is not vanquished.
        Seizing his head in her mighty arms,
        She is about to fly with him
        High into the air.

        Again the sword flashes.
        She shrinks before it,
        Leaping to the highest crag.

        But down he pulls her,
        Down,
        And yet once more
        Does the flashing sword pierce her,
        Pierce her
        To the very heart.

        And in the flash of his sword
        Are they overwhelmed,
        These fearsome demons.
        And nought remains
        But the terrifying power of bravery. . . .

(*After* KOREMOCHI *places his sword against her breast, the* DEMONESS
exits by the hurry door, indicating she has been killed. KOREMOCHI
*then shoulders the sword, strikes a pose for a moment at the name-
saying-seat, and exits in long, gliding strides along the bridge. He is
followed by the musicians, while the* CHORUS *exits by the hurry door,
and the stage is left bare.*)

D

THE DOLL THEATRE

THE Nō theatre enjoyed a revival after 1945 and continues to thrive. Playhouses in the larger cities give regularly scheduled weekly performances, and Nō plays have been presented on television. The doll theatre, on the contrary, has been slowly declining since the eighteenth century, shows no sign of regaining its former popularity, and survives today only in the Bunraku Theatre of Osaka, where the box-office has not paid the cost of production for some fifty years. The Bunraku troupe dates from 1845, when Uemura Bunraku opened a doll theatre in Osaka; the subsidizing of the theatre was taken over in 1909 by the Shochiku Company, the largest theatrical enterprise in the country. At its height in the eighteenth century the doll theatre had a popularity such as only films and television enjoy today, and it produced some of the greatest Japanese playwrights. When in the late nineteenth century the Japanese thought it necessary to produce a playwright comparable to Shakespeare, they found him in Chikamatsu Monzaemon (1653–1725), the most brilliant writer for the doll theatre. Despite its decline, the influence of the doll theatre remains considerable today. Its best plays are alive in the repertory of the Kabuki theatre, the foremost Kabuki actors continue to study the performance of the dolls, and the Bunraku Theatre has been declared a 'cultural property', subsidized and preserved by the Government.

Although in the fifteenth and sixteenth centuries the Japanese commoner, by paying an admission fee, could see an occasional performance of 'subscription' Nō and could probably understand a good deal of its complicated literary language, he had, strictly speaking, no formal theatre of his own. His other professional entertainers were strolling players—dancers, acrobats, puppeteers, and story-tellers—a sort of casual, street-corner amusement reminiscent of that which existed in Europe after the disappearance of the Roman theatre and before the rise of the liturgical drama. It was largely out of such materials that the doll theatre was fashioned at the end of the sixteenth century.

Writers of the ninth to the twelfth centuries mention travelling puppet-show operators, *kugutsu mawashi*, who were apparently foreigners and led a precarious existence. By the end of
the twelfth century, however, some of the puppet troupes had
become somewhat more respectable and were permanently
attached to shrines and temples, where, on festival days, they
gave performances dealing with religious history. At about the
same time another didactic religious form developed which had
rudimentary elements of drama. Sermons explaining Buddhist
doctrine, *sekkyō*, doubtless with the intent of attracting larger
audiences, introduced passages in dialogue, and eventually
added a musical accompaniment. As late as 1665 a theatre for
the performance of *sekkyō-bushi* (*sekkyō* music) was set up in Edo,
the present Tokyo. This combination of music, declamation,
and chant was very much like that of the Buddhist priests and
blind musicians who, at the end of the twelfth century, performed passages from historical romances, accompanying
themselves on the *biwa*, a four-stringed plucked instrument of
gentle, lute-like quality, shaped like the mandolin, which was
said to have been imported to Japan from China in 735. About
the middle of the fifteenth century appeared an increasingly
popular historical romance, *The Tale of Jōruri*, which was
eventually to supply the name for the vocal and musical elements of the doll theatre. Some time between 1558 and 1569
a new musical instrument, the three-stringed samisen, was
introduced to Japan and gradually supplanted the *biwa* in the
favour of the musician-reciters. The samisen, having greater
dynamic range and plangency than the *biwa*, made possible more
striking and dramatic effects in the performance of *The Tale of
Jōruri*, and so it happened that the word *jōruri* came to be used
to describe this style of narrative and dialogue declaimed and
sung to a samisen accompaniment.

It is not clear just when the puppets were added to *jōruri*,
but it is thought that puppet *jōruri* performances were given in
1596 in the city of Kyoto. Puppeteers from Kyoto went to Edo
in 1616 and afterwards and enjoyed great popularity there,
but towards the end of the seventeenth century the centre of
doll-theatre activity shifted to Osaka, some thirty miles from
Kyoto, where it has since remained. The great success of the

doll theatre in Osaka was due largely to the collaboration of two men: Takemoto Gidayū (1651–1714), so accomplished a *jōruri* performer that his name, *gidayū*, became another word for *jōruri*, and Chikamatsu Monzaemon, who was, in reality, the first unabashedly professional playwright in Japan. The Takemoto Theatre, the scene of their joint triumphs, was opened in 1684, and during that year played three previously-written *jōruri* by Chikamatsu. With *Kagekiyo Victorious* (1686), a play written by Chikamatsu especially for Takemoto, they began a series of constantly successful works, and three to five new *jōruri* by Chikamatsu were produced annually.

The puppets used by the *kugutsu mawashi* seem to have been crude clay figures operated from below like the contemporary Punch and Judy, the manipulators hidden by a curtain. Just when string-operated marionettes appeared has not been established; they are described as being 'common' in 1617 and continued to be used, by one troupe at least, well into the nineteenth century. But the marionettes, however widely they were used in the seventeenth century, were gradually supplanted after 1690 by hand-operated puppets, the kind used by those most influential in formulating the doll theatre. Satsuma Jōun, for example, who went from Kyoto to Edo and established a theatre there in 1635, used hand-operated puppets of wood in preference to the cruder ones of clay. His puppets did not have hands or feet, but these were added about 1690. Takeda Izumo of the Takemoto Theatre made improvements in the articulation of the arms and legs of the dolls, and their history thereafter is one of increasing mechanical refinement. The present-day doll, which attained its form around 1736, is about half life-size. It is not manipulated by strings in the fashion common in the West, though it is not quite accurate to say that the doll has no strings attached. Its chief manipulator, handsomely dressed in formal nineteenth-century costume, holds the doll up, and, standing behind it, operates a system of strings and pulleys concealed within the head to move the doll's mouth, eyebrows, and eyelids. In addition, he controls the right arm and the hand, which is also moved by hidden strings. His two assistants, both dressed in black, their faces covered, animate the rest of the doll. The one to the chief manipulator's left operates the left arm, and the one to the right the legs and feet. This practice of having the manipulators appear in full view of the audience dates from the first decade of the eighteenth century.

The earliest stage was no more than the box in which the puppets were carried. Some operators attached the box to the end of a pole which they stuck in the ground, so that they were free to stand behind the box and manipulate the puppets. The earliest theatre consisted simply of an area surrounded by a bamboo fence, within it a box-like structure with a head-height opening in which the dolls were displayed. The two *jōruri* performers, a chanter and a samisen player, occupied positions behind a curtain upstage of the operators and thus were hidden from the audience. There was no scenery in this theatre, but the dolls were brilliantly costumed. The curtain concealing the *jōruri* performers fell into disuse towards the end of the seventeenth century, although at this time the doll manipulators were still concealed. The *jōruri* performers remained in their position behind the dolls until 1728, when at the Takemoto Theatre they were seated at stage-left, the position they now occupy. Other theatres copied this practice. The reason for moving them was that more and more scenery was being introduced at this time and upstage space was needed to accommodate it. At the front of the stage, and extending the width of it, was placed a flat about 2½ feet high whose upper edge served to indicate the non-existent surface on which the dolls walked. The area upstage of this, in which the operators moved, was free of scenery, but the area directly behind it was used for interior, though floorless, settings. The operators thus used two distinct playing areas, the downstage one generally being used for exteriors. Another acting area, not used in the doll theatre before 1724, was the *hanamichi*, a narrow passageway between the rear of the auditorium and the stage, which was used for important entrances and exits. The *hanamichi* no longer exists in the doll theatre today, but it remains an important acting area in the Kabuki.

Since the doll theatre and the Kabuki appeared at about the same time and attracted the same audience (the increasingly wealthy commoners called 'townsmen'), their history during the seventeenth and eighteenth centuries is one of complicated interaction. Both had something of a common point of origin in their drawing freely on the Nō, using its music, plays, and methods of staging. When the Osaka doll theatre achieved its greatest brilliance in the first half of the eighteenth century, the Kabuki theatres of that city found it necessary for survival to imitate its popular innovations, and these in turn were adapted by the theatres of Edo, which from that time on were the stronghold of the Kabuki. The use of a scenic background, as opposed to the 'fictional things' used in the Nō and in the early Kabuki, was a doll-theatre innovation, introduced by Takeda Izumo after he became manager of the Takemoto Theatre in 1703. Between 1727 and 1758 appeared a remarkable variety of theatre machines in Osaka, among them the elevator stage in 1727, a trap-lift for actors in 1744, an elevator stage in three independent sections in 1757, the revolving stage in 1758. All these machines for producing spectacular scenic effects were taken over by the Kabuki theatre and are used today. The highly stylized, non-realistic movement of the dolls was adapted by the Kabuki actors, and it is possible that the static attitude, the *mie* (pronounced *mee-ay*), which is the Kabuki actors' most expressive moment, also derives from the doll theatre. On the other hand, the doll manipulators studied the movement of the living actors and introduced it into their performances. The samisen, essential to the performance of *jōruri*, was not used in the Kabuki until 1663, but thereafter it quickly became the basic musical instrument of the Kabuki and remains so today. Plays and plots were frequently exchanged. The love story of *Yūgiri and Izaemon* was first played as a Kabuki piece by the actor Sakata Tōjūrō (1647–1709) in 1678; in 1708 Chikamatsu wrote his *jōruri* on the same subject. The story of the death of Lord Asano and his revenge by his forty-seven faithful retainers was dramatized by the popular Kabuki actor Sawamura Sōjūrō (1689–1758) and played in Kyoto in 1747; Takeda Izumo saw the production, and the following year, with the help of two collaborating playwrights, presented his version, based obviously on Sawamura's play, copying the last act almost exactly, and using the stage business of the actors for the dolls.

The earliest doll-theatre plays were concerned with historical and quasi-historical matters, but towards the end of the seventeenth century the *jōruri* writers began to introduce into their pieces what can only be described as a love interest, which was in part derived from the contemporary Kabuki plays. The *jōruri* writer and performer Uji Kaga-no-jō (1635–1711) was considered to be the inventor of a new form of play in which material from the lives of the commoners was combined with the exaggerated exploits of historical characters. The desire of the commoner to see contemporary life on the stage gave rise, in 1688, to dramatizations of current events (*kiri-kyōgen*) and the popularity of idealized and romanticized portrayals of the townsman's affairs resulted in the 'domestic play' (*sewamono*) as a separate dramatic genre from the 'historical play' (*jidaimono*). Chikamatsu wrote both kinds of plays with equal success. His *The Battles of Coxinga* (1715), a piece compounded of history, legend, patriotism, and exoticism, broke all previous records by running for seventeen months at the Takemoto Theatre. In many ways the play is representative of the materials from which the 'historical' plays were fashioned, setting gory and improbable incidents beside complicated lyrical passages of great beauty, and requiring physical violence of a sort possible only when using non-human actors. Chikamatsu's success with *The Battles of Coxinga* was repeated in 1720 with a domestic play, *The Love Suicide at Amijima*, probably based, as were many of his domestic plays, on an actual occurrence. The play deals with a paper merchant, Jihei, whose love for a courtesan, Koharu, leads inevitably to their double suicide. The atmosphere of the play, when compared with that of *The Battles of Coxinga*, is one of striking, though obviously stylized, realism. This is no world of battles with tigers and gouging out of eyes, but one of business accounts, irate fathers-in-law, and medicine for the children. The *jōruri* is, of course, couched in highly literary language, the dolls move generally in stylized fashion, and the 'realism' of the performance is therefore wholly relative.

In 1703 the Government forbade the dramatization of current events, but it was concerned rather with forbidding plays in which the affairs of the warrior class might be held up to criticism than with restricting the use of innocuous materials drawn from the townsman's life. In 1723 it did, however, proscribe plays about double suicides, for an inordinate number of couples, seemingly prompted by the example of Chikamatsu's lovers, chose to imitate them. When dealing with current events in the lives of the samurai, the *jōruri* writers used the simple expedient of slightly changing the names of those involved and setting the incidents in the past. Thus the affair of Lord Asano and his forty-seven loyal followers, occurring in the years from 1700 to 1703, was set by the playwrights five centuries earlier with the names of the participants only slightly disguised.

Although the Japanese continue to speak of historical plays and domestic plays as distinct forms, many of the qualities of the domestic plays were introduced into the historical ones, and in the latter part of his career Chikamatsu rarely dealt with such bizarre, grotesque, and exaggerated materials as those of *The Battles of Coxinga*, nor did other *jōruri* writers. Commoners began to play important roles in historical plays, a love interest appeared in them, current events were anachronistically combined with remote history and legend, greater emphasis was placed upon the emotions of the individual than upon external event. The doll theatre was in the business of attracting as large an audience as possible, and its historical plays, like the present-day 'historical' film, provided something for everybody—spectacle, elaborate costuming, music, violence, amorous adventures—the *mélange* contriving to be at once thoroughly contemporary yet curiously remote and exotic.

Chikamatsu's successor as chief playwright at the Takemoto Theatre was Takeda Izumo, who had grown up in his father's doll theatre in Kyoto, where he was a manipulator of the dolls. Although he had managed the theatre after Takemoto Gidayū's retirement and was responsible for introducing scenic innovations, he did not turn to playwriting until 1723, when, in collaboration with Matsuda Bunkōdō, he wrote an historical *jōruri* which was edited by Chikamatsu. Takeda, like most of the doll-theatre and Kabuki playwrights of his time and later, collaborated with others in his compositions, and together with Miyoshi Shōraku and Namiki Senryū, he wrote in successive years three remarkable historical plays which have continued to be among the most popular pieces in the repertoires of both the doll theatre and the Kabuki: *The House of Sugawara* (1746), *A Thousand Cherry Trees* (1747), and *The Loyal Forty-seven Rōnin* (1748).[1]

The House of Sugawara, like the others, is an ingenious blend of legend, history, and contemporary event. Sugawara Michizane was an historical character born in 845. Coming from a respectable, though not outstanding family, he became its most illustrious member, achieving early fame through his great scholarship. Imitating the Chinese example, Japan at that time elevated its foremost scholars to positions in the Government, and Sugawara rose rapidly from an administrative assistant to governor of a province. His success in the post brought him to the attention of the Emperor Uda who installed him at the court in Kyoto, gave him important assignments, and consulted him on all significant matters. The friendship of Uda and Sugawara was further enhanced when Sugawara's eldest daughter was brought to the palace as *nyōgo*, the second wife of the Emperor. When, according to the custom of the time, Uda decided to abdicate the throne in favour of a son, he conferred with Sugawara upon his successor. The choice fell upon Uda's eldest son, who, in 898, ascended the throne at the age of thirteen as the Emperor Daigo. His father retired to a Buddhist monastery, ostensibly practising religious and artistic pursuits, but, in actuality, paying close attention to affairs of state. Shortly after Daigo's enthronement, and doubtless by Uda's doing, Sugawara was appointed Minister of the Right, an office superior to that of the Minister of the Left, which was held by Fujiwara Tokihira. No one who was not of royal blood or of illustrious family had attained so high a position in over two centuries. In 900 Uda secretly offered Sugawara an even more eminent post, that of Prime Minister (*kampaku*). Knowledge of the offer came to the powerful Fujiwara clan, and they decided that Sugawara would have to be got rid of.

The Fujiwara house, which had come into political

---

[1] The Japanese titles of these plays are *Sugawara Denju Tenarai Kagami, Yoshitsune Sembonzakura,* and *Kanadehon Chūshingura.*

prominence towards the end of the seventh century, was in
fact the real ruler of Japan. The Fujiwara gained their importance by a relatively simple device: they attached themselves to the Imperial Court and married their relatives to as
many members of the Imperial family as possible, with the result that none but the son of a Fujiwara woman could possibly
gain the throne. Towards the end of the ninth century the
position of the family was further strengthened by having a
Fujiwara occupy the office of Prime Minister. This person
could nominally be Minister either of the Right or the Left, but
his power was actually such that he was in complete command
of the Emperor, though he gave every external evidence of
being submissive to the Emperor's wishes. The twin facts of
Sugawara's daughter being second in rank only to the Empress
and of Sugawara having been offered a post traditionally
occupied by the Fujiwara were sufficient to outrage the clan.
Fujiwara Tokihira and his parents levelled various accusations
against Sugawara, the principal of which was that he plotted
to dethrone the present emperor, replacing him with Daigo's
younger brother, Tōkiyo, to whom one of Sugawara's daughters
was married. For centuries the Fujiwara had attained their
objectives by intrigue rather than violence; their opponents
were usually not killed, but persuaded to enter a monastery or
take up residence in a remote spot. They decided that Sugawara should be exiled to Dazaifu, a town on the island of
Kyūshū. Though he attempted to resist their demands, Daigo
was at last forced to submit to the Fujiwara, and in the first
month of 901 he issued a decree which stripped Sugawara of
all his positions and ordered his exile. When the retired
Emperor Uda heard of this, he set out for the palace, but the
Fujiwara had placed their guards at the entrance and refused
to admit him to his son. Sugawara left Kyoto under heavy
guard, taking with him into exile only a son and daughter. His
wife and his twenty-one other children remained in the capital.
At Dazaifu Sugawara lived quietly in the small Enoki temple
and occupied himself with writing poetry. In 903, after two
years of exile, he died.

The threat which the Fujiwara felt Sugawara offered them
seemed to disappear. Tokihira married his sister to the

Emperor, and the traditional power of the family appeared secure. But the Fujiwara failed to reckon with the power of superstition and the force of legend. A series of catastrophes began to afflict both the city of Kyoto and the Fujiwara, and these were widely interpreted to be caused by the angered spirit of Sugawara. The spirits of the dead had a way, in those times, of appearing to Buddhist priests, and monks occasionally made journeys to the other world, where they saw Sugawara and returned to report upon his condition and his intentions. In 908 there were exceptionally violent thunderstorms in Kyoto, and the story spread that Sugawara, having become the god of thunder, was beginning to take his vengeance. It was said that during a storm the enraged spirit of Sugawara appeared to the terrified Tokihira, who died the following year. In the 920s and 930s there were further disasters. Royal children died almost annually; there were storms, droughts, epidemics; lightning struck the palace, and many died in the ensuing fire. The Emperor, apparently believing these prodigies to be the work of the vengeful Sugawara, destroyed the decree banishing Sugawara, abdicated the throne in 930, and died shortly thereafter. Messages from the other world regularly reported Sugawara's increasing strength and divinity. He had now become a god, and the Fujiwara, wishing to placate him, contributed to the building of temples erected in his honour. The principal of these temples was built in the north-west section of Kyoto, where Sugawara was deified under the name of the god Tenjin. The Sugawara cult spread rapidly. Shrines were established throughout the country, and Tenjin became the patron deity of calligraphy, scholarship, schoolchildren, and the city of Osaka, the latter office making him a likely subject for a play at the Takemoto Theatre. (Chikamatsu had written a play called *The Chronicle of Tenjin* [*Tenjinki*] in 1713.) In Japan there was, and still is, a close connexion between art, poetry, and calligraphy, for the writing of the language becomes a graphic art in its own right; consequently, the matter of Sugawara's selection in the play of the heir to his style of calligraphy was, even to the meanest member of the audience, a subject of great moment.

Another widely known aspect of Sugawara's historical and legendary character utilized by the playwrights was his love of trees, in particular the three trees which he cultivated in his gardens and which in Japan have the greatest poetic value— the pine, the plum, and the cherry. After his banishment, Sugawara wrote poems of regret and farewell to each, poems which today are commonly known in Japan. The cherry-tree (*sakura*), deprived of its master, withered and died in his absence. The plum-tree (*ume*), adjured in a poem not to forget Sugawara, uprooted itself and flew miraculously to its master in distant Dazaifu. Sugawara then, in poetry, gently reprimanded the pine (*matsu*), pointing out that the cherry-tree had died in sorrow, the plum had flown to his side, but that the pine had shown no such love for him. Thereupon the pine, following the example of the plum, followed its master into exile. It was the belief that a grove of pine-trees had suddenly and miraculously appeared in the north-west of Kyoto which prompted the building of the temple dedicated to Sugawara on that spot. The legend of the flying plum and the flying pine was made the subject of the Nō play *Oimatsu* (*The Pine Which Followed*). Sugawara's love of his trees and his poems about them were, of course, well known to the audiences of the Takemoto Theatre. The playwrights happily hit upon a way of taking dramatic advantage of this knowledge and giving it a contemporary piquancy. Shortly before the play was written, an Osaka woman had given birth to triplets. This was such an unusual event in Japan that it was talked of throughout the country, and the mother was honoured by the Government. Takeda combined the legend of the trees with the well-known triplets by inventing triplet brothers with the names of plum, pine, and cherry as retainers of Sugawara, and their fates in the play follow the pattern of their poetic, legendary, arboreal prototypes.

The ideological basis of the play, its concern with loyalty to Sugawara and the extraordinary sacrifices made to maintain it, is a typical anachronistic imposition by the playwrights of contemporary attitudes upon the tenth century. The idea that the warrior should display unquestioning fidelity to his master appears in the earliest Japanese writings, but its influence was confined, naturally, to those for whom military pursuits were a way of life. The Fujiwara, as has been suggested, held their power by cleverness rather than by military prowess and standing armies. When a rebellious chieftain in an outlying province became unruly, the prestige of the Fujiwara and the court honours they could award were sufficient to gain them the services of a military clan in the vicinity to quell the disturbance. But by about 1100 the military clans had become a strongly consolidated class, increasingly conscious of their power, while the Fujiwara grew progressively weaker. The shift in actual power grew out of a complicated web of economics, land-holdings, and clan affiliations, but shortly after the middle of the twelfth century the strength of the Fujiwara had disappeared and two strong military clans had emerged— the Taira, to which Koremochi of *The Maple Viewing* belonged, and the Minamoto. The rivalry of the two clans, which had adherents in every part of the country, culminated in epic battles in 1156 and 1160, and in the decisive one at Dannoura in 1185, which established the superiority of the Minamoto and gave Japan what is probably its most fertile source of literary materials. From that time on, until 1868, the rulers of Japan (*shōgun*) were in essence military dictators, though the emperors, however neglected and impoverished, continued to be treated as the traditional heads of the country. Japan was again involved in intermittent war between military clans throughout the sixteenth century, and at the conclusion of this great civil conflict the victors were the Tokugawa, descendants of the Minamoto line, who occupied the office of *shōgun* from 1603 to 1867.

Under the Tokugawa the code of the warrior, stressing fidelity, obedience, sacrifice, and hierarchy, which in previous times had been an admirable method of instilling unswerving loyalty in troops, gradually gained wider circulation, became in varying degrees the ethical code of the commoners as well as the warriors, and was one of the means by which the Tokugawa ensured their ascendancy. This code was not, of course, one which governed society at the time when Sugawara lived, but when *The House of Sugawara* was written it constituted the constant ethical framework of historical plays. Thus in the play

Sakuramaru is required to take his life in 'apology' for having unwittingly contributed to Sugawara's exile, and Matsuōmaru, his brother, makes his heroic sacrifice to save the life of Sugawara's son because of his sense of 'obligation'. The life of the townsman throughout the Tokugawa period was increasingly dominated by governmental efforts to maintain the social hierarchy, and, judging by the admittedly idealized picture of the townsman in the contemporary plays, the code of the warrior, now become a kind of ethical propaganda designed to ensure the social stability possible when social obligations were carefully defined, gradually came to be part of the ideological framework of even the domestic plays which dealt with the townsman's life. Strictly speaking, the three brothers in *The House of Sugawara* are commoners, and their story was apparently of more interest to the contemporary audience than that of Sugawara himself, who, about half-way through the play, ceases to play an active role.

The play, like others of the contemporary doll theatre, established its rapport with the audience, one might say, in depth, glamorizing commonly-known history and giving it a contemporary feeling, using a touch of the supernatural, which seems always to delight Japanese audiences, romanticizing the behaviour of the commoner, and providing, towards the end of the play, scenes of the utmost pathos, which then and now wring tears from the most hard-hearted in the audience. The curious aspect of all this, to the Westerner, is that this effect was and is achieved through the highly stylized medium of the doll theatre, with the manipulators in sight of the audience, the lines of the characters spoken by the *jōruri* performer, their thoughts also revealed by him. In the West the marionette theatre has never been seriously considered, except by a handful of people, an important form of dramatic expression, but rather something suitable for the amusement of children. This attitude seems engrained in foreigners, for it is not unusual to see a foreign couple in Japan taking their small children to the Bunraku Theatre, having heard, doubtless, about the marionette plays, and determined to give the children a jolly afternoon. After an hour or so they leave in bewilderment, if not in anger, at not having seen the Japanese version of a Punch and Judy show.

It is scarcely surprising, however, that a nation which created the Nō theatre, where the actor moves, gestures, and speaks within an aesthetic system which controls him like a marionette, should also create a theatre in which the stylized activity of dolls is the centre of visual interest. A high degree of stylization and a consequent avoidance of realistic reproduction is common to all forms of Japanese art. The invention of the camera, for example, had no such far-reaching effects upon native Japanese art as it had upon the graphic arts of the West, where the photograph for the first time freed painting from its chore as a medium of representation and permitted it to deal with less realistic expression. Until modern times Japanese artists have rarely voiced an opinion about the non-realistic quality of their work; there was, in fact, little or no motivation to do so, for this quality was traditionally inherent and seemed a prerequisite to any artistic statement. When someone, an untypical Japanese surely, presented the argument to Chikamatsu that plays should be realistic and that Kabuki actors should look as much like real people as possible, Chikamatsu replied:

Your view seems like a plausible one, but it is a theory which does not take into account the methods of art. Art is something which lies in the slender margin between the real and the unreal, . . . if one makes an exact copy of a living being, . . . one will become disgusted with it. Thus, if when one paints an image or carves it of wood there are, in the name of artistic licence, some stylised parts in a work otherwise resembling the real form; this is, after all, what people love in art. The same is true of literary composition. While bearing resemblance to the original, it should have stylisation; this makes it art, and is what delights men's minds.[1]

[1] Donald Keene, *The Battles of Coxinga; Chikamatsu's Puppet Play, Its Background and Importance*, London, 1951, pp. 95–96. The author translates Chikamatsu's words from Hozumi Ikan, *Naniwa Miyage*, ed. Ueda Kazutoshi (Tokyo, 1904).

An attitude not unlike Chikamatsu's has also been stated in the West: '. . . in all imitation two elements must coexist, and not only coexist, but must be perceived as coexisting. These two constituent elements are likeness and unlikeness, or sameness and difference, and in all genuine works of art there must be a union of these disparates. . . . If there be a likeness to nature without any check of difference, the result is disgusting, and the more complete the delusion, the more loathesome the effect.' Coleridge, 'On Poesy or Art,' 1818 Lectures, Lecture XIII.

Gordon Craig is one of the few Westerners who has made a plea for the artistic validity of the marionette. He contends that the theatre can never become an art until the actor forsakes realism and becomes as controlled an object as the marionette. His arguments are based on the idea that art is created by design out of 'calculable' materials, and that the human being, 'at the mercy of the winds of his emotions', is not one of these materials. Craig holds that acting will be an art only when it has worked out a system of 'symbolic gesture', a kind of rigid choreographic vocabulary of movement which allows no possibility for the observer to be 'swamped by the personality, the emotion' of the actor, a control of the kind, one gathers, to which the Nō actor is subjected. It seems a pity that Craig did not know the doll theatre of Japan at first hand, for he would have found in it an artistic control of the 'actor' such as he never dreamed of. The genesis of the performance is in the 'libretto', the script placed on the stand of the narrator-singer. At his side is the samisen performer, playing a constant accompaniment to lines and narration, and maintaining the closest rhythmical accord with the *jōruri* performer. On the stage are the manipulators of the dolls, three, usually, to each of them, the men's movement growing out of the samisen music and the *jōruri* and synchronized to the ultimate degree with that of each other. The doll is the ultimate recipient of the force of this delicately balanced ensemble, and the perfection of its stylized movement and gesture derives from the interacting power and control of five men, working within a predetermined and exact form. The winds of individual emotion which Craig finds inimical to art cannot blow in this environment to agitate the inanimate figure which embodies a character. There is no room for accident, no possibility of the personality of an actor being confused with that of the character, no escape from the living mechanism which has given the doll its theatrically controlled existence.

The French playwright Paul Claudel, who served as ambassador to Japan, greatly admired the doll theatre for much the same reasons that Craig admired the marionette:

The living actor, whatever his talent, always bothers us by mingling an extraneous element with the fictional drama he

E

embodies, something from actuality and from daily life; he remains always a person falsified. The marionette, on the other hand, has no life or movement except that which it derives from the action [of the play]. It takes on life under the influence of the recitative; it is like a shade which is brought back to life by being told all it has done and which little by little changes from a memory to a being. It is not an actor who speaks, it is speech which acts. The figure of wood embodies personification. It floats in a vague region between the action and the words. The audience sees in it all that the narrator declaims at his desk, supported by the samisen, that instrument which vibrates like plucked nerves, and by the companion at his side who by his inarticulate cries and his outbursts makes evident not only the emotions of the scene, but the desire to exist, the effort of the imaginary being to live again. The marionette is like a ghost. Its feet do not touch the earth. It cannot be touched and it cannot touch anything. Its whole life, its whole movement comes from the heart—and from this mysterious conclave of animators behind it, masked or not, this collective destiny of which it is the expression. The dramatic expression has been split up so cleverly that the story takes place entirely in imagination and reverie, without the aid of any disenchanting materiality. By other means the *Jōruri* achieves the same results as the *Nō*.[1]

The exquisite control of the doll theatre, the element which binds together the composite efforts of narrators, musicians, and doll manipulators and assures their artistic calculations, is delicately balanced and subtly shared rhythm.

The House of Sugawara: The play is never performed today in its entirety either in the doll theatre or in the Kabuki, for the occasional 'complete' production invariably omits several of the scenes, particularly the final one, in which the spirit of Sugawara, in the guise of thunder and lightning, descends upon the Imperial Palace and destroys the villains of the piece. The original script is in five acts, the traditional form for Japanese plays from about 1675, each act consisting of several scenes. Of the scenes omitted in the present version, the only one which is not omitted in Japan, and is frequently performed independently from the rest of the play, is that called 'Pulling the Carriage Apart' ('Kurumabiki'), which would be placed, in the

---

[1] Translated from Claudel's letter to Tsunao Miyajima in the latter's *Théâtre Japonais de Poupées*, Troisième Edition (Osaka, 1931).

present arrangement, between Acts Two and Three. The scene
is mostly dance and has little dramatic content. In it Sakuramaru and Umeōmaru confront their brother, quarrel with him
in dance, and are vanquished by the forbidding aspect of
Shihei. The incident is referred to here in Act III, Scene i.
The last scene of the present version, 'The Village School', is
one of the best-loved and most frequently played passages in
Japanese dramatic literature, so well known that it is never
rehearsed. In the doll theatre all the lines of the characters are,
of course, read by the narrator-singer; in the Kabuki the
majority of the lines are read by the actors, unless they are
engaged in dance movement. The passages here assigned to a
chorus are those which are performed by the narrator in the
Kabuki. The stage directions are derived from both doll-
theatre and Kabuki contemporary performances, as well as
from the first production of this script in English.

THE HOUSE OF SUGAWARA

(Sugawara Denju Tenarai Kagami)

A play written for the doll theatre by

TAKEDA IZUMO, MIYOSHI SHŌRAKU, AND NAMIKI SENRYŪ

(1746)

Translated by Albert Miyasato and Shigeru Yamaguchi
English version by Louis M. Steed aud Earle Ernst

ACT I

The curtain rises to sacred music. The scene is a bank of the Kamo River. On stage-left is a court carriage, an ox harnessed to it.

SHIROMATA *and* KUROMATA, *low servants, have been drinking* sake *from a rice bowl. Since* sake *is usually sipped from small cups, both are somewhat drunk.*

SHIROMATA (*excessively polite*). Come now, Kuromata, have a drink!

KUROMATA (*equally polite*). Oh, no, Shiromata, you drink first!

SHIROMATA. No, no, no, Kuromata! You first.

(KUROMATA *again declining,* SHIROMATA *begins to drink. At that,* KUROMATA *snatches the bowl from him and drinks himself.*)

KUROMATA (*wiping his mouth*). Ah! The more *sake* I drink, the better the scenery looks.

SHIROMATA (*looks offstage, starts in terror, then relaxes*). I thought I saw Kiyotsura coming! (*In drunken confidence.*) Kuromata! Our master, the honourable Shihei, is short-tempered, but he is by nature generous. Whereas his representative Kiyotsura is not only short-tempered, but also by nature a son of a bitch. We'd better not get caught.

KUROMATA (*frightened*). Hey, don't say such a thing about our master. It's Prince Tokiyo, the representative for Lord Sugawara, who is really a bastard. (*Shakes his head.*) I don't understand it. Lord Sugawara makes such a man his pupil and sends him to the shrine as his representative.

SHIROMATA (*pondering it, mysteriously*). There must be some reason we don't know.

(*They nod solemnly in agreement.*)

KUROMATA (*suddenly*). Let's drink. (*They do.*) Prince Tokiyo was seen at the shrine, so Sakuramaru should be coming along pretty soon.

(*There is sacred shrine music, and* SAKURAMARU *enters wearing the formal dress of a warrior.*)

SAKURAMARU (*disgruntled at their being there*). So this is where you are!

KUROMATA *and* SHIROMATA (*in unison; not concealing their dislike of him*). Oh, it's you, Sakuramaru. We were just talking about you!

SAKURAMARU. I see you're enjoying your *sake*. The ceremony is already half over. Don't you think you'd better go before you're called?

55

KUROMATA (*suspiciously*). Sakuramaru, what d'you mean *we* should go? It's you who should go, because once the ceremony's over, your prince will be leaving first. What are *you* doing here?

SAKURAMARU (*at a loss*). Oh . . . well . . . ah . . . (*He improvises.*) My prince is resting at the shrine-keeper's house, and I don't know how long he'll be there. But your representative seemed anxious about some business at the Imperial Court. You'd better hurry if you don't want to be scolded.

SHIROMATA. Eh! You're right. (*Gloating.*) There's a difference between a prince with no office and the busy Kiyotsura who is the representative of the honourable Shihei.

SAKURAMARU. Certainly, certainly.

KUROMATA and SHIROMATA (*in unison*). I guess we'd better be going.

SAKURAMARU. Hurry up!

(*Music, as* KUROMATA *and* SHIROMATA *exit hurriedly.* SAKURAMARU *intently watches them leave.*)

SAKURAMARU. That did it! There they go!

CHORUS. He claps his hands in signal.
 Then comes the gentle Princess Kariya,
 A young lover, shy and hesitant,
 Her beauty like spring perfume on the air.
 And following her, the charming Yae,
 Beloved wife of Sakuramaru.
 These loyal servants have arranged
 The meeting of the Princess
 And he who loves her,
 The Prince Tokiyo.

(*During this,* PRINCESS KARIYA *appears on the* hanamichi, *followed by* YAE. *They move to the stage.*)

YAE. My good husband, is everything arranged?

SAKURAMARU. Of course, of course. Welcome, Princess. (*She hides her face with her sleeve.*) Now, now, don't be so shy. A countenance more stately than that of the Buddha will soon appear before you.

(SAKURAMARU *raises the bamboo blind of the carriage. Within is* PRINCE TOKIYO, *magnificently dressed.*)

CHORUS. As the blind of the carriage is lifted,
 The Princess sees the bashful face of the Prince.
 A glance at him,
 And she must hide her blushes
 In her flowing sleeve.

SAKURAMARU. My good wife, it's too bad they're not lowly people like us. They're just too noble to be indiscreet. If they could only have a moment of complete darkness!

YAE. But that's easily done, even in broad daylight. Look! (*She points meaningfully at the carriage.*)

SAKURAMARU. Yae, you're smart! If they let down the blind of the carriage . . . (*Before he can finish,* YAE *pushes him as a hint that he should leave. Awkwardly.*) Well, I think I'll go to take a rest for a while. (*He leaves.*)

YAE. Be off, be off. Men are a nuisance at a time like this. Come, Princess, you can be quite at ease now. (*Pause.*) If you have anything to say, say it now. (*Pause.*) Go ahead.

CHORUS. Even though beside her lover,
　　　　Overcome by the joy of her first love,
　　　　Not a word could she say.

YAE (*more and more urgently*). Oh, Princess! This short spring day will soon be over. You're not the first one to feel like this! Look, Sakuramura has gone, and even I'm faced the other way. Hurry, hurry, and say something, anything.

KARIYA (*after a pause*). I was both happy and thankful when I received your long answer to my note, and you asked me to come at the first opportunity. I have been anxiously awaiting this opportunity, and now I have come as bidden.

TOKIYO (*shy and embarrassed*). Sakuramaru has been very useful. (*Pause.*) With each day my desire to see you has been greater. (*Pause.*) I'm very happy you are here. (*Pause.*) But we are so near the river. Don't you find the spring breeze cold?

CHORUS (*tongue in cheek*). This tender inquiry
　　　　　　　Filled her with a delicate passion
　　　　　　　That made her forget
　　　　　　　The chill spring breeze.

　　(SAKURAMARU *suddenly jumps up from behind the carriage.*)

SAKURAMARU (*exasperated*). In heaven's name, wife! Do something!

YAE (*suddenly inspired*). My, it's cold. Brrrrr. Princess, you must be cold there. (*A happy idea.*) But fortunately, as protection against the chilly wind, you can take shelter in the carriage.

KARIYA (*horrified*). But, Yae, it is a sacred court carriage. It wouldn't be right if I——

YAE (*pushing* KARIYA *into the carriage*). This is no time for scruples! Get in, get in, get in, get in!

CHORUS. By this skilful manœuvre of Yae,
　　　　The interior of the sacred court carriage
　　　　Was at once
　　　　Transformed
　　　　To a setting for tender love.

SAKURAMARU. Thank heavens, you got her in.

(He lowers the blind. Sacred shrine music accompanied by samisen. YAE *keeps careful watch in all directions.)*

TOKIYO. Come a little closer, Princess Kariya.

KARIYA. Won't the wrath of the gods fall upon us for being in this sacred carriage?

(While YAE *is looking the other way,* SAKURAMARU *creeps up to her and kisses her.)*

YAE *(giggling)*. Now, now, control yourself.

SAKURAMARU. Yae, how can I, with all this going on?

YAE. Hush, hush, not so loud. You'll be heard!

SAKURAMARU. Who cares?

YAE. But we might attract attention.

SAKURAMARU. What of it?

YAE. But what if someone comes along?

(During the foregoing, YAE *has been cuddling up to* SAKURAMARU. *Now she kisses him, using her sleeve to hide their faces. At this moment, the ox gives a great bellow. They jump apart in surprise.)*

SAKURAMARU *(laughing)*. I think the ox is jealous. *(A glance at the carriage.)* Congratulations, my dear. You've done a marvellous job!

YAE. Oh, it was nothing. I just followed your instructions. I dressed as a court lady and went to Princess Kariya. When I said I was Sakuramaru's wife, Yae, she said, 'I've been expecting you. Shall we go now?' Then she sent her ladies-in-waiting off, and we slipped out the back way.

SAKURAMARU. I had no trouble either. These last few days, Lord Sugawara has not left his study: he's preparing to give his secrets of the art of calligraphy to one of his pupils. Since I haven't been busy, I asked Lady Sugawara for a few hours of freedom to visit the shrine. And the servants—I bribed them with *sake*. Oh, that reminds me. *(Indicating the carriage.)* They'll probably be thirsty and need a drink.

YAE. The idea of such a thing! They're two pure, innocent souls.

SAKURAMARU. Hmmm. Don't be so naïve.

YAE *(giggles)*. Well . . . I'll get some water from the river. *(She starts off.)*

SAKURAMARU *(with mock concern)*. Oh, don't go there. The river bank is slippery from the rain. Suppose you fell and got hurt. What would I do if such a thing happened?

YAE. Oh, you! *(Thinks a moment.)* But there isn't any other water.

SAKURAMARU *(a sudden idea)*. You can get some of the sacred water from the shrine.

YAE. Why of course! The sacred water. *(Stops abruptly.)* Oh, why can't you be more reverent! The idea of using the sacred water!

SAKURAMARU. It's perfectly all right. Nine virtues has God and ten virtues has the Emperor. Now since the Prince is the younger brother of the Emperor, the Prince must have nine virtues—just like God. Go and get the sacred water.

YAE (*with exaggerated ceremoniousness*). Yes, dear, I'll go and get the water.

SAKURAMARU (*in the same tone*). Thank you very much, dear wife.

YAE. It's quite all right.

(*She goes off, and* SAKURAMARU *sits down before the carriage*.)

CHORUS. Just as Sakuramaru is relaxing
    After this trying experience,
    (*Violently*.) There comes the follower of Shihei,
    There comes Miyoshi no Kiyotsura,
    Accompanied by his guards.

(KIYOTSURA *wears white hunting attire*. FOUR GUARDS *follow him*.)

KIYOTSURA (*belligerently*). So there you are, Sakuramaru! I know you escorted the Prince Tokiyo from the shrine even before the ceremony was finished. What have you done with him?

SAKURAMARU (*insolently*). How should one of lowly rank know the actions of a lordly personage? Why not look for him in a more likely place?

KIYOTSURA. Don't try to fool me! I've heard of your shady dealings in the past. Today, when prayers are being offered for the speedy recovery of our Emperor, acts defiling the shrine, even though committed by the Prince, will meet with severe punishment. If you don't speak, we'll get the truth out of you by torture. Men, tie him up!

GUARDS. As you say, sir.

(*They move towards him, and he rises*.)

SAKURAMARU. Once I say I don't know, I don't know.

KIYOTSURA. Impudent scoundrel, stop your acting. (*To guards*.) The carriage looks suspicious. Tear off the blind!

GUARDS. Yes, sir.

(*They rush at* SAKURAMARU, *who strikes a pose and glares at them*.)

SAKURAMARU. I, Sakuramaru, am responsible for this carriage. Stay away if you love your lives.

KIYOTSURA. Boaster! We'll fix you.

(*There ensues a dance in which fighting is mimed in conventional attitudes and movements*.)

CHORUS. Sakuramaru, seizing a spear,
    Falls upon his attackers savagely
    And beats them away.

(KIYOTSURA *and the* GUARDS *flee from the stage,* SAKURAMARU *following them.*)

CHORUS. The Prince and the Princess,
          Fearful of being discovered,
          Leave the carriage.
          In their confusion,
          In the rashness of their youth,
          They start on an aimless journey.

(TOKIYO *and* KARIYA *exit hand in hand. A pause, and* KIYOTSURA *returns and looks into the carriage.*)

KIYOTSURA. I was wrong. (*A frightening notion.*) When Sakuramaru comes back, he'll be angry. I'd better leave. (*He starts off, hesitates, then goes the other way.*)

CHORUS. Off goes Kiyotsura.
          A moment later, Sakuramaru comes running back.
          He is shocked at the disappearance of the two.
          Then he finds a note left by the Prince.

(SAKURAMARU *picks up* TOKIYO's *fan, on which a message has been written.*)

SAKURAMARU. What? 'Rather than be discovered and cause a scandal, we will leave.'

CHORUS. Shocked and bewildered,
          Sakuramaru stands frozen to the spot.

SAKURAMARU. I must go after them. They need my protection.

(*As* SAKURAMARU *runs on to the* hanamichi, YAE *appears carrying a wooden pail.*)

YAE. Here you are. I've got the water.

SAKURAMARU. Don't bother with water now. Kiyotsura came snooping around, and now the Prince and Princess have disappeared.

YAE (*dropping the pail*). What! Where could they have gone?

SAKURAMARU. I don't know, but I have an idea. The Princess is an adopted daughter of Sugawara, but her real mother lives in Kawachi. That's a likely place for them to go. Take the carriage back to the Prince's palace. It may cause trouble if we leave it here.

YAE. Certainly, certainly. I'll masquerade as you. (*She takes his white jacket and puts it over her shoulders.*) Go immediately. I'll take care of it.

(SAKURAMARU *runs from the* hanamichi.)

CHORUS. Yae impatiently prods the ox.
          Pull as she may,
          Urge as she may,

The ox
Just plods
Lazily along.
YAE. Ohhh! This is maddening!
CHORUS. Every day that passes may bring news of failure.
Oh, will this day be a fatal day for the couple?
'A day of darkness for my husband?'

Praying to God for forgiveness,
She beseeches Him to crown them with happiness.

But the ox,
The spotted, stubborn ox,
The ox
Just plods
Lazily
Along.

CURTAIN

ACT I

SCENE II

A handsome room in the castle of LORD SUGAWARA. *The upstage wall consists of beautifully painted sliding doors. At the centre of the stage,* MAREYO *sits at a writing-desk.*

CHORUS. There are three essentials to success:
Natural ability, practice, and interest.
And of these, interest is the key to proficiency.
This is an adage for students of the arts.
Lord Sugawara, the foremost calligrapher of his day,
Spent all his time between official duties
Pursuing the art of calligraphy.
Court nobles, servants, samurai, merchants,
From all classes,
Students flocked to his school of calligraphy.

So great was the art of Sugawara
That his Imperial Majesty suggested
The art should not die with him
But be transmitted to his most gifted pupil.

Seven days have passed, and now
Mareyo, one of the most advanced pupils,

Sits before his writing-desk at break of day,
Egotistically thinking it a matter of time
Before he will receive the secret art.
Boisterously he demands tobacco and tea,
To the utter despair of the chambermaids.

(MAREYO *is unpleasant and lecherous. He claps his hands impatiently, and* KOSHIJI *appears in haste,* KATSUNO *following her.*)

KOSHIJI (*calling offstage*). Isn't there anyone there? Master Mareyo is demanding service.

MAREYO (*domineering*). Well, it's about time, Koshiji! I've been clapping until my hands are sore, and yet you ignore me! Do you find my daily presence such a nuisance? I've been here for seven days, but I tell you I'm not here merely for my own good. Kan Shūsai, our master's son, is only a child and cannot be entrusted with the secret art at this time. But after he is of age I will impart the secret art to him. So you see, in serving me you will really be serving the lord, our master.

KOSHIJI (*placating him*). Take notice, Katsuno. I'm being held responsible for your inattention. Please be more careful hereafter. All that is required is that you be obedient at all times. Isn't that so, Master Mareyo?

MAREYO (*fatuously*). Certainly! That's very good advice. Trials and tribulations day after day, all for the sake of the house of Sugawara. Koshiji, will you please present my finished copy to the master?

KOSHIJI. Please, not again! Let me off today!

MAREYO (*shrilly*). Why?

KOSHIJI. Well . . . Lord Sugawara has not been satisfied with your work. (*Hastily.*) The fault is really not yours, but rather the way I present your copies to him. (*Brightly.*) So today we'll have Katsuno do it.

MAREYO. Katsuno! That would be sacrilege! Since Lord Sugawara has been fasting, his study has been converted into a sacred place. How could I send a sensual woman like her? Now he may not have been satisfied with my past work, but this copy is quite extraordinary. This one is radiant with the life which flows from my body through the tip of my brush. Now, please do me the favour of presenting it to him.

CHORUS. Not having the heart to refuse,
Koshiji reluctantly consents.

(MAREYO *carefully watches* KOSHIJI *as she leaves.*)

MAREYO (*rubbing his hands*). Now, Katsuno, I hope you understand the significance of Koshiji's advice about being obedient.

KATSUNO (*a wide-eyed innocent*). Yes, I do.

MAREYO. Well, that's fine! Fortunately there is no one around. Come. Let's go behind that screen and have some most interesting amusement.

(*He seizes her, and she attempts to fight him off.*)

KATSUNO. Don't! Don't behave so horribly, or I'll scream!

MAREYO. Scream if you like. I'm so desperate for you I've lost all discretion. Come now, don't resist me. (*He chases her about.*)

KATSUNO (*loudly*). Help! Help!

MAREYO. Who do you think will hear you?

KATSUNO. Lady Sugawara will hear me. Help! Help!

(MAREYO *seizes her again.*)

CHORUS. Help! Help!
Echoes of the frantic cries
Resound through the halls,
As Lady Sonō, wife of Sugawara, appears,
Leading her young son by the hand.

(LADY SONŌ, *gracious, aristocratic, warm, appears just as* MAREYO *is about to kiss* KATSUNO. *Her child,* KAN SHŪSAI, *is a boy of seven.*)

MAREYO (*talking rapidly*). Lady Sonō. I hardly expected you to honour me with your presence. What you just saw was simply one of my attempts to cure Katsuno's hiccups. I'm a jack of all trades. My very name, Mareyo, signifies that I am gifted with rare intelligence and aptitudes. Just as the young prince is intelligent beyond his years. Take his name, Kan Shūsai: *shū* means to excel, *sai* means intelligence, and *kan* signifies the family name. There you have it. Perhaps I'm too talented for my own good. I hope you don't object to my playing the part of a masseur.

SONŌ. There is really no need for apologies. I'm quite familiar with your daily conduct.

CHORUS (*ironically*). A most magnanimous and tactful reply.

MAREYO. Well, I'm relieved to hear that. (*Advancing towards her in an insinuating manner.*) By the way, may I ask what happened to the Princess Kariya? I've heard rumours that she has had a scandalous affair with Prince Tokiyo, and that she has been gone from the household for seven days. Although I thought the rumour to be just idle talk, I visited her quarters and found she has not been there. And since nothing has been done about her absence, can it possibly be that she has eloped—with your consent?

CHORUS. Confused by this embarrassing question
Lady Sonō cannot immediately answer.

SONŌ (*sits*). It seems pointless to keep the secret any longer. It is a pity that the helpless Princess is the target of public ridicule, and that Prince Tokiyo must wander about, unable to return to his palace for fear of being punished. No doubt there will be a searching party for the Prince, organized by his own worried servants. As for our daughter, her mother by birth is Kakuju of Kawachi, who is also the aunt of Lord Sugawara. We adopted her before the birth of Kan Shūsai. Knowing that she would be unable to return to the palace, I secretly dispatched a messenger and learned that she had gone to Kawachi, the place of her birth. I have purposely withheld knowledge of this scandal from my husband. Since he received the Imperial message concerning the secret art of calligraphy, he has confined himself to his study for the past seven days. He is completely ignorant of what has been happening outside. I am afraid he will be terribly upset when he hears of this scandal. Please try to understand my predicament.

CHORUS. In these circumstances,
    A foster mother seeking sympathy
    Is understandable.
    At this moment a servant enters.

SERVANT. Madam.

SONŌ. Yes?

SERVANT. After a frantic search we have finally found Takebe Genzō, who was formerly a member of this household. As directed by the master, he is now here, accompanied by his wife. Shall they be brought to you?

SONŌ. Let them come at once. I have been anxiously awaiting them.

SERVANT. Yes, madam.

    (*He leaves.*)

SONŌ. Run along now, Kan Shūsai. Go in and play with Katsuno. Mareyo, if you don't mind. . . .

MAREYO (*insulted*). I understand, Lady Sonō. I'll go where I won't be in the way.

CHORUS. They leave the room,
    But curious Mareyo goes unwillingly.

    (*Music.* GENZŌ *and* TONAMI *appear at the end of the* hanamichi, *he first.*)

CHORUS. Four years ago, Takebe Genzō
    Fell in love and married Tonami.
    In doing so, he incurred his master's displeasure
    And was banished forever from the house of Sugawara.
    With him went his wife,
    To share his fate as a masterless retainer
    In the depths of poverty and deprivation.

Now, at his former master's summons,
Genzō comes. Remembering his past conduct,
Which broke the code of a loyal retainer,
He anxiously approaches his former home.
And when he sees his former mistress
He instantly bows in reverence.

(GENZŌ *and* TONAMI *bow from the* hanamichi.)

SONŌ. It gives me great pleasure to see both of you again. Four long years have passed since my husband banished you from the palace. Unfortunately, he is still as strict in obedience to his code as he is compassionate in other ways. But it must be pleasing that he has summoned you.

GENZŌ. We are deeply grateful, Lady Sonō.

SONŌ. Come, come now, don't be so stiff and formal. Come closer and let us talk together.

(*Music. They move to the stage and bow before her.*)

SONŌ. Oh, how you have changed, even in the clothing you wear. It is a pity to see you, Genzō, as you are now. But Tonami, your embroidered silk is beautiful. I must commend you on preserving your delicate taste even in such trying circumstances.

CHORUS. Showered with these words of kindness,
Tonami sheds tears of gratitude.

TONAMI. O my mistress, we do not deserve these kind words. After betraying the trust of our master, it is only proper that we should suffer. In the first days we suffered untold agonies, watching our beautiful clothing being transformed into our daily meals. But even in our most trying days, when I had to sell my tortoise-shell comb, I couldn't bear to part with this dress, which I treasure as a token of your kindness. Otherwise, even the clothes my husband wears have been rented for the occasion. Oh, but it is shameful of me to bother you with our problems. Please do not mention this to the lord.

CHORUS. The proud desire of the warrior
To retain his sword,
Though blunt and rusted,
Is the symbol of his sincere loyalty.

GENZŌ. As my wife has said, our present discomfort is truly the result of our past sins. We must bear it with fortitude.

CHORUS. Genzō and Tonami, again in this house,
See the shape of the past rise before them,
And pained by recollection, quietly weep.
Koshiji enters silently,
Rousing them from their sad reminiscences.

KOSHIJI. The lord wishes to see Genzō alone in his study, and has instructed me to let no one disturb them until the interview has ended.

SONŌ. I understand his wishes. Go to him, Genzō. And Tonami, come with me to the inner rooms.

(SONŌ, TONAMI, *and* KOSHIJI *exit.*)

CHORUS. Trembling with fear and anxiety
      Genzō approaches
      The presence of his lord.

(*Music. The upstage sliding doors open, revealing Lord* SUGAWARA's *study. He is seated at his desk, a figure of great calmness and dignity.* GENZŌ *kneels.*)
      Imparting the secret art of calligraphy
      Is an act of divine grace,
      And the serenity of the study of Lord Sugawara
      Is a fitting place for a sacred rite.

      Solemnly the lord sits
      At a plain unadorned desk
      In a study made holy
      By sacred decorations.
      Awed by the stately figure of his lord,
      Genzō is tense with anxiety and reverence,
      Waiting to be told the reason
      Of his master's summons.

SUGAWARA. I have tried to find you because of an urgent problem which has beset me. Now I am deeply satisfied to see you here before me. From the time you first came to me as a child, you showed an inherent talent for the art of calligraphy. You advanced so rapidly in the art that you surpassed even the older students. But just at the time I saw a brilliant future for you, an unexpected break in our relations occurred, and my dreams were shattered. It is my hope that your skill in the art was not also destroyed on that unfortunate day.

GENZŌ. Since the time of my childhood, my master, I have continued to serve you. I have never forgotten your sage advice: 'The art of calligraphy is the mother of all the arts.' I have poured my soul into my study. To make a living, my wife and I have started a school near Naritake village, and there I teach the children the art of calligraphy. But in spite of my daily practice in correcting the work of my pupils, my skill in the art shows no sign of improvement. I am greatly honoured by your summons, and I deeply regret my incompetence.

CHORUS. Understanding and sympathizing with
     Genzō's difficulties,
     Lord Sugawara says:
SUGAWARA. Teaching is an honourable profession: it makes of art a
     virtue. Despite your admirable modesty, I feel that your skill in
     the art of calligraphy must have improved with the years. In-
     deed, it is unnecessary that I see your writing to determine your
     skill, but for the sake of formality, I ask you to write something
     from the copy-book on my desk. I will later explain my reason
     for asking this. (*He rises from behind the desk, moves to the opposite side
     of the stage and sits.*)
CHORUS. This kindly gesture fills Genzō with warm emotions.
     He bows, but instinctively hesitates
     To use the materials
     Of his former master.

     The wily Mareyo, villain that he is at heart,
     Suddenly appears on the scene.
MAREYO (*moving indignantly to* GENZŌ). The master is free to say what
     he will, but Genzō, have you no sense of shame? From your toad-
     like appearance I take it you intend to accept his generous offer.
     You presumptuous fool! What do you expect to gain by it?
GENZŌ. I am honoured that you still remember me, Mareyo. I
     may be presumptuous, but I am not such a fool that I am un-
     aware of my present position. At the moment I am trying to de-
     cide whether I should write or not. For the past four years, living
     in the country, I have used nothing but cheap brushes, crude ink
     sticks, and inferior paper. How can I write with such fine
     materials as these?
MAREYO. Of course, of course! Now you are seeing things properly.
     You should take your leave immediately.
GENZŌ (*pausing*). You know, Mareyo, I have been banished. I
     thought perhaps I might impose on your good nature, and ask
     you to aid me in restoring myself.
MAREYO. I am not adverse to making apologies to the master on
     your behalf. But I could not think of troubling him with such
     trifles at present. The situation is this: Life and death are un-
     predictable in this transient world of ours, but it is only natural
     that the old should go first. Now that Lord Sugawara is fifty-two
     years of age, the Emperor has suggested that he impart the secret
     art of calligraphy to his ablest pupil before it is too late. In com-
     pliance with the Imperial wish, the master has been fasting for the
     past seven days in preparation for selecting that pupil. Now when

all this is settled, I will speak favourably to him about your ignoble
position. Be on your way now. Hurry!

(GENZŌ *stands up slowly, not knowing what to do.*)

SUGAWARA. Genzō! Do not leave. Remain here and write as I
have asked you.

GENZŌ. Yes, my lord.

CHORUS. No more felicitous order than this
　　　　　Could Genzō receive.
　　　　　But it adds fire to the anger of Mareyo,
　　　　　Who fumes, and glares at his happy rival.

MAREYO. You don't mean to insult me by daring to write?

GENZŌ. I cannot disobey the order of our master.

MAREYO. I've never heard of such impudence!

GENZŌ. Now if you will be good enough to excuse me——

CHORUS. Moving from Mareyo,
　　　　　The humble Genzō sits before the desk,
　　　　　Offering a prayer to the gods,
　　　　　Imploring their watchful guidance.

　　　　　Solemnly he mixes an ink
　　　　　Rich in fragrance,
　　　　　Rich in hue.
　　　　　Then with his accomplished brush,
　　　　　With ink,
　　　　　With paper,
　　　　　He creates the visible form of beauty.

MAREYO. A cunning rascal like you would undoubtedly take ad-
vantage of the transparent paper and trace from the copy-book.
But I'll see that you don't! Look at your disgraceful appearance!
You look exactly like a priest in a poor country temple. (*Laughs.*)

CHORUS. Mareyo, raging with jealousy,
　　　　　Heaps slanderous abuse on Genzō.
　　　　　Then he jars the writing-desk
　　　　　And purposely jostles Genzō's arm.

　　　　　But Genzō, patient and self-possessed,
　　　　　Reveals no sign of reproach,
　　　　　While from the book he calmly copies poems,
　　　　　Pouring his heart and soul into his brush.
　　　　　Completing his task,
　　　　　Respectfully he takes his work to the master,
　　　　　Retreats a step, and bows with reverence.

SUGAWARA (*reading*). The grass encroaching on the sandy beach

Is but a few inches deep,
And the mist caught in the treetops
But a few feet.

This verse I composed myself.

Only yesterday we welcomed the new year
And now the mist of spring
Envelops Mount Kasuga.

This was composed by Hitomaro. Both of these poems depict the spirit of early spring. However, that is not the point at the moment. Your manner of writing the characters is excellent—there can scarcely be any better form. Much of the skill in writing requires technical excellence—the eight master strokes, the sixteen points in handling equipment—but technique remains technique. In the Sugawara style, calligraphy becomes art, and writing is therefore a sacred ceremony. Splendidly done, Genzō, splendidly done! On this seventh day of my fast you have received the blessings of the gods. To you will be imparted the secret art.

GENZŌ (*joyfully*). Praised be the gods for their most generous blessing! The honour of inheriting the secret art is mine! And perhaps I have also been forgiven? O my lord, may I not again address you as my master?

SUGAWARA. What! Master? You have no master. Banishment is banishment. Receiving the secret art is another matter. Because of the Imperial order, I could not ignore you—so excellent a calligrapher—no matter how rash you were in the past. My personal displeasure is, and will remain, a personal displeasure. But I sincerely desire that my art live after me. I do not think the Emperor will see any partiality in my judgement. No, Genzō, your banishment is irrevocable. Our relationship is broken. Henceforward I shall allow no interviews.

GENZŌ. Forgive my impertinence, my lord, but I would rather be forgiven than receive the secret art.

MAREYO. You have my sympathies, Genzō. What's the good of it if you are to remain banished? I think it would be wise for the master to forgive you and give me the secret art. Then both of us would be satisfied.

CHORUS. As Mareyo finishes,
A warrior-guard enters.

GUARD. I bring a message.

MAREYO. What is it?

GUARD. A royal messenger from the Imperial Palace has just arrived with an urgent request that his lordship come to the Imperial Court immediately.

MAREYO (*insolently*). Did you hear that, my lord?

SUGAWARA (*puzzled*). My seven days of fasting are not yet over. What can the urgent matter be? Tell my followers and guards to make preparations to leave at once.

GUARD. Yes, sire.

(*He leaves.*)

CHORUS. Lord Sugawara, mindful of the summons,
    Goes to prepare for the
    Imperial Court.

(*Music.* SUGAWARA *moves into the upstage area, and the sliding doors close.* GENZŌ *and* MAREYO *remain downstage.*)
    Then Lady Sonō comes from the inner rooms,
    Carefully concealing Tonami beneath her flowing robe,
    So that the banished Tonami
    May have a final glimpse of her lord.

SONŌ. Mareyo, I sympathize with your feeling in not being chosen. The fortunate one is Genzō. (*She turns to* GENZŌ.) However, it is a great pity that your former ties could not be restored. This may well be the last time that you will ever be here. It is best to bid your final farewell to your former lord when he departs for the Imperial Palace.

SAMURAI (*offstage*). The lord's departure!

(*Drums. Two samurai and six porters appear. The drumming dies down. The sliding doors open, revealing* SUGAWARA.)

CHORUS. Now comes the noble Sugawara
    In stately ceremonial robes,
    A figure of grace and elegance.

SUGAWARA. Come to me, Genzō.

GENZŌ. Yes, sire.

(GENZŌ *moves to* SUGAWARA, *who hands him a scroll carefully wrapped in silk.* GENZŌ *wipes his hands with paper, takes the scroll, and raises it reverently to his forehead.*)

GENZŌ. Great is this blessing, which I do not deserve. Now it is my honour to transmit this art to posterity.

CHORUS. In this act
    Is the origin of the famed village schools,
    Revered through the ages
    For teaching the art of calligraphy,
    The art which has come down to our time.

SUGAWARA. Now this ceremony is ended. You will take your leave, and we shall not meet again.

MAREYO (*moving to* GENZŌ). Genzō, there's no use begging any

more. Your pleas are useless. If you can't stand up and leave by
yourself I'll gladly drag you out.

(*He is about to do so when* SONŌ *stops him.*)

SONŌ. No, no, Mareyo. For Genzō this is the end of all worldly
relations with the lord. You must appreciate that he is sad and
hesitant to leave.

CHORUS. From beneath the Lady's robe
Tonami steals a last glimpse of her former master.
This Lord Sugawara sees,
But pretending not to,
Says nothing.
Then, for no apparent reason,
The coronet falls from his head.

SUGAWARA (*catching the coronet in his hand, disturbed*). What thing is
this? The coronet has fallen from my head.

CHORUS. For a moment the lord stands rigid,
Caught up by a foreboding of evil.

SONŌ (*eagerly*). It is but the sign of Genzō's grief, my lord. Grief
brings the falling of tears, and the coronet has fallen like his tears.

SUGAWARA. No. No. It cannot be. At the Imperial Court I will
know why it fell. Genzō, take your leave at once.

MAREYO. The lord's departure!

ALL. The lord's departure!

(*Drums. With* SUGAWARA *at the head, the procession moves on to the*
hanamichi. MAREYO *follows with a sneer on his face, stopping on*
the hanamichi *as the procession disappears.*)

TONAMI. Oh, Genzō, you had the great fortune to be addressed by
the lord and to look upon his noble face, while I could steal only
a glimpse of him. Our offence has been equal, yet I, the woman,
have had to suffer more. (*She weeps.*)

CHORUS. Then comes Mareyo, affectedly casual,
Showing all his malevolence,
Swaggering in his brazen manner.

MAREYO (*having returned to the stage*). Lady Sonō, you are neglecting
your duty to the lord by permitting Genzō to stay. The lord has
repeatedly ordered that Genzō leave immediately. It is clearly my
duty to eject him from the premises. But I'll allow him to remain
a little longer, on one condition. Although I have no desire to read
the scroll you received, Genzō, I would like to hold it in my
hands so that hereafter my writing will be blessed by the gods.
For the sake of our friendship, let me do reverence to the scroll.

GENZŌ. But how can I permit that, when it has been entrusted to
me?

MAREYO (*grovelling*). For the sake of my future, let me do reverence
to it.

GENZŌ. Well . . . then hold it for a moment.

(*He hands the scroll to* MAREYO.)

MAREYO (*raising the scroll to his forehead*). I am deeply grateful to you.
I'm certainly fortunate to be here just at this time so that I can pay
reverence to this sacred object. I'm fortunate, I'm fortunate.

(*He runs off on to the* hanamichi, GENZŌ *after him.*)

CHORUS. Genzō seizes him,
Throws him down,
Recovering the precious scroll.

GENZŌ (*putting the scroll in his kimono*). Conniving, thieving scoundrel!
Would you dare steal this sacred scroll? If you try to escape I will
kill you!

SONŌ. Here, here, Genzō! Tonami, stop him!

TONAMI. Genzō, Genzō, listen to Lady Sonō!

GENZŌ. Though you should be severely punished, I will let you live.
But you cannot be let off too easily: you must be punished a little.
Tonami, this child must be punished as unruly children in our
school are punished. Bring me the desk!

(*Music.* TONAMI *brings* GENZŌ *the small writing-desk, which he
ties to* MAREYO's *back with* MAREYO's *obi. Then with dance
movement,* GENZŌ *pushes* MAREYO *along the* hanamichi. *Finally,*
GENZŌ *kicks him, and* MAREYO *falls.*)

MAREYO. Damn it! It's like a dirty thief stealing from a bath-house
for court nobles. You'll live to rue this day, you filthy beggar.

GENZŌ (*facing him menacingly*). What?

MAREYO (*snivelling*). Nothing. Nothing at all.

CHORUS. Mareyo, fearing to lose his life,
Slinks away utterly crushed,
Wincing with pain and shame.

(*Music.* GENZŌ *returns to the stage.*)

CHORUS. Genzō and his wife
Bow reverently to Lady Sonō.

GENZŌ. I should like to stay until news is received from the Imperial
Palace. But by remaining, I fear I would only make matters
worse.

TONAMI. My lady, could you not put in a good word for us, so
that the lord will be less displeased?

SONŌ. Do not worry, my dears. I will do what I can. I regret that I
cannot offer you a night's lodging. But keep up hope: fate may
still bring us together.

GENZŌ. May the gods preserve you, my lady.

SONŌ. Take good care of yourselves, both of you.

BOTH. Good-bye, Lady Sonō.

(GENZŌ *and* TONAMI *move to the* hanamichi. SONŌ *pauses a moment, then exits.*)

CHORUS. Now must this unfortunate couple
Forever bid farewell
To the home of their master
And return to the barren life of banishment.

(*Music and drums. The scene changes, before the eyes of the audience, to the exterior of the Sugawara estate. A high wall with a centre gate.*)

CHORUS. Just after the dejected couple
Have passed through the gate of the Sugawara household,
Umeōmaru, brother of Sakuramaru,
Comes running in reckless haste.
Stumbling and falling, he calls out to Genzō:

UMEŌMARU. Wait, Genzō, wait! Lord Sugawara has been arrested by the Imperial Guard and is surrounded by bamboo spears. They are returning now. Tell Lady Sonō at once! Hurry!

(GENZŌ *and* TONAMI *return to the stage and run through the gate.*)

CHORUS. Within the Imperial Court, disorder and confusion,
Outside the Court, a band of Imperial Guards
Surrounded Lord Sugawara, and with menacing gestures
Took him prisoner.
Leading the group is
The follower of Shihei,
Miyoshi no Kiyotsura.

(*Enter* KIYOTSURA *on the* hanamichi. SUGAWARA *follows him, now dressed in ordinary clothes.* CHIKARA *is behind him wearing two swords. Behind them, a host of samurai. The procession stops on the* hanamichi, *and* SONŌ *appears through the gate.*)

KIYOTSURA (*oratorically*). Let it be known that Lord Sugawara has been discovered plotting against the Imperial Throne. After the Prince Tokiyo and Princess Kariya disappeared from the banks of the Kamo river a thorough investigation was conducted. All evidence indicates that Lord Sugawara has been planning to marry his daughter Kariya to the Prince. He intended later to elevate the Prince to the throne, thus making his daughter Empress. Therefore Lord Sugawara is to be banished from the land. But until the place of his exile has been determined, he will be put under heavy guard. My retainer, Arajima Chikara, will be in charge of the guard.

CHIKARA. Yes, sire.

(SONŌ *runs to* SUGAWARA *on the* hanamichi *and falls before him*.)

SONŌ. Oh, what have they done to you? Why do you not prove your innocence? Tell them you have been fasting for seven days, that you know nothing of the Prince and Princess. An innocent man sent to exile! This is an unbelievable judgement!

SUGAWARA (*calmly*). The charge against my name is false, yet I bear no malice against the Emperor. That I received his blessing yesterday, that I am condemned by him today, these are the works of the gods, and I can bear no anger towards them. When the coronet fell from my head it was a sign from the gods that I was to be a penniless, rankless man. I have no regrets. Now let me go.

CHORUS. As he frees himself from his lamenting wife,
Mareyo comes swaggering back.

MAREYO (*appearing on stage-left*). Kiyotsura, you have done a splendid job. Although I was a pupil of Sugawara, of course I had no part in his doings, I offer no resistance. Take him away. Be sure to remember me to the honourable Shihei!

KIYOTSURA. I will do that. (*To* CHIKARA.) Imprison Lord Sugawara within his house!

CHIKARA. Yes, sire!

(*Music, and the procession moves on to the stage. There* SUGAWARA *pauses.*)

CHIKARA. Move on! (*He threatens to strike* SUGAWARA *with a bamboo spear.*)

MAREYO (*with relish*). Wait! Wait! Let me perform that duty. (*He takes the spear from* CHIKARA.) Now, you conspirator, our relationship is different. My loyalty now belongs to Shihei, and I will prove it by striking you. Scoundrel! (*He raises the spear.*)

UMEŌMARU. Scoundrel indeed! *You* dare call anyone a scoundrel? I'd like to spit in your beady eyes. Who do you think you're going to strike?

MAREYO. This fool of a conspirator!

UMEŌMARU. Who's a conspirator, you ungrateful swine? If Lord Sugawara will not raise his hand against you, I, Umeōmaru, will. (*He moves towards* MAREYO.)

SUGAWARA. Wait, Umeōmaru! Your actions are impertinent. I have been arrested by Imperial Order. Resistance to Mareyo or any of the others is comparable to disobeying the word of the Emperor. Umeō—and all the rest of my household—if you do not obey my wish in this matter I will banish you eternally.

UMEŌMARU (*kneeling before him*). But my lord——

SUGAWARA. Do not speak.

MAREYO. Come, Umeō, you bragging weakling, let me see you carry out your threats. (*He strikes* SUGAWARA.)

CHORUS. Lord Sugawara is rudely forced through the gate,
Made a prisoner in his own house.
Guards surround the estate,
The gate is made fast
So that none can escape.

KIYOTSURA (*to* CHIKARA). Have guards placed at all the entrances. Keep alert, Chikara! They may make an attempt to climb over the wall. (*Greatly satisfied.*) Well, Mareyo, I shall be going home.

MAREYO. As you wish. I'll keep Chikara company.

(KIYOTSURA *leaves*.)

CHORUS. Takebe Genzō, the loyal retainer,
Hid in the shadow of the trees.
Now, with Kiyotsura gone,
He rushes from his hiding-place
Towards Mareyo, the traitor,
And Chikara, captain of the guard.

(GENZŌ *and* TONAMI *run on to the stage.* GENZŌ *strikes* MAREYO *in the stomach, then throws* CHIKARA *to the ground.*)

CHIKARA. Guards! Guards!

CHORUS. Guards! Guards!
Kill! Kill!
Cries fill the air.

MAREYO (*doubled up in pain*). You've caused enough trouble today, Genzō. You'd better be more cautious. What you do may be credited to your lord, and his exile may be changed to death.

GENZŌ. Fool! I am still banished—I have no lord. Umeōmaru has a lord and must obey him. But I can act for him.

(GUARDS *appear*.)

MAREYO. Guards! Slash him to pieces!

GENZŌ. Slash away! And the devil take your souls!

(*To music, sword fighting is pantomimed, in dance movement.* GENZŌ *drives the* GUARDS *and* CHIKARA *from the stage and the* hanamichi. *Meanwhile,* MAREYO *has attacked* TONAMI, *who sword-fights with him. Seeing this,* GENZŌ *returns to the stage, kills* MAREYO.)

CHORUS. The enemy is routed as darkness falls.
Genzō and Tonami knock at the barred gate,
And breathlessly wait for an answer.
Piercing the stillness of the air
Comes an angry challenge:

UMEŌMARU. Who's there?

GENZŌ. It sounds like the voice of Umeōmaru.

UMEŌMARU. Is it Takebe Genzō?

(He appears above the wall.)

GENZŌ *(quiet, intense).* It is. Listen to me, Umeō! If we do not take action, the house of Sugawara will disappear forever. It would be a simple matter to seize Lord Sugawara and take him away to safety. But if you did that he would banish you. My plan is this: my wife and I will escape with the young prince, Kan Shūsai. We will hide him away and care for him until this trouble is over. Now, run, run, and bring him at once.

UMEŌMARU. Good! Good! If we were to ask Imperial permission to release Kan Shūsai we would be refused. It is better this way.

GENZŌ. Yes, it is. Now make haste.

CHORUS. Umeōmaru noiselessly disappears.
But a moment later he returns,
Bearing in his arms
The heir of the house of Sugawara,
Kan Shūsai.

UMEŌMARU. Here he is. Take good care of him, Genzō.

GENZŌ. I will. I will.

CHORUS. Genzō raises his hands
To receive the precious burden,
Yet higher than his hands
Reaches his loyal heart.
And though the cold wall of Imperial order
Stands between them,
The warm hearts of these loyal retainers
Meet in this act of love.

Out rushes the Captain of the guard,
Arajima Chikara.

CHIKARA. You there! You curse of the guards! We can't get a moment's peace because of you. Don't you dare move from there until I report that you've stolen Kan Shūsai.

GENZŌ. Come back here! If you have any reports to make, you will make them to me. On guard, Chikara!

CHORUS. Genzō attacks!
Swinging and countering,
Charging and retreating,
They fight to and fro.
Then suddenly
A scream of agony
And Chikara lies dead.

Now the way is clear for their escape.

UMEŌMARU. Take good care of the prince, Genzō.

TONAMI. The lord and his lady within the house——

GENZŌ. Take good care of them, Umeō!

UMEŌMARU. You may trust me. I will. I will.

CHORUS. The unselfish action
　　　　Of these three fearless souls
　　　　Is a living example
　　　　Of the virtue of loyalty,
　　　　Transmitted
　　　　From generation to generation
　　　　In the teaching
　　　　Of the famed village schools.

　　(TONAMI *leads* KAN SHŪSAI *by the hand on to the* hanamichi, GENZŌ
　　following. UMEŌMARU *watches them go, then strikes a pose of
　　defiance.*)

CURTAIN

ACT II

*The estate at Kawachi of Kakuju, the Princess Kariya's mother. Two
rooms, enclosed with sliding doors, on either side of the stage, a platform with
a low railing between them. Before the stage-left room is a garden pool, in
the form of a blue cloth laid on the stage floor.*

The curtain rises to koto *music. Three maids are seated on the central
platform, the oldest one making an arrangement of pine branches in a tray.*

MAID I. Well now, I've just about finished this.

MAID II. You know so much about flower arrangement! That
branch is so beautifully set!

MAID III. That's the result of daily cultivation of good taste for
such things. The mistress is very particular in her taste about
everything.

MAID I. Stop chattering, you two. (*Pause.*) I hear that our visitor
is to leave tomorrow.

MAID II. Oh? Is he? Is the beautiful princess leaving with him?

MAID I. No, I think not. (*Confidentially.*) She is Princess Kariya,
Lord Sugawara's adopted daughter, but for some reason or other,
she is denied audience with her father.

MAID III. Oh! What a pity! I heard that her poor father is going to
be exiled to a far-away island. And they say his stay here was
made possible only by the pleadings of our mistress.

MAID II. My, my, what unfortunate people! (*Pause.*) Do you know
what the mistress intends to do with this arrangement?

MAID I (*snubbing her*). No, I can't say that I do, but we'd better take it to the mistress. Don't you think so, Kogiku?

MAID III. Yes, I think so. Let's do it right now. Come.

(*The* MAIDS *leave the stage.*)

CHORUS. Under the protection of Sakuramaru
　　　　The Princess Kariya fled to Kawachi.
　　　　By sheer chance, Lady Tatsuta,
　　　　Sister of the Princess, found the Princess
　　　　Wandering disconsolately by the pier.
　　　　Secretly the Lady Tatsuta brought
　　　　The Princess back to her home.
　　　　Now the Lady Tatsuta slides open the door
　　　　Of the room in which the Princess has been hidden,
　　　　Hidden even from her own mother.

(LADY TATSUTA *enters from the stage-left room, leading* PRINCESS KARIYA.)

TATSUTA. My dear sister, you must be terribly lonely. I've wanted to come and keep you company, but mother always has me by her side.

CHORUS. Coming from her room of hidden loneliness,
　　　　Desolate and forlorn,
　　　　Princess Kariya sheds tears afresh
　　　　At the tender concern of her sister.

(*They sit facing each other.*)

KARIYA. You have been so kind to me since . . . since I left Prince Tokiyo. There is nothing for me now—I must resign myself to fate. I should kill myself, but when I think of my dear mother and of Prince Tokiyo, my heart cries out for them, and I have not the courage to kill myself. Oh, if I could only see Lord Sugawara and beg forgiveness for what I have done, I would not suffer so.

CHORUS. The sorrow of this frail flower,
　　　　Torn by an undeserved, relentless fate,
　　　　Brings tears of tender sympathy
　　　　To the eyes of gentle Tatsuta.

TATSUTA. Do not weep, Princess Kariya. Be patient, my sister. At mother's request Lord Sugawara is now in this house, and there may yet be a way for you to meet him. (*Pause.*) Perhaps if I were to talk to mother, explain your remorse, perhaps she would go to him and—— But no, she will not. She will not break her code of behaviour. Since you were adopted into the house of Sugawara, she says you are no longer her child but owe all your loyalty to your foster parents. (*Hesitantly.*) There has been a re-port from the pier that the storm has subsided. Terukuni has sent word to mother that they will come for Lord Sugawara tomorrow at dawn. The servants are already making preparations. We must do something quickly, my sister. Do not weep. Help me to think.

CHORUS. As they struggle hopelessly for a solution,
    Sukune Tarō suddenly appears.
    (SUKUNE TARŌ, *husband of* TATSUTA, *wears the costume and swords of a samurai. He is rough, swaggering, and not very intelligent.*)

SUKUNE. Here behind you stands a man of ability and discretion.

TATSUTA. Why! It's you, Tarō! I did not hear you coming.

SUKUNE (*angry*). What do you mean, you didn't hear me coming? Does your husband have to be announced? What kind of wife have I got, deceiving her husband by hiding someone and carrying on secret conversations. (*Looking at* KARIYA.) Hmmm. I heard you had a sister adopted as a child by Lord Sugawara, but this is the first time I've had the pleasure of seeing her. I never dreamed anybody could be so beautiful! I don't blame Tokiyo, or whatever his name is, for falling in love with her. (*To* TATSUTA.) Shall I tell you something? Before meeting the princess I imagined you to be the most beautiful woman in the world, but now I've decided we'll have to change that.

TATSUTA. Oh, is that so? Change it to what, pray?

SUKUNE. To Lady Next Best, of course.

TATSUTA. Oh, my lord, you are merry. But, I beg you, do not let mother know that the Princess is here!

SUKUNE. Don't worry about that. Kakuju has asked me to go to Terukuni's lodging to thank him for his kindness in allowing this 'member of the nobility' to stay here. Terukuni's party is to leave tomorrow morning at the first crow of the cock. Well, if I get any ideas I'll let you know . . . Lady Next Best.

TATSUTA. Oh, stop that nonsense.

SUKUNE. Well, good-bye.

CHORUS. As informally as he speaks
    He takes leave of the two.
    The Princess Kariya wistfully watches
    As the sprightly Sukune leaves.

KARIYA. Forgive me, Tatsuta. I was so occupied with my present predicament, I did not act with proper formality before your husband.

TATSUTA. Oh, that is unimportant! But we cannot waste any more time. Now! Even if we talk to mother, she will not help us. So come! My husband has gone, mother is not here, I'll take you to see Lord Sugawara myself. Come, my sister.

CHORUS. As the kindly Tatsuta takes Princess Kariya's hand,
        A sound of sliding doors,
        And there is their mother, Kakuju.

KAKUJU (*to* KARIYA). Undutiful girl! Where are you going?
Where?

CHORUS. Kakuju
        Raises her staff
        To strike the Princess.
        Tatsuta, shocked by the unfamiliar sight
        Of her mother's rage,
        Rushes between them.

TATSUTA. Mother! No! If you are displeased because her being
here was kept secret from you, it is I who should be punished, not
the Princess. Haven't you yourself said she is no longer your
child? Should you punish the Princess who is no longer your
child, but the daughter of Lord Sugawara?

KARIYA (*to* TATSUTA). No, no, you have done nothing wrong!
Strike me, mother, I am the undutiful one!

TATSUTA. No, Princess Kariya. It cannot be——

KARIYA. Please——

TATSUTA. No——

KARIYA. Let fall——

BOTH. The rod of punishment upon us!

CHORUS. Unrestrained in their display of love,
        Each sister
        Stubbornly refuses to yield
        To the entreaties of the other.
        But Kakuju,
        Unmoved by their love,
        Is not softened.

KAKUJU. Tatsuta, she is not my daughter, but since she is the
daughter of my nephew, Lord Sugawara, she is yet a member of
our house. (*Turning on* KARIYA.) And who caused the exile of my
nephew? Who behaved in a shameless manner? Never can I
beg Lord Sugawara's forgiveness unless I punish this loathsome
creature. . . . I am an old woman, and my hair is white. When
my husband died I should have cut off my white hair and become
a nun, but you, Tatsuta, you begged me to stay with you. So I
took only my holy name, Kakuju, and did not become a nun.
This I have regretted until today. But now I am glad. If my
head were shorn and I wore the robes of a nun I could not
chastise you. But now I must, I must. Both of you must be
punished.

(*In stylized movement,* KAKUJU *strikes* TATSUTA *and* KARIYA *with her staff.*)

CHORUS. With every blow
    Both chastised and chastiser weep.
    From the eyes of the sisters
    Fall tears of pity,
    From the eyes of Kakuju
    Fall tears of pain.

(*From the enclosed room on stage-right, a voice is heard.*)

SUGAWARA. Forgive them, Kakuju. Forgive them, my dear aunt. The pain of my daughter will also touch Prince Tokiyo, and that would be pity indeed. Now let my daughter come to me.

CHORUS. As she hears the calm voice of Lord Sugawara,
    The aged woman
    In a flood of tears ·
    Drops her staff
    And stands bewildered
    Her heart overwhelmed with reverence and gratitude.

KAKUJU. A true mother punishes her child to fulfil her obligations to the foster father. The foster father fulfils his obligations to the true mother through his forgiveness. Both punishment and forgiveness are the visible signs of parental love. That you will see the Princess is more a blessing to me than to her. For this I give you the undying gratitude of an indulgent mother. Princess Kariya is fortunate indeed in such a father. Come, Princess Kariya, dry your tears and rejoice. Go to your father, who waits for you.

(*The sliding doors are pulled open by stage assistants.*)

CHORUS. Look!
    A wooden image
    Carved in the likeness of Lord Sugawara!
    But nowhere to be seen is the lord himself.
    Transfixed by confusion, surprise, and fear,
    Princess Kariya herself
    Stands like a wooden image.

KARIYA. He must have said he would see me to stop the punishment of my mother. But now perhaps he does not wish to see me. The words spoken a moment ago were unmistakably those of my father. But how can a wooden image speak? Or is it that he is hidden somewhere?

(KARIYA *moves into the room.*)

KAKUJU. Wait, Kariya! Since Lord Sugawara has been with us, he has lived in the other wing of this court, which is quite far from here. When I heard his voice a moment ago, overcome by

G

surprise and gladness I forgot that. Now I realize that Lord Sugawara has not been here at all. This is a strange and wonderful event, but I can explain it. When Lord Sugawara arrived here I requested him to make a likeness of himself to leave with me. On the very first day he began making a wooden image. When he finished it he immediately destroyed it. Then he made another image. That, too, he destroyed. Then he made a third image—the one that stands before you—and this he gave to me. The first two images were merely pieces of sculpture, he said, but this one contains his heart and soul. He told me not to think of it as a mere image, but as his real self. Then, too, he said that although he wished to speak to his daughter, he could not, for such action might anger his Imperial Majesty. And so it happened that although you cannot see your father, you have been able to hear his voice. This is a happy day for you, my daughter, and for me as well.

CHORUS. The happiness of the mother and daughters
    Seems to shed a joyous light.

    Leisurely walking in
    Upon this touching and delightful scene,
    Comes the father of Sukune Tarō,
    Haji no Hyōe.
    (*A sly old man, dressed in samurai clothes. Behind him is* SUKUNE TARŌ.)

HYŌE (*excessively agreeable*). Ah, here you are, Kakuju! Since the honourable guest is to leave early tomorrow morning, you must have many household duties. Although I'm sure I'll only be in the way, I've come to offer my services in whatever way possible. On my way here I stopped at Terukuni's lodging, and I was very happy to learn that most of the preparations for tomorrow's departure have been made. I thought of returning home tonight and coming again early tomorrow morning for the departure, but since I am an old man, I will take the liberty of imposing on your kindness and will stay here for the night if I may.

KAKUJU. This is the home of your daughter-in-law, and you should consider it as your own. Do not hesitate to ask for anything you may need. Go, Tatsuta, prepare a room for Hyōe. Excuse me, Hyōe, we will meet again this evening.

    (*The three women exit.*)

CHORUS. Father and son
    Now left to themselves
    Converse quietly
    So as not to be overheard.

HYŌE (*complete change in manner*). Tarō! Be careful! Nothing must go wrong with our plans.

SUKUNE. Don't worry, father. There won't be any mistakes.

(*They exit.*)

CHORUS. The rooms are brilliantly lit with candles,
There is the bustle of last preparations,
For the last festivity
On the last night
When Sugawara
Must bid his last farewell.

Into this radiant, solemn night,
Comes Haji no Hyōe,
Stealthily creeping,
Making his way to the low garden gate,
He opens it and signals.
Then from the darkness come sinister figures
Who give to Hyōe
A travelling chest.

HYŌE. No slip-ups, understand! At the appointed time, be sure that the required number of men, in the proper dress, come for Lord Sugawara with a covered palanquin.

MEN. We understand you, sir.

HYŌE. Be off now!

MEN. Yes, sir.

(*They leave.*)

CHORUS. Back to the garden sneaks the plotter,
Travelling chest in hand,
As if in fear of the very moon that lights his way,
In search of his son,
His partner in the crime.

(SUKUNE *enters.*)

SUKUNE. Father! Is everything ready? Has it arrived?

HYŌE. Son, be quiet! Everything went perfectly. Now there's something of vital importance I must discuss with you if our plan is to succeed. Come this way!

(*They move to the pool. Presently* TATSUTA *appears on the upstage platform.*)

CHORUS. Father and son
Move stealthily
In the stillness of the night
To the pool in the shadow of the trees.
There they whisper

> Beside the darkness of the pool
> Unaware they have been followed,
> Unaware that Tatsuta listens to every word.

SUKUNE. Now, father, I understand the plan. Before Terukuni arrives, we come with the false escorts. We take Lord Sugawara away, and then we kill him. It's all perfectly simple. But this is what I don't understand: everybody knows that Terukuni will not come until the first cock crow. Kakuju knows that. And she certainly won't let us take Lord Sugawara before the cock crows. What do we do about that?

CHORUS. Hyōe,
> Unmoved by his son's excitement,
> Quietly draws out
> A cock
> From the travelling-chest.

SUKUNE. Oh! What a fine bird! It's past midnight now—we may as well make it crow. Come on, crow! (*Pause.*) Father, why doesn't it crow?

HYŌE. Fool, it won't crow whenever you want it to! The laws of nature make it crow at dawn. We can't force it. But there is a secret way of making it crow before dawn. You put some steaming hot water in a large bamboo and put the cock on the bamboo. The heat makes it think the day is breaking, and then it'll crow. I have the bamboo in this travelling-chest, and the water should be boiling by now. Go fetch the pot. Quietly, now!

CHORUS. Horrible was the plot
> To the listening Tatsuta,
> Hardly believable
> And yet so likely.
> 'Should I go to mother and tell her?
> Yes, I must. No, I mustn't. Yet I should.'
> She struggles within herself.
> Fighting her confused emotions,
> She finally manages
> To calm herself.

TATSUTA. Sukune! Where are you, Tarō?

CHORUS. Panic stricken
> At the thought of being discovered,
> The plotting criminals,
> In utter confusion,
> Thrust the cock
> Into the travelling-chest,

Slip on the cover,
And face the unwelcome Tatsuta
With empty indignation.

SUKUNE. Why are you yelling like that? Has something happened? You frightened the wits out of us. You shouldn't come on us unannounced if you've nothing important to say.

CHORUS. Gazing at the brazen face of her husband,
  Who plots a horrible crime against Lord Sugawara,
  Tatsuta feels a wave of nausea sweep over her.

TATSUTA. Frightened you! You frightened me, dear husband, and dear father. I overheard your plot to murder Lord Sugawara. What enmity do you bear him?

CHORUS. 'Or perhaps the loathsome Shihei
  Has promised you a reward.
  For money
  Would you betray
  Your loyal and loving wife?'

TATSUTA. Have you forgotten all that mother has done for you? Do you feel no obligation towards her? Do not betray her faith in you, Tarō. Father, consider well, and turn back from this ugly deed.

CHORUS. The immeasurable depth of this woman's feelings,
  Her purity,
  Her respect for her father and husband——
  She seems to embody pure conscience.
  But unmoved,
  The sly father
  Winks roguishly
  At his brutish son.

HYŌE. Well . . . ah . . . such a pure feeling must be met with a feeling of extreme disgrace on our part. Ah . . . we're certainly ashamed of ourselves for thinking such thoughts. We will not let this happen again, daughter, so . . . ah . . . forget all about this, will you?

TATSUTA. Oh, thank you, thank you! Since you realize the folly and impropriety of such an act, I shall wipe the incident from my mind. Tarō, not only will I be a faithful wife in this world, but in the world to come I will serve you and your father with loyalty and affection. Now let us go in out of the cold.

  (*As she turns,* HYŌE *whispers to* SUKUNE.)

HYŌE. Now's your chance!

  (SUKUNE *stabs* TATSUTA *in the back. She writhes in pain, then turns to face him.*)

TATSUTA. Oh! You beast! You coward! I should have known better than to trust you! Help! Help!

SUKUNE. Quiet, you bitch!

CHORUS. Tatsuta desperately clings to her husband,
But he mercilessly shakes her off.
Tearing a strip of cloth from his sleeve,
He gags her with it.
Then he strikes a final blow,
To her heart.

HYŌE (*standing guard*). Is she finished?

SUKUNE. Don't worry, father. We won't hear from her again. (*He wipes the dagger and puts it into the scabbard.*) What shall we do with her body?

HYŌE. What better place than this murky pool? We can put some rocks in her sleeves—that will keep the body from bobbing up. Now dump her into the depths of the pool.
(*They put the body in the pool.*)

CHORUS. The bloody corpse
Sinks
To the bottom of the pool,
A crimson film
On the surface of the water
Flickers weirdly
In the cold February moonlight.

SUKUNE. The intruder is out of the way. I'll fetch the hot water.

HYŌE. No need for that now, Tarō! There's yet another way to make the cock crow.

CHORUS. Then he places the cock
On the cover of the travelling-chest
And gently guides it
To the centre of the pool.

SUKUNE (*watching incredulously*). What kind of nonsense is this? Making a boat out of the cover of the travelling-chest and floating the cock on it! You're crazy!

HYŌE. My son, you have a thick head. Don't you know that if there is a corpse on the bottom of a deep river, and a boat with a cock in it passes over, the cock will crow when it is directly over the corpse? I just recalled this peculiar characteristic of cocks, so you see we will make good use of Tatsuta's body. Look, Tarō! The cock is flapping his wings. It's over the corpse now! There! It's crowing! It's crowing!

SUKUNE. Listen! Other cocks are crowing too!

CHORUS. The wily father and son

Seeing their plan succeed
Beam in delight,
As though the gates of heaven
Were suddenly swung open
For them to enter.

HYŌE. We must hurry now, so that we can come back for Lord
Sugawara. We can't lose another second. Come!

CHORUS. Hyōe leaves by the garden gate.
Sukune pauses for a moment,
Then suddenly turning,
He scurries off.

Within the house
The cock crow has been heard.
The time has come to finish preparations,
To perform the final ceremony of farewell
For Lord Sugawara
On his way to exile.

(SUGAWARA *enters, followed by* KAKUJU *and a* MAID *with the
arrangement of pine branches.*)

KAKUJU. This is the inevitable moment of life, the time from which
there is no escape, the death of parting. There is no delaying—
we can but hope for the Imperial pardon. This pine symbolizes
our constant longing for your safe return and our best wishes for
the future.

CHORUS. At the bleak moment of parting
All the unsaid things
Come welling up,
And parting becomes more painful still
Because we cannot say
The unsaid things.
Lord Sugawara
With reverence sadly bids his aunt farewell
With more unsaid than would have been
Had not the parting been so sorrowful.

(SUKUNE *appears from stage-right, followed by four officials led by*
YATŌJI, *who carries a mace.*)

SUKUNE. The time of departure has arrived. Already the escorts are
waiting outside the gate. Hangandai Terukuni has left his lodging
to prepare the roads for the Imperial train. He will soon be here
with his retainers. Bring on the palanquin.

MEN. Yes, sir.

(*Music. A covered palanquin, carried by four men, is brought on.*

SUGAWARA *enters the palanquin, and the procession exits on the* hanamichi.)

SUKUNE. Well, I'm glad that's over. You must be sad, Kakuju, but it must also be a relief. Perhaps you would like to go back to bed.

KAKUJU. No. No. I can no longer sleep.

SUKUNE. What's the matter? Don't you feel well?

KAKUJU. Oh, how strange this is! Within the same household the departure of Lord Sugawara creates both joy and sorrow. Here is my son-in-law feeling nothing but joy at seeing the guest depart, while the unfortunate Princess weeps in desperation because she could not bid farewell to her father. I did not call Tatsuta, for I thought she would wish to comfort the Princess. However, it showed a want of taste on her part not to have appeared at the leave-taking. Somebody bring Tatsuta to me.

MAIDS. Yes, madam.

(*They leave.*)

CHORUS. At Kakuju's order
    Sukune shows signs of dismay.
    Almost at once the maids of the household return.

(*They are accompanied by two menservants.*)

MAID I. We looked into the Lady Tatsuta's room, and also all the other inner rooms.

MAID II. But only Princess Kariya is there.

MAID III. The Lady Tatsuta is nowhere to be seen.

KAKUJU. What? Not here? That cannot be! Go and look again.

MAIDS. Yes, madam.

(*They leave, followed by* KAKUJU.)

SUKUNE. Here, men. Go and help to look for the Lady Tatsuta.

MEN. Yes, sir.

(*They exit.*)

CHORUS. From room to room,
    From house to garden,
    The search is made for Tatsuta.
    In the flower garden,
    Over the miniature hill,
    Maids and menservants,
    Lanterns in hand,
    Spread out through the garden.
    Then suddenly near the pool,
    One of the servants, Takunai,
    Sees a stain of blood.

TAKUNAI (*a clown, in great excitement*). Wait! Wait! Hold on! Hold on! *One,* I look around here; *two,* I think there's something suspicious; *three*, I know I've found something; *four*, and the dawn's about to break; *five*, I don't understand, but *six*, I believe I'm afraid; *seven*, I really wonder, *eight*, if I should, *nine*, take a dive, *ten*, into the pond!

ALL. Dive in! Dive in!

CHORUS. The chill morning air
　　　Vibrates with the cry,
　　　Search the pool!
　　　Search the pool!

　　　Then out wades the sturdy servant
　　　In his arms
　　　The mutilated body
　　　Of the once beautiful Tatsuta.

　　　Tarō stands stolidly alone
　　　In the midst of the whispers of horror.

SUKUNE. The cowardly murderer must still be here. Close the gates and let no one enter or leave until the fiend is found.

CHORUS. Disturbed by the cries of excitement
　　　Kakuju and the Princess
　　　Appear in haste
　　　To see what is happening.

KARIYA (*by the body*). Who did it? Tatsuta! Who did it? I wondered why you didn't come to me, but I thought you were with mother . . . and now you lie dead before me. Oh, can there be one more unfortunate than I? But now a farewell to my father in life, and now a farewell to my sister in death.

　　　(*The samisen repeats the sound of her weeping.*)

KAKUJU. Alas, my poor child! I thought she was with you, while you thought she was with me. It is my fault, it is my fault that she lies dead before us.

SUKUNE. Tears don't do a dead person any good. We've got to find the murderer and kill him for the repose of Tatsuta's spirit. I'll question every last one of you, man and woman. Takunai! Come here before me!

TAKUNAI (*cringing before* SUKUNE). Oh heavens! I didn't do it! Of all people, I should be the last to be suspected. I . . . I . . . If I'm to be called up first, it should be to present me with a reward for finding the body. If you would give me a reward, I would be extremely, extremely grateful.

SUKUNE. What? You greedy pig-head! What do you mean, asking for a reward? Now how did you know that Tatsuta's body was in the pool? Answer me that!

TAKUNAI (*terrified*). Well, sir, I couldn't possibly have seen the body in the pool, but when I saw the trail of blood leading there, I knew there must be something in the pool. That's a good explanation, isn't it?

SUKUNE. Hah! How could you see the blood in the weak light of that lantern? You killed her and sank her body in the pool. That's why you found the body when the others couldn't. You knew where it was from the beginning.

TAKUNAI. Oh, but master! Don't say such a thing! I tell you I just saw the trail of blood to the pool and that's all. I don't know anything else about it.

SUKUNE. You lie! You lie! A blood trail to the pool! Have you gone crazy to expect me to believe that? Take the fool and throw him in the water. I'll make him confess.

CHORUS. Mercilessly
    Takunai is dragged towards the pool.
    Sukune is about to follow
    But Kakuju interrupts him.

KAKUJU. That is not necessary, Sukune. While you were conducting your investigation, I discovered the murderer.

SUKUNE. You certainly have remarkable insight, mother dear. We'll cut the dog to pieces to revenge my wife. Hold his arms. (*He draws his sword.*)

KAKUJU. Wait! He must not be killed with a single thrust of the sword. For the death of my daughter, the murderer must die slowly, slowly, the pain eating up his soul. Let me first wound the animal that killed my daughter. Give me your sword, my son, give me your sword.

CHORUS. Kakuju takes the sword of Sukune,
    She slowly raises her arm
    To strike to the heart of the murderer:
    Sukune!
    Tarō!
    'Devour his heart, sword, let stream his blood.'
    Fatally wounded,
    Tarō,
    Gasping,
    Writhing,
    Moaning in agony,
    His eyes
    Black with hatred
    Turn on Kakuju:

SUKUNE. Why have you done this to me? Why?

KAKUJU. You are the murderer! You silenced the cries of Tatsuta with a cloth torn from your sleeve. There it is, yet in her mouth. O clever villain, your cleverness has been your undoing. Suffer, animal, suffer, here before the body of my daughter. Look, my daughter, look!

(SUKUNE, *in agony, crawls up on the centre platform.* SAMURAI *enters.*)

SAMURAI. Madam, Hangandai Terukuni has just arrived from his lodgings and waits outside.

CHORUS. Completely bewildered by this message,
The aged woman can only state the facts:

KAKUJU. Lord Sugawara has already departed with an escort, and therefore I don't know—— But let Terukuni be brought in.

SAMURAI. Yes, madam.

(*He goes. The servants remove the body of* TATSUTA.)

KAKUJU. Princess Kariya, retire to the inner chamber.

(*As* KARIYA *leaves*, TERUKUNI *appears in ceremonial clothes, carrying a mace.*)

TERUKUNI. The time of departure has come, madam. If everything is in order I should like to leave at once.

KAKUJU. What? What are you saying, Terukuni? Your servants arrived some time ago and Lord Sugawara left with them.

TERUKUNI. Now, now, dear lady! My servants did not come for Lord Sugawara. I told you I would come for him at the first cock crow, and it is now the promised hour. It is not likely that you would let him go a moment before the appointed time, even if I had come earlier. Dear lady, I know this parting is painful to you, but there is nothing to be gained by delaying it. You cannot save Lord Sugawara from exile; you can bring only misfortune on us all. Now forgo your plan, whatever it may be, and ask the Lord to prepare to leave.

KAKUJU. Oh, sir, there is no plan, there is no evasion. I am speaking the truth. The cock crowed in the garden, and Lord Sugawara left with the escort. (*Pause.*) My daughter's murder . . . my son-in-law . . . all this may be—the escort must have been a trick of some kind, a ruse to lead Lord Sugawara——

TERUKUNI. You may be right, my lady. They cannot have gone far. I must go after them at once. (*He moves towards the* hanamichi.)

VOICE OF SUGAWARA. Wait, Hangandai Terukuni, wait! I, Sugawara Michizane, am here.

(*The doors of the stage-right room slide open, revealing* SUGAWARA *sitting calmly within.*)

CHORUS. Kakuju
Stands aghast

At seeing Lord Sugawara before her,
But Terukuni,
The true escort,
Is overcome with glee.

TERUKUNI (*laughing*). The sincere manner of Lady Kakuju had convinced me. I thought you were really gone. How relieved I am to see you! (*To* KAKUJU.) I sympathize with your grief. If I had my way I would do everything possible to keep you together; but I am under Imperial orders and cannot act as I wish. Come, it grows late, let us make haste and depart.

(*A* SAMURAI *rushes in.*)

SAMURAI. The escorts who came for Lord Sugawara a while ago have returned. They are just outside the gate.

KAKUJU. What's that? They have returned? That is fortunate. Let them be brought before me. They shall serve as proof of my loyalty to the Imperial throne.

(*Exit* SAMURAI.)

TERUKUNI. These are villains, indeed! By impersonating my men they have involved my name in their foul deeds! But wait! If they see me they may run off. I'll hide myself to find out what they are up to. May I use your room as a hiding-place, Lord Sugawara?

CHORUS. Before Lord Sugawara has time to answer,
Terukuni closes the sliding doors behind him
And crouching there
Awaits the impostors.

(YATŌJI *and the escort run on to the* hanamichi *with the palanquin.*)

CHORUS. Seething with anger,
As he sees Kakuju calmly smiling,
Yatōji bellows:

YATŌJI. Hah, old woman! What do you mean by trying to deceive us, the representatives of the honourable Terukuni, by passing this thing off on us. You can't fool me with such a trick!

KAKUJU. What is the cause of your shouting? Lord Sugawara went with you. What do you mean by 'this thing'?

YATŌJI. What! Still trying to play innocent, eh? Sugawara is Sugawara. We don't want a Sugawara made of wood! What'll I do, what'll I do? I'll tell you what I'll do! I'll exchange this wooden image for the real flesh and blood Sugawara—if you don't mind.

CHORUS. A flash of comprehension
Lights up the face of Kakuju.
Can it be

That the spirit-filled image of Sugawara
Entered the palanquin?

KAKUJU. I do not understand what you are talking about. Let me
see the wooden image.

YATŌJI. Sure! I'll show it to you! Old wooden image! (*He pulls
back the screen of the palanquin.*)

CHORUS. The screen is opened,
And look!
Here is no wooden image,
But the stately figure
Of Lord Sugawara himself.
The false escort,
Aghast at the sight,
Kakuju,
Amazed at her miscalculation,
All stare incredulously at Lord Sugawara.

KAKUJU. Oh, thank you, thank you, for returning him safely.
(*She moves towards* SUGAWARA, *but* YATŌJI *holds her back.*)

YATŌJI. Hold on! Hold on! Don't go near! But who am I to say
that? I take away Lord Sugawara, and find an image. I return
to get the real Sugawara, and what do I find? The flesh and
blood Sugawara again. Are my eyes deceiving me, or is it the
change in altitude? Hey, it's uncanny.

KAKUJU. It makes no difference what form Lord Sugawara may
choose to take. Let me go to him.

YATŌJI. What the——! Where do you think you're going?

CHORUS. Pushing Kakuju aside,
Yatōji forces Lord Sugawara
Back into the palanquin.

YATŌJI. You men have just seen a strange happening. Lord Sugawara
transformed into an image and back to himself again. We can't
leave without solving the mystery. Now, men, search the house!

MEN. Yes, sir!

CHORUS. As he rushes to the house,
Yatōji discovers Sukune Tarō
Hovering between life and death.

YATŌJI. By the treasures of Buddha! Tarō has been wounded!
(*He turns.*) Master, master! It's Tarō. He's hurt!

CHORUS. Hearing the cry
The father Hyōe,
Forgetting his disguise,
Rushes from the group of escorts
To the side of his son.

HYŌE. Tarō, my son! Who did this to you? Name the scoundrel!

KAKUJU. Hyōe! I, Kakuju, am his slayer!

HYŌE. What! Why are you proud at slaying your own son? What has he done?

KAKUJU. Deceive us no more, Hyōe. You and your son killed my daughter Tatsuta. You and your son plotted Lord Sugawara's death. Confess to your crime, Hyōe!

HYŌE. Ha! We were so close to success, and now—— Filthy old woman! Yes, I made the cock crow before dawn. By killing Sugawara my son could have joined the ranks of the noble Shihei, he could have risen in the world. But now, my son—— Ah, Kakuju, you have killed my son. You have destroyed my hopes——

(HYŌE *draws his sword and moves towards* KAKUJU.)

CHORUS. But just at this moment
          A figure appears.
          It is Hangandai Terukuni
          Come to protect Kakuju.

HYŌE. Don't try to stop me, Terukuni! I will have my revenge.

CHORUS. Reckless with rage
          He lunges forward,
          But Terukuni quickly steps aside.
          Wresting the sword from Hyōe's hand,
          Pinning him down with his mighty foot,
          Terukuni shouts in stern command:

TERUKUNI. Come, men! Tie up the impostors!

YATŌJI. Come, men! Tie up the impostors!

A GUARD. But sir! You are one of the impostors.

YATŌJI. Eh? Why so I am!

CHORUS. At the command
          'Tie up the impostors!'
          The members of the false escort
          Scamper away helter-skelter.

          Concerned for the comfort of Lord Sugawara
          Kakuju opens the palanquin.
          But to her amazement
          She finds the wooden image.
          Doubting her eyes,
          She goes to the house
          And slides open the door.

(SUGAWARA *is seated within the room.*)

SUGAWARA. My dear aunt! All is well. Do not disturb yourself.

KAKUJU. Terukuni, can you tell me which is Lord Sugawara himself?

SUGAWARA. Since the escorts of Terukuni did not appear, I fell asleep while waiting. Then the clamour outside awoke me. Now, waking from my dream, I find Hyōe's plot against me discovered, and Lady Tatsuta dead. Oh, Aunt Kakuju, this is a sorrowful day for you indeed! And I, Michizane, have brought this evil upon you, by staying in this house.

KAKUJU. No! No! Had I a hundred daughters, their lives would be less than yours. You have been saved from death, and I am content. So why should I weep . . . why should I weep . . . (*She sobs.*)

CHORUS. Though firm in her loyalty to Sugawara
Her mother's heart is torn with grief.

KAKUJU (*calming herself*). There is the cause of all this evil—Haji no Hyōe! (*She goes to* HYŌE.) Look, you beast, at Lord Sugawara, alive and well before you. Look at him, and my daughter's spirit will find rest.

CHORUS. Then moving to Tarō
She pulls the sword of vengeance
From his side.
As if the blade
Tore the last breath from his body,
He sinks
Into death.

KAKUJU. Loathsome as you are, this death exceeds my revenge. This is the blade that cut off my daughter's life; now, blade, cut off my white hair, symbol of earthly sins.

CHORUS. Then with the sword of vengeance
She cuts off a strand of silver hair.

KAKUJU. Long, long ago, this hair should have been cut from my head. But I clung to life, hoping one day to see my grandchildren. Now the future is barren, my lineage ends with me. My daughter has gone before me into the land of Buddha, while I must yet enter the way of Buddha as a nun. (*In anguish.*) What Karma is this? (*Pause.*) Namu Amida Butsu.

CHORUS. As Kakuju murmurs the holy words
The eyes of Sugawara are wet with tears.
Hangandai Terukuni, deeply moved,
Watches the reverent scene.

TERUKUNI. Now that you have bid farewell to this fleeting world, I, Terukuni, will complete your revenge. The villain has lived long enough. (*He kills* HYŌE.)

KAKUJU. Without the mystic powers of this image, the murderous plot of Hyōe would not have been discovered.

SUGAWARA. Many are the legends of pictures and images that have come to life. I carved this image out of the depths of my heart and soul; it received my spirit and saved my life. Now, in disgrace, my body is being sent into exile, but . . .

CHORUS. The image of Sugawara,
          Who after death became the god Tenjin,
          This sacred image
          Containing the soul of its creator
          Remains to this day
          In the village of Kawachi
          In the temple Dōmyō.

TERUKUNI. Forgive me, my lord, but the hour grows late. See, the sun rises over the hills.

KAKUJU. But wait, my lord. Accept from me a parting gift.
          (*She claps her hands and a maid appears.*)

KAKUJU. Bring me the things I have prepared.

CHORUS. Kakuju orders her maid
          To bring a silken cloak of Princess Kariya
          Laid over a basket of incense.
          (*The* MAID *returns with the cloak.*)

KAKUJU. The voyage may be cold and windy, and so I have brought a cloak fragrant with the incense of my good wishes. Take it with you, my lord, and wear it to the isle of exile. Terukuni, will you hand it to him?

TERUKUNI. Here is a thoughtful gift. An incensed cloak both to please the senses and to keep out the cold. (*He goes to* SUGAWARA *and gives him the cloak.*)

SUGAWARA. I appreciate the cloak which expresses your kind feelings. But the incense? Am I not familiar with it? Can it be the fragrance of the Princess Kariya? (*Pause.*) Alas, my aunt, this is a woman's garment, and I cannot wear it. But I shall take it with me, and treasure it as I treasure the memory of my daughter.

CHORUS. Thus Sugawara let Kakuju know
          That he understood the significance of her gift.

KAKUJU. Forgive me, forgive me, but before you depart, see her, even for a moment . . . please grant your aunt's request.
          (*She clings to* SUGAWARA. KARIYA *appears.*)

SUGAWARA. It may be that my ears deceive me, but I thought I heard the cry of a young bird in pain. And if the young bird cry, will not the heart of its parent cry also? (*Pause.*) I leave behind me this poem:

CHORUS. Look forward
  And face the dawn of the distant land,
  And hurry your parting
  At the cry of the bird.
(*As* SUGAWARA *turns to leave,* KARIYA *timidly approaches him and takes his sleeve. He shakes her hand off, not looking at her, and starts towards the* hanamichi. *She sadly follows her father and bursts into tears as he walks on to the* hanamichi. SUGAWARA *moves to the rear of the* hanamichi *throughout the speech of the chorus.*)
CHORUS. This,
  Then,
  The last farewell.
  Sadly
  He touches his daughter's garment.
  It seems to him a wingless bird,
  Quietly perched on the incense basket,
  While he,
  The father,
  Is a captive bird,
  Caged
  By the plots of wicked men,
  Caged
  By his code of behaviour.
  Now,
  Though the dawn flames on the hill,
  Within his soul
  All is darkness.
  Yet in this darkness
  Shines a light
  To guide his steps
  On the unknown path before him,
  A light
  Now clouded by mortality
  But soon to shine more radiant than the sun,
  The light
  Of the way
  Of the gods.
  Hence the name of the temple
  That honours his image:
  Dōmyōji.
  Dōmyōji,
  The temple of the enlightened path.

H

One last look.
And now,
The end of his story.
He departs
On the journey of no return,
The journey of no return.

CURTAIN

ACT III

SCENE I

The home of SHIRODAYŪ *of Satamura. The interior of a thatched hut is raised above the stage floor. On stage-left, a small room enclosed by paper sliding doors. In front of this are three young trees, each enclosed by a low bamboo fence: a pine, a plum, and a cherry-tree. On stage-right, a gate marks the entrance to the garden in front of the house. In the upstage wall of the house is a curtained door and to the side of it a household Buddhist shrine.*

The curtain rises to folk music.

SHIRODAYŪ, *seventy years old, is working in the garden.*

CHORUS. The months before spring
Are times of leisure
For the peasants
Who use the hoe and the plough,
But not for the industrious Shirodayū.
In the village of Sata,
On Lord Sugawara's estate,
Lives Shirodayū,
A peasant,
The oldest of Sugawara's followers.
He has spent his life
In loyal devotion to his lord,
Tending the gardens,
Loving all green, growing things.
His greatest care
He gives to the pine,
The plum,
And the cherry,
The favourite trees of his kind master,
Who in days past
Came often to this distant farm.
But on this day

He sets aside his rake and hoe
To gather round him
His triplet sons and their wives,
And with them celebrate
A memorable occasion:
His day of birth,
Now seventy times returned.

Bundle in hand,
Walking merrily,
Comes Sakuramaru's wife,
The gentle Yae.

YAE (*at the gate*). Good day, father. I've finally arrived!

SHIRODAYŪ (*going to her*). Yae, wife of Sakuramaru! The other
two wives should be coming soon. Now, come in, come in, and
rest a while.

(*They go into the house.*)

YAE. Oh, the others haven't come yet?

SHIRODAYŪ. No, I'm still waiting for my sons and the other two
wives. It will be nice to have all of you here together, to celebrate
this great day.

YAE. You have lived to a rare age, father.

SHIRODAYŪ. Yes, when I went to pay my respects to Lord Sugawara
this spring, he was surprised to learn I was almost seventy years
old. And he was so pleased that I have taken good care of his
land all these years, he ordered me to have a celebration on my
birthday. So I made my plans. I felt that for such an occasion it
would be proper to have my triplet sons and their wives with me.

YAE. We are very glad for you, father. I am so happy we can be
with you to honour the month, the day, and the exact hour of
your birth. Oh, I was so excited this morning! I was afraid I'd
be late, then I got on the big ferry on the banks of the Yodo, then I
hurried to get here.

(CHIYO *and* HARU *appear on the* hanamichi. *They are carrying hats
filled with flowers.*)

CHORUS. Then come the wives of Umeō and Matsuō.
They have been lingering on the way,
With womanly delicacy
Picking the early spring flowers
To take to the house of Shirodayū.

(*The women arrive at the gate.*)

CHIYO. It took time to pick the flowers, but it was time well spent.
You go in first, Haru.

HARU. Oh, no, Chiyo, after you!

CHORUS. The wives of Umeō and Matsuō
　　　　Exceedingly careful to preserve courtesy
　　　　Urge each other to enter first,
　　　　And neither enters.
　　　　Shirodayū,
　　　　Privately amused,
　　　　Settles this momentous problem.

SHIRODAYŪ. Here, here, it doesn't matter which of you enters first.
Waste no time, and come on in.

(*They do, quickly, and* YAE *goes to greet them.*)

HARU. You certainly got here early, Yae. I thought perhaps you
would stop at my house on your way over, and so I waited there.
But then it got later and later, and I decided I'd better go.
Fortunately I met Chiyo on the way, and we picked these flowers
to enliven this gay occasion.

YAE. That was so thoughtful of you! I wanted to stop at your house,
but I was late myself. It's so nice that you met Chiyo!

CHIYO. Oh it was fortunate for me to have met Haru. We had such
a pleasant trip. Now, father, have you prepared the food?

SHIRODAYŪ. No, I haven't. I want you three to do it. No need for
anything fancy. There's some rice left from this morning. I
boiled some seaweed, so we won't have to waste time on that. The
radishes are right there—oh, well, you don't know your way about,
so, arrrh, I'll get up.

CHIYO. Oh, no, don't get up! You're the honoured one at this
happy anniversary. Don't worry about the food. You just rest
until it's all ready.

HARU. Yes, yes, we may not know our way about, but we'll manage.

SHIRODAYŪ. Well, that's very nice of you. But since I'm up, I may
as well get some of the things off the shelves for you. (*He takes
down some trays and plates.*) Look here! These plates have been in
our family for generations. There are ten of them, and they're
very sturdy. Just as sturdy as I am. But don't handle them too
roughly. (*Pause.*) I wonder what's keeping my three sons? I
might as well take a short nap until they come.

CHORUS. And the kind and generous father of the triplets
　　　　Lies down
　　　　And goes to sleep.

HARU. Now really, even if he says there is no need for anything
fancy, we can't just serve these things! We must cook some rice,
and we simply must have some fish and some vegetables. And we
really ought to make some soup, too.

YAE. Yes, certainly. I'll make the soup.

HARU. And I'll prepare the rice. Chiyo, Yae, will you help me?

CHIYO. Let's begin, let's begin the preparations!

(*To music, a little ballet of the kitchen.*)

CHORUS. Rice is poured
Into the pot
Water carried
The fire started
Grind
Grind
Goes the mill
Chop
Chop
The kitchen knife
Happy women
Preparing food
Pleasant task
Happy women . . .

But Shirodayū can sleep no longer
And rises from troubled dozing.

SHIRODAYŪ. Haven't my sons come yet? There's no reason for
their being late, they've known about my birthday celebration
since New Year's Day. Now let's see. Oh, yes, my neighbour was
telling me the other day that he heard the triplets had a big fight
in front of Shihei's carriage. You three must know something
about it. Matsuō's wife! Since Matsuō is in the service of Shihei,
you come here and explain everything.

CHORUS. To her embarrassment
Unhappy Chiyo is singled out
To tell of the quarrel of the husbands.

(*The three women look at each other.* CHIYO, *having no choice,
approaches* SHIRODAYŪ.)

CHIYO. Well, we didn't want to tell you about this now, before the
celebration, but . . . well, my husband happened to lose his
temper with Sakuramaru and Umeōmaru, and they had a fight.
But it's nothing to worry about. No one was hurt . . . and the
affair was settled . . . for the moment. But my husband is still
grumbling about it. (*To the women.*) Isn't it the same with your
husbands? These men and their unfortunate tempers!

HARU. Yes, that's so. But we hoped this gay celebration might
smooth over their ill-feeling.

YAE. Yes, father. If this happy day could only bring them together again!

CHORUS. With tender feelings for their husbands
The wives plead for help from Shirodayū.

SHIRODAYŪ. I had a feeling it was something of the sort. Born at the same time, yet so different in nature. Generally triplets look alike and think alike. But not so with mine. Nobody would believe they were even brothers. The easy-going Sakuramaru, the practical Umeōmaru, and the ill-natured, wicked-looking Matsuōmaru. Oh, forgive me, Chiyo! Don't take me seriously. Well, I'm glad to hear that no one was hurt. But it's getting late, it's almost the exact hour I was born. Has everything been prepared? Hurry! Bring out the food!

HARU. But what can be keeping the men? It's so late! Shall we go out to the roadside and see if they are coming?

CHIYO. Yes, rather than wait here, we may as well go and look for them.

(*They move towards the gate, but* SHIRODAYŪ *calls to them.*)

SHIRODAYŪ. Ah, ah, wait, wait! The men are here. They've been here all the while.

THE THREE WOMEN. Our husbands here? Where? Where?

SHIRODAYŪ. Oh, you dull women! Can't you see them right there? The three trees are my three sons. Umeō, the plum, Matsuō, the pine, Sakura, the cherry. All three are there. Now Lord Sugawara told me to celebrate my birth exactly to the minute—we mustn't offend such a great lord. So make haste with the trays of food. Hurry! Hurry!

CHORUS. Prompted by Shirodayū
The wives wait no longer
But busy themselves
To prepare the trays.

(YAE *takes a tray to* SHIRODAYŪ *in the house.*)

YAE. First, dear father, please be seated here.

SHIRODAYŪ. No, I'll go down there and be served.

YAE. No, the ground is too cold; it is not good for you. Please dine here.

(SHIRODAYŪ *sits.*)

CHIYO. And now we'll each serve our husbands.

(*The three women bring trays and place them before the trees.*)

HARU. This plum-tree represents my husband, Umeōmaru.

YAE. This shapely cherry-tree is very much like Sakuramaru of Yoshino.

CHIYO. Strong and faithful is this pine, symbol of Matsuōmaru. This makes the party complete.

(*The women move to the right and sit before their trays.*)

THE THREE WOMEN. Happy birthday, dear father.

SHIRODAYŪ. Thank you, thank you. But I must make some sort of speech before we begin.

HARU. No, no, there's no need to be so formal. Please eat your food before it gets cold.

CHORUS. Then he moves from the room
Into the garden,
And there before the three trees
He bows.

SHIRODAYŪ. My sons, I appreciate your coming here on this happy occasion. I know you would like to make congratulatory speeches, but you can't talk. Never mind, just stay as you are. (*He returns to his food.*) Here, women, give the children another serving of rice. Mmmm. This is delicious. Who made it? I guess you all did. I suppose I'll have to have three servings of everything, so I won't offend one of you, eh?

(*He chokes on some food. The wives gather around him, pounding him on the back and giving him water.*)

SHIRODAYŪ. Ohhh! I almost committed suicide on that.

(*Pause. Then he notices a little stand which* YAE *has put in front of him.*)

SHIRODAYŪ. Well, what's this? A brand new stand! Who brought it?

HARU. That's Yae's present for you.

SHIRODAYŪ. Well, this is a surprise! Thank you, thank you. Haru, are you giving me something too?

HARU. Oh, yes, I almost forgot! (*She takes three fans from her sleeve.*) Here are three fans, with pictures of the pine, the plum, and the cherry. In the same way that these fans spread out, so may the lives of your sons.

SHIRODAYŪ. Thank you, Haru. This is a joyous present. (*Then he quickly puts down the fans.*)

CHIYO. And I have made this head-band for you. Please wear it and remember me.

SHIRODAYŪ. Thank you, Chiyo. You are all very thoughtful. Well, now that I've had my food, you might clear away the trays. (*Pause.*) The children's food is probably cold by now. (*Pause.*) But why don't you all have some more to eat?

CHIYO. No, thank you. We'll wait for our husbands.

HARU. Then we'll all eat together.

SHIRODAYŪ. Well, do as you wish. Now I'll go and pay reverence to the village shrine. (*He gets up, picking up the fans, and moves down into the garden.*)

HARU. Very well, father.

SHIRODAYŪ. Please hand me the coins I have prepared for my offering. (*He looks at the fans.*) I will show the gods these three fans, symbols of the well-being of my three sons.

(*Pause.* YAE *hands him the coins. Pause.*)

SHIRODAYŪ. Yae, would you like to come along with me?

CHIYO. That's a fine idea, Yae. Haru and I have already seen the shrine; why don't you go with him?

YAE. Yes, I think I will.

SHIRODAYŪ. Shall we go?

(*They move through the gate,* SHIRODAYŪ *walking with a cane, and go off right.*)

HARU. Don't rush, father. Take your time. (*Pause.*) I wonder what's keeping Umeōmaru? He should be here by now!

CHIYO. And Matsuōmaru! It can't be that he doesn't intend to come. How could he stay away on such an occasion?

(*She moves to the gate.* MATSUŌMARU, *wearing ceremonial clothes, appears on the* hanamichi. *Music.*)

CHIYO. Well here he comes. It's Matsuō.

(*He comes through the gate.*)

CHIYO. Where have you been? Don't you know it's way past the promised time?

MATSUŌ (*he sits. Roughly*). Be quiet! I had to carry out an order of Shihei, and I couldn't leave until I was finished. Didn't you tell father that, or did you forget? Where's Umeō and Sakura? Where's father?

CHIYO. Father has gone to the shrine with Yae. Your brothers haven't arrived yet.

MATSUŌ. What? Not here? Then why are you complaining about me being late? I, who have a lord to serve. Umeō and Sakura have no lord. Those rascals have no reason at all to be late.

(*Music.* UMEŌMARU, *wearing plain clothes, runs the length of the* hanamichi *and comes through the gate.*)

CHORUS.   Then Umeōmaru,
           Weary after his long journey,
           Comes rushing in,
           Almost falling in his haste.
           He pretends not to notice Matsuōmaru.

UMEŌ. It's nice to see you, Chiyo. (*He sits on the opposite side of the stage from* MATSUŌ.) Where are the others?

HARU. Matsuō just asked that. Sakuramaru hasn't arrived yet, and the others have gone to the shrine.

UMEŌ. Sakuramaru hasn't come yet, eh? The ones you wish to

see don't come, but somehow the ugliest faces are always there to greet you.

CHORUS. Goaded by Umeōmaru,
Matsuōmaru can no longer be silent.

MATSUŌ. If you have anything insulting to say, say it to my face like a man!

UMEŌ. Ahhh! I can't say anything to your face. Every time I look at it I get sick in my stomach.

MATSUŌ. Your hardships have unsettled your brain. I feel sorry for you. It must be a difficult life, being a masterless retainer. I have a lord to serve.

UMEŌ. A lord! Do you think you're serving a lord? It takes a dirty bastard to receive support from dirty hands.

MATSUŌ. Hold your foul tongue! You dare repeat that word again and I'll——

UMEŌ. Of course I will! You bastard! You bastard! How's that? You dirty bastard!

MATSUŌ. You'll be sorry for that!

CHORUS. Matsuōmaru,
His pride gone,
Reaches for his sword.
And Umeōmaru
Repeats the action of his brother.
The wives,
Astonished,
Rush between them.

CHIYO. Wait, wait! Have you gone crazy, Matsuō?

HARU. Umeō! You've come here to celebrate your father's birthday, and look! How can you do this? Stop it, and listen to me!

CHORUS. Deaf to the pleading of his wife,
Who clings to his sword,
Umeō throws her from him.

UMEŌ. Birthday or no birthday, this thing must be settled here and now. Come on, Matsuō! (*Pause.*) What's the matter, are you scared? You coward! Now you'll want to use your wife as an excuse for not fighting!

MATSUŌ. I'm not making excuses! I'm thinking of what your wife said. It's true, we can't duel until after we've seen our father. But if I can't kill you now, at least I can give you a beating. Here, Chiyo, hold my swords.

UMEŌ. All right! Until Sakuramaru comes, I'll let you live. (*He gives his swords to* HARU.) Without swords there can't be much bloodshed. Stand back, you two, and don't get in the way.

(*They fight in stylized dance movement.*)

CHORUS. They rush on each other
    Come to grips
    Matsuō falls
    Umeō jumps upon him
    A tangled mass of arms and legs
    Grabbing, punching, scratching, slapping,
    Gouging, pulling, turning, twisting,
    Rolling on the ground.
    Together, apart, together, apart,
    He drags him!
    He pins him down!
    He kicks him!
    Two brothers in the prime of life
    All their strength directed against each other.

    Chiyo and Haru,
    Swords in hand,
    Horrified at their husbands' quarrel,
    Not daring to come close,
    For fear the two might seize the swords
    In a moment of frenzy.

HARU. Umeō, don't you think you've had enough?

CHIYO. Dear husband, please stop it. That's enough!

MATSUŌ. Be quiet! One of us has to win.

CHORUS. Matsuō with all his strength
    Lunges at Umeō to lift him up.
    Umeō with furious resistance
    Turns and twists his mighty shoulders.
    Evenly matched with equal strength
    Like the powerful pine-tree
    And the stubborn plum-tree
    They stand unmoving for a breathless second.
    Then a sudden twist
    And they both fall
    Against the cherry-tree.
    The wives are shocked:
    A branch of
    The once proud tree is broken.
    The brothers
    All vigour gone
    Pant in weary agony.

HARU. Stop it! Stop it! Here comes father!

MATSUŌ. What? Father?

UMEŌ. He's come home?

CHIYO. Yes, and look! The cherry-tree your father has been tending all these years!

UMEŌ. I didn't do it!

MATSUŌ. I didn't either!

THE WOMEN. What a terrible thing you have done!

CHORUS. There is scarcely time to recover their swords
Before the return of their father.
Though grown men
They cower
Like frightened schoolboys
At the thought of being scolded.

(*Music.* SHIRODAYŪ *and* YAE *enter.* SHIRODAYŪ *looks at the brothers, then goes up the steps into the house. He gazes at the broken cherry-tree for a moment, then down at the brothers, who are frightened and bow at his feet.* YAE *sits near* SHIRODAYŪ.)

MATSUŌ. Dear father, on your happy seventieth anniversary——

UMEŌ. ——we bring you our heartfelt felicitations.

SHIRODAYŪ. Your wives came on time, so we're all finished with the ceremonies. You knew about this celebration long ago, so when you didn't come at the appointed hour I knew you had urgent business to attend to. Umeō, Matsuō, I am very happy you could come.

CHORUS. Although he had seen the broken tree,
There were no words of anger from Shirodayū.
He seemed to take no further notice of the tree,
Nor did he ask who broke it.
In former times
Their father would have punished them.
Now since he says nothing,
The brothers are puzzled.
They sense a hidden reason
For his mild manner,
His unusual behaviour.

Then Umeō brings forth a paper,
A formal request to present to his father.

UMEŌ. Since the celebration is finished, will you please grant this request of mine?

MATSUŌ (*producing a paper*). I also have a request to make.

SHIRODAYŪ. I thought everything should be informal among members of a family. You could tell me what you want, but here you are giving it to me in writing. Well, I'll pretend I'm a government official and act formal too. Now let's see . . .

CHORUS. Taking up the letter
Shirodayū reads,
Mumbling to himself,
Scarcely audible.
And Yae,
Understanding none of this,
Fears all is not well,
Fears what may come. . . .

YAE (*aside, to the other women*). Chiyo, Haru, what is the meaning of all this? Can't we bring the brothers together as we planned? Oh, if only my husband were here!

CHORUS. The other wives sympathize with Yae,
Anxious about her husband.
Meanwhile Shirodayū has read the letters.

SHIRODAYŪ. Umeō, you request permission to travel. You want to go to the island where Lord Sugawara lives in exile, is that it?

UMEō. Yes, father. It must be difficult for the lord to live in a thatched cottage after living in a palace. Please grant me leave to go so I can serve him there.

SHIRODAYŪ. It is said that if you have no sense of obligation to one who has done much for you, you may have the outward appearance of a human being, but within is the heart of a beast. Your request shows that you have a human heart. Are the lord's wife and son safe and taken care of?

UMEō. I haven't seen Lady Sugawara since the exile; I don't know where she is. But she's only a woman. As for the young Prince Kan Shūsai, I know definitely that he is—— (*A glance at* MATSUō.) ——well, that he is safe—according to rumours—but I don't know where he is exactly.

SHIRODAYŪ. What! How can you claim to be loyal when you don't care where the young prince is? And saying the lord's wife is only a woman! She's your master as much as he is, if you don't happen to know it! I'd better go to the island and attend to the lord myself. You're probably afraid of your life. How can I depend on a coward like you to protect him? I reject your request!

CHORUS. Striking Umeō with the letter,
Shirodayū glares at his son and daughter-in-law,
And before his wrath
Husband and wife bow in fear.

SHIRODAYŪ. Matsuō, you have requested banishment from this

household. If ever there was an unfilial, irreverent rascal, you are the one. But—I grant your request.

MATSUŌ (*solemnly*). Thank you, very much. I hope you understand that I made the request because I want to be loyal to my lord.

SHIRODAYŪ. *You* speak of loyalty? Loyalty is honourable only when you walk the right road. You would cut yourself off from your blood relations to serve an enemy of this household, eh? When you act against your parents, you act against the will of the gods. I've granted your wish, now leave before I thrash you. Get out of my sight. Go!

CHIYO. Oh, you fool! What a thing to do to father! Father, father, do not forget your grandchild!

SHIRODAYŪ. I no longer love a child of his! Now go! (*Pause.*) Why don't you go? Or do you want me to return the present you gave me today? Here! Take it and go!

(*He throws the head-band at* CHIYO.)

CHIYO. Oh, don't, don't!

MATSUŌ. Take it back, then. If he won't use it, I will.

SHIRODAYŪ. Why, you——! I'll beat you till——

(*He is about to strike* MATSUŌ.)

MATSUŌ (*rising*). You'd better not! Tomorrow I will shave off my forelock and become one of the samurai in the service of Shihei— as Matsuō Harima no Kami. If you raise your hand against me, you will be punished. Come, Chiyo.

(*He exits, right.*)

CHORUS. Innocent of this quarrel,
　　　　Chiyo is torn between father and son.
　　　　Blinded by tears,
　　　　She silently bids farewell
　　　　To Haru and Yae.

(CHIYO *follows* MATSUŌ.)

SHIRODAYŪ. I'm glad to be done with that villain. (*To* UMEŌ). Well, foolish one, why are you still here? Take your leave and look for Lady Sugawara and the young prince. Go!

UMEŌ (*rising*). Then you mean I can't go to the island?

SHIRODAYŪ. No! I am the one to go. Now get out of my sight.

(UMEŌ *and* HARU *move towards the gate.*)

HARU (*aside*). Yae, please reason with him later on, won't you?

YAE (*aside*). Don't worry! After he's calmed down, I'll talk to him.

SHIRODAYŪ. I ordered you to leave! Now get out!

(*He chases them from the garden with a broom.*)

CHORUS. Husband and wife
　　　　Pause outside the gate.

Reluctant to leave,
They decide to hide themselves
And return later.

Shirodayū,
Shaking with anger,
Goes within the house.

(SHIRODAYŪ *disappears into the curtained doorway.* YAE *stands by the
gate looking for* SAKURAMARU.)

CHORUS. Left all alone,
Yae ponders the strange events of this day,
Hoping her husband
Will soon come through the gate
And put an end to her sorrows.
But he will not come through the gate.
The curtain of the inner room parts,
And there stands Sakuramaru,
Sword in hand,
Quietly smiling.

SAKURAMARU. Dear wife, you have been waiting for me a long time.

YAE. Sakuramaru! Where did you come from? Here I've been
worrying about you, and all the while you were inside the house.
Father lost his temper at your brothers, and you just stayed there.
(*She goes to him.*) What is the meaning of this? Why did you hide
yourself? Tell me! Why?

CHORUS. And then comes Shirodayū
Bearing the full weight of his years,
An old man,
Weary of living.
He carries a ceremonial stand,
And on it,
A naked sword.
Comes slowly,
Slowly,
And places the stand before his son,
Sakuramaru.

SHIRODAYŪ. Here it is. If you are ready, wait no longer.

CHORUS. And horror
Sets its talons
In the heart of Yae.

YAE. Sakuramaru, what are you doing? This sword——! You are
going to kill yourself! Father, why must he kill himself? Why,
father? (*To* SAKURAMARU). Tell me why!

SAKURAMARU. You are my dear wife, and you must know. (*He sits.*)
My master is the Prince Tokiyo. I was given the honour of serving
the Prince because of the influence of Lord Sugawara. We owe
all our good fortune to the lord: he has been kind to our father,
he named me and my brothers after his most treasured trees, he
raised us in rank to serve at his palace. Of the three brothers, I,
Sakuramaru, was the most fortunate. I served a prince of royal
blood, and brought him and his beloved Princess Kariya together. But the treacherous Shihei has turned their innocent love
into a scandal, and both she and Lord Sugawara have been
branded conspirators to the throne. Now the house of Sugawara
is crumbling. The Prince and the Princess are in good hands;
they no longer need my clumsy services. But to atone for the
misery I have brought upon them, and upon Lord Sugawara, I
must end my miserable life. Early this morning I came to see my
father and received his blessing. He understands that I must do
this. So, dear Yae, thank him for me, and take care of him when
I am gone.

YAE. Have you forgotten that I, too, helped bring the Prince and
Princess together? If you must kill yourself to atone for this, then
I also must die. You cannot ask me to live without you. Father,
don't just sit there with bowed head. You must stop him. Have
you no feelings at all?

CHORUS. Half crazed with anguish
     Her soul in hell
     Pleading with Shirodayū
     He must speak
     He must tell her . . .

SHIRODAYŪ. Yae, Yae, don't think me a heartless father! Today was
to be a day of happiness for me. I got up early this morning, and
when I opened the door, Sakuramaru was standing there. I
thought he had walked all night long, or got a special boat, just
to be with me a little longer today. I felt great tenderness and joy.
But when he told me why he had come so early, my joy was gone.
Ah, I tried to argue with him, but he wouldn't listen. Since the
rest of you were coming soon, I asked him to wait in the house
until the celebration was over. Then I tried to decide whether he
should kill himself. But I couldn't. And so I asked the gods to
decide for me. Yae, those three fans Haru gave me—— I pretended I was going to the shrine to pray for the happiness of my
sons, but I took you along so that the gods could decide your
husband's fate. I prayed for a long time that his life might be
spared. Then I placed the three fans before the altar. I asked the

gods to let my hand fall on the cherry-blossom fan if Sakuramaru
was to be saved. I closed my eyes and prayed fervently as I
picked up a fan. On it was painted the plum blossom. In my
despair, I dared to doubt the decision of the gods and I picked up
another fan. It was the pine-tree. But even then I was not willing
to believe that this was the undeniable decision of the gods. I
came home, and I found a branch of the cherry-tree broken. It
was the gods' final warning not to disregard their decision. There
was no other way: I had to grant my son's last wish and bring to
him the sword. . . . I am suffering too, Yae. Do not cry. I will
not cry either.

SAKURAMARU. Now, Yae, you know everything. My only regret
is that I must leave this life before my father. But I know my
disgrace, and I must fulfil my obligation.

CHORUS. Solemnly
　　　Sakuramaru lifts the sword,
　　　The sword
　　　Whose sharp edge undoes life,
　　　The sword
　　　Whose blade moves
　　　Between the now
　　　And the hereafter.
　　　No tears
　　　Dim the image of the sword
　　　In the eyes of Sakuramaru,
　　　But Shirodayū
　　　Cannot see the sword . . .
　　　Cannot . . .
　　　See . . .

SHIRODAYŪ. Your father will assist in the noble death of his son. See,
this is what I will use. (*Reaching into his kimono, he brings out a small
bell-hammer.*) If I help him with this 'sword', he will forever, for
all eternity, be at peace. With this 'sword' he will become a
Buddha.

　　　(SHIRODAYŪ *sits before the shrine, repeating the prayer, 'Namu Amida
　　　Butsu, Namu Amida Butsu', while striking the bell.* YAE *seizes her
　　　husband's arm, and he gently removes her hand.*)

CHORUS. As if
　　　In rhythm
　　　With his father's chant
　　　Sakuramaru
　　　Raises
　　　The sword

Steel pierces flesh
And it is done.
(SHIRODAYŪ *strikes the bell more loudly.*)

SAKURAMARU. Father, father, help me!

SHIRODAYŪ. Yes, my son.
(*He goes behind* SAKURAMARU *and chants.*)

CHORUS. Devoutly he repeats the parting chant:
Namu Amida Butsu
Namu Amida Butsu . . .
Then Sakuramaru
Slowly
Raises
The sword
Cuts his throat.
(YAE *seizes the sword, intending to kill herself. At this moment,* UMEŌ *and* HARU *rush in.* UMEŌ *wrests the sword from* YAE, *then bows before his father.*)

UMEŌ. We knew something was wrong. That's why we didn't go away.

CHORUS. The life of Sakuramaru now ends.
Sharply
Suddenly
Like the snapping of a branch of the cherry-tree.
Silent tears
Regret
Prayers for his soul.

UMEŌ. That so young a man should die——!

CHORUS. Umeō and Haru,
Feeling limitless pity,
Yae,
Separated by death from her husband,
The old man,
Dazed by grief,
All their passions
Locked within their hearts,
All their pain
Transmuted to fervent prayer
For the soul of Sakuramaru.

SHIRODAYŪ (*rising*). I must go now, to the island of Lord Sugawara. Care for his body, Umeō and Haru. He is safe now. Our prayers carry him to the other world. Namu Amida Butsu.

ALL. Namu Amida Butsu.

CHORUS. Wearing the robe of prayer,

I

The soul of Sakuramaru
Begins the long journey.
Away to the west
Across a hundred thousand years
To the land of no return.

UMEŌ. Farewell to his spirit, and farewell, dear father.

HARU. Loyal while living——

YAE. ——a loyal warrior in death.

SHIRODAYŪ. One tree has withered and gone forever——

ALL. ——the cherry-tree, with its fleeting beauty.

CHORUS. At the shrine of Sata,
At the birthplace of the three brothers,
Still stand the two trees,
The plum and the pine,
Telling us of fate,
Telling us
Of the unbending will of the gods.

(SHIRODAYŪ *moves towards the gate, then turns to look back.* UMEŌ *raises the body so that* SHIRODAYŪ *can see the face of his dead son.* SHIRODAYŪ *weeps and, beneath the weight of his grief, falls to the ground.*)

CURTAIN

ACT III

SCENE II

Genzō's school of calligraphy. On stage-left is Genzō's home, the upstage area a platform, with entrances centre and left. On the right of the platform, KAN SHŪSAI *is seated at a small low desk. The other pupils are at desks downstage of the platform. A gate, right of stage centre, indicates the entrance to the house.*

The curtain opens to folk music.

CHORUS. Reading and writing
Is the treasure of the world,
A single word
More precious than all its gold.
Among the pupils
Who come to share in this treasure
Is Kan Shūsai,
Whom Genzō and Tonami pretend is their own son.
In the remote mountain village of Serifu
Genzō and his wife
Gathered the children of the village,

Teaching reading and writing to the bright,
And
Of course
The dull.
Study may be pain for the dull student,
But what is his pain,
Compared to the pain of the teacher?
One boy in particular,
The oldest of the lot,
Is the worst of them all.

CHUCKLEHEAD (*a tall, awkward boy*). Hey, kids, what's the use of studying when the teacher isn't here? Look, I've drawn the bald head of a priest! (*He shows them his drawing.*)

CHORUS. This is Chucklehead,
A fifteen-year-old rascal.
Meanwhile
The well-behaved Prince looks quietly on.

SHŪSAI. If you learn one character a day, in a year you will know three hundred and sixty-five characters. Stop your silly doodling and study your lessons.

CHUCKLEHEAD. Yaah! You smart aleck! Ya, ya, yaah!

CHORUS. The children all rise to defend the Prince,
Who neither asks for nor hopes for their aid.
(*The children mill about, shouting.* TONAMI *enters.*)
Hearing the rowdy noise,
The mistress of the house
Hastily enters.

TONAMI (*exasperated*). No! Not fighting again! Now, now, stop it! Stop it and be quiet! The master is returning soon, so you'd better behave yourselves! Oh, you're the worst children I've ever seen! I can't take my eyes off you a minute. Now listen! The master may excuse you from school this afternoon, but you must be quiet and finish your studies.

CHUCKLEHEAD. Yippee! Another holiday!

TONAMI (*turning on him*). Chucklehead, you're the oldest and biggest boy here, and yet you cause the most trouble. I'll have to punish you again today. Come here!

CHUCKLEHEAD (*pouting*). Yes, ma'am.
(TONAMI *makes* CHUCKLEHEAD *stand on his desk, holding a water-filled saucer in one hand and a saucer of burning incense in the other.*)

TONAMI. The rest of you, back to your studies!

CHORUS. So the children go back to their work,
Reading aloud from their copy-books.

(*The boys read louder and louder,* 'Thank you for your . . .' 'Dear Sir : I hope . . .' *and so forth.*)

(CHIYO *enters on the* hanamichi, *leading* KOTARŌ *by the hand.* SANSUKE, *a servant, follows, balancing a writing-desk and other school supplies on his shoulders and carrying a bundle in one hand. They stop outside the gate.*)

CHORUS. A lady appears,
> Leading her son by the hand,
> A child with clean-cut features
> And eyes that sparkle with intelligence,
> Quite unlike
> The stupid servant who follows behind.

SANSUKE (*an older counterpart of* CHUCKLEHEAD). Hello there! Is this the home of Genzō of the bamboo rod?

CHIYO. Pardon me. Is this the residence of Takebe Genzō?

TONAMI (*opening the gate*). Yes, it is. Will you please come in?

CHIYO. Thank you. Please forgive me for taking up your time.

(*They enter the house.*)

CHORUS. The women come face to face:
> Two women whose hearts are nothing but love,
> The love of a son,
> The love of a son of her lord.

(*Throughout the following scene it is subtly apparent that* CHIYO *is under great strain.*)

CHIYO. My husband and I live a simple life just outside the village. When we heard of your school, we sent a messenger to see whether you would receive our boy, and were given a most gracious answer that you would.

TONAMI. I am so happy you have come! Is this the child?

CHIYO. (*Pause.*) Yes, he is the one.

TONAMI. My, what a handsome boy!

CHIYO. You are very kind to pay compliments to my naughty boy. (*Pause.*) I have heard that you have a son who is my boy's age. Is he here?

TONAMI. Yes, he is over there. Come here, son! Come here, for a moment.

(KAN SHŪSAI *goes to her side.*)

TONAMI. This is our own son, Genzō's heir.

(CHIYO *looks at the two boys, as if comparing them.*)

CHIYO. (*Pause.*) You have a lovely child.

TONAMI. You are most kind. What is your boy's name?

CHIYO. Kotarō. (*Pause.*) I hope he doesn't cause you trouble with his naughtiness.

TONAMI (*to* KAN SHŪSAI). Run along now.

CHIYO (*handing her a package*). Will you please accept this as a token of my appreciation?

TONAMI. Thank you very much. You are so considerate. It is really too bad that my husband isn't at home just now. He was . . . invited out and hasn't returned.

CHIYO (*with sudden fear*). Then the master is out?

TONAMI (*a little taken aback*). Yes, but if you wish to see him at once, I shall send for him.

CHIYO. No, no, don't bother. I must go on an errand, and I'll stop here on my way back.

TONAMI. Please do. He should be back any time now.

CHIYO. Then I'll leave the child in your care.

(CHUCKLEHEAD *suddenly breaks into loud crying*.)

CHIYO. Oh, my! He frightened me! What is he being punished for?

TONAMI. He's been very naughty. He takes advantage of the master's absence and annoys the other children when they're trying to study.

CHIYO. Oh? It's really not my affair, but—won't you please forgive him this time?

TONAMI. Please don't worry about him. He's been naughty so much that if I don't punish him he'll never behave.

CHIYO. I know how you feel, but please forgive him just this once. (*To* CHUCKLEHEAD). Come, come now. I'll apologize for you, and from now on you'll be a good boy and do your studies, won't you?

(CHIYO *helps him off the desk and holds a handkerchief to his nose*.)

CHUCKLEHEAD (*blubbering*). Yes . . .

CHIYO. Please forgive him.

TONAMI (*smiles*). Here now, thank the lady.

CHUCKLEHEAD (*bowing awkwardly*). Thank you, lady.

CHIYO (*laughs*). Go now. Go and study hard.

(*As* CHUCKLEHEAD *goes to his desk, he passes behind* SANSUKE, *lifts the lid of a box* SANSUKE *has been carrying, takes a piece of candy, and puts it in his sleeve*.)

SANSUKE. Here, here, what did you do?

CHUCKLEHEAD. Nothing.

SANSUKE. You little crook! You took a piece of candy and put it in your sleeve!

CHUCKLEHEAD. I did not!

SANSUKE. No? Let me see your sleeve, then.

CHUCKLEHEAD. Well . . . uh . . .

SANSUKE. Let me see it!

CHUCKLEHEAD. No . . . don't . . .

SANSUKE. Come on now. Give me that candy!

CHUCKLEHEAD. Aw! Why did you have to go and catch me!

SANSUKE. You're a bad boy. And I ought to take it away from you. Right now. But since this is Kotarō's first day at school, I'll let you keep it.

CHUCKLEHEAD (*dancing around awkwardly and singing*). La, la, la, la, la, la, la!

TONAMI. Be quiet now!

CHIYO. Kotarō, I have to go to the village for a while, so you be a good boy while I'm gone. Good-bye. I'll hurry back.

(*She goes to the gate.* KOTARŌ *runs over and clings to her.*)

KOTARŌ. Mother! I want to go with you!

CHIYO (*freeing herself from the child, almost in tears*). Now, behave yourself, dear. A big boy like you! You ought to be ashamed. (*To* TONAMI.) You see, he's really quite a baby.

TONAMI. It's only natural for a child of his age. Here, I have something sweet for a sweet little boy. (*She gives him candy and takes him to her side.*) I'll wait for your return, madam.

CHIYO. Yes, I won't be long. Good-bye.

CHORUS. The mother goes,
> But she pauses,
> Turns,
> And looks longingly
> At the little boy she leaves behind.

(SANSUKE *leaves with* CHIYO, *stage-right.*)

TONAMI. Now let's go inside, until your mother returns. (*To* KAN SHŪSAI). You come too.

(*She takes them into the stage-left room.*)

CHORUS. Leading the boys by the hands,
> Tonami takes them to the inner room,
> Hoping to amuse the little boy,
> Until his mother returns.

(GENZŌ *appears on the* hanamichi.)

CHORUS. Then home comes Genzō,
> The schoolmaster,
> Pale with fear,
> Almost insane with worry.

(*He pauses on the* hanamichi, *looking towards the stage. Then he hurries on, enters the house. All the children bow before him.*)

CHORUS. He looks a moment at his pupils,
> Then sighs with disgust.

(TONAMI *enters with* KOTARŌ.)

GENZŌ. Ah! The faces of the parents show in the faces of the children. None of these will serve my purpose! They are peasants with the faces of peasants.

(*The children return to their desks.* GENZŌ *sits, dejectedly.*)

CHORUS. Concerned at her husband's unusual behaviour,
    Tonami hurries to his side,
    Her heart beating rapidly
    With sudden fear.

TONAMI. What is the matter? Please don't be so unpleasant to the children. It's true, they are poor and shabby, but it isn't like you to take out your troubles on them. Besides, you'll frighten the little boy who has just come to school today. Please be gentle with him.

CHORUS. Tonami pleads with the sullen Genzō,
    Then leads the child before his master.
    Kotarō politely bows and says:

KOTARŌ. Dear teacher, I will be a good and obedient pupil from this day, obeying your every command.

CHORUS. Suddenly Genzō's face brightens.

GENZŌ. Well, well, what have we here? A noble child, fit to be a prince! My boy, you are a handsome child, and well mannered, too!

CHORUS. Puzzled,
    Though pleased,
    By her husband's sudden change in mood,
    Tonami looks thoughtfully at the child
    And says:

TONAMI. Yes, yes, he certainly is! And I'm sure he's a good pupil, too.

GENZŌ. I should say so! A perfect pupil! (*Sudden pause.*) And where is his mother?

TONAMI. She said she had some business in the village.

GENZŌ. Well, well, that's fine, that's excellent! (*Change in tone.*) Now let the child go in and enjoy himself with the other children.

TONAMI. There now, children, go in and play. Kotarō, go in with the rest of the children.

(*The children leave by the centre door.* TONAMI *sits near* GENZŌ.)

TONAMI. Dear husband, what is the matter? Just a moment ago you were worried and unhappy, but as soon as you saw the new child, you changed completely.

GENZŌ. Yes, yes. I will tell you what has happened. This meeting at the village master's home—it was nothing but a trick of Shihei's followers, Matsuōmaru and Gemba. Matsuōmaru is ill, but even so, he was ordered to conduct an investigation. Now he has discovered that we are hiding Lord Sugawara's son. He demanded that I behead the young Prince, or if I would not, he would bring a hundred men and take the child away. I agreed to behead the Prince, and give the head to Matsuō. (TONAMI *cries out.*) I thought I would be able to substitute one of the other pupils and kill him in place of Kan Shūsai. All the way home I tried to think of a suitable child. But how could a child born in a thatched hut bear even the slightest resemblance to one of noble birth? I was about to resign myself to fate, when I saw that child! Such stateliness, reserve, and good breeding! Surely, I thought, God must have sent him to us! So he must be sacrificed, and then we will flee to Kawachi with the Prince.

TONAMI. But wait! That Matsuō, the evil one of the triplets, he must surely know the face of the Prince. He'll discover the truth!

GENZŌ. There is the danger. Kotarō looks somewhat like the Prince, and we can only hope that Matsuō doesn't recognize the difference. But if he does, I will kill him and fight it out with his men. If there's no other way, we'll die with the Prince and be his escort into the other world. But there's a more immediate danger—the mother of the child. What can we do when she comes for her son?

TONAMI. Let me think. Perhaps I could . . .

GENZŌ. (*Pause.*) If there is no other way, she, too, may have to die.

TONAMI. Oh!

GENZŌ. There is nothing more important than the welfare of the Prince. You know that. You know that.

TONAMI. Yes, yes, we can't be weak. If we must play the devil, we must play him completely.

GENZŌ. (*Pause.*) My pupils are my children.

TONAMI. Oh, how cruel is the law of Karma! Can it be the sins of the child or the sins of the mother that sent him here, on this day?

GENZŌ. And we are the unfortunate ones who must be the instrument of punishment.

TONAMI. Then our turn, too, will come, and we will be punished.

GENZŌ. There is none so innocent in this——

BOTH. ——as the lonely servants in the courts.

(*They hear, from the far end of the* hanamichi, *the cries of the fathers of the children and go into the room on stage-right.*

GEMBA, *a red-faced, cruel man, appears on the* hanamichi, *carrying the box for the head. Following him, a palanquin and ten* GUARDS. *Behind them, the peasants, who kneel, bowing, on the* hanamichi.)

CHORUS. Then suddenly appears
      Shundō Gemba,

Chancellor of Shihei.
Behind him,
Ill,
Carried in a palanquin,
Matsuōmaru,
Whose task it is
To confirm the death of Kan Shūsai.
And as the palanquin stops by the gate,
A group of village peasants gathers about.

FIRST PEASANT. Oh, master, all the people here have children in this school!

SECOND PEASANT. We don't want you to make a mistake and behead one of our children.

THIRD PEASANT. Please, please, look at the children carefully before you behead the Prince.

FOURTH PEASANT. If you would please let them come home——

ALL. ——we would greatly appreciate it!

GEMBA. Stop your yapping, you worthless dogs! I don't care about your filthy brats. Take them away if you want.

MATSUŌ (*from the palanquin*). Wait a moment, Gemba! (*He gets out slowly, leaning heavily on his sword.*) We must be careful even with such scum as this. I am the only one who knows the face of Kan Shūsai, and so in spite of my illness I am here, and I must fulfil my duties. (*He coughs.*) These peasants are undoubtedly sympathizers with Sugawara. That they have harboured Kan Shūsai in their village may mean that they will try to slip him away by disguising him as a peasant's son.

(*Protests from the peasants.*)

MATSUŌ. Be quiet, you filthy peasants! Call out your brats one at a time. You may have them after I've had a good look at each one of them.

FIRST PEASANT. Chomatsu! Come here, Chomatsu!

FIRST CHILD. Yes, Grandpa, I'm coming!

(*The boy, his face smeared with ink, comes through the centre doorway and then through the gate.* GEMBA *makes him kneel, his fan at the child's throat.* MATSUŌ *shakes his head.*)

CHORUS. The prince is pure white snow,
But the little rascal before him,
Coal,
Dull even in its blackness.
And away he sends the boy.

(GRANDFATHER *and* CHILD *exit on the* hanamichi.)

SECOND PEASANT. Where are you Iwamatsu, my boy? Iwamatsu!

SECOND CHILD. What is it, Grandpa?

(*The business of inspection is repeated.*)

MATSUŌ. There's no need to inspect him. Take him away.

SECOND PEASANT. Thank heavens! (*They go.*)

(CHUCKLEHEAD *comes out, grinning and singing, and strikes a Kabuki attitude, using a broom in lieu of a spear. As he goes through the gate,* GEMBA *kicks him in the shins, and* CHUCKLEHEAD *falls before him.* GEMBA *looks at him, gives a snort of disgust, and hits him on the head with the fan.* CHUCKLEHEAD *bawls and goes on to the* hanamichi *snivelling.*)

THIRD PEASANT (*beckoning to* CHUCKLEHEAD). Here, my precious baby, come!

CHUCKLEHEAD. Papa, I want to go piggy-back. Please, Papa, can I go piggy-back?

THIRD PEASANT. Yes, yes! Here you go.

(CHUCKLEHEAD *jumps on his father's back. The father takes a few steps, falls on his face.* CHUCKLEHEAD *picks up his father, carries him off piggy-back.*)

FOURTH PEASANT. Please be very careful when you look at my boy. I am afraid you might mistake him for the Prince.

CHORUS. Out comes the child
　　　　At the call of the proud father,
　　　　Fair of complexion,
　　　　Clean cut of features,
　　　　The best looking one of the lot.
　　　　Seizing him by the neck,
　　　　Gemba looks at him:
　　　　But oh!
　　　　Could the Prince have a dirty neck like this?
　　　　Gemba casts him aside.
　　　　It's only natural that children from a peasant home
　　　　Should look like potatoes freshly dug from the ground.

(FATHER *and* CHILD *leave, and in rapid succession the remaining four children are quickly inspected and go with their fathers.*)

(GENZŌ *and* TONAMI *come out from the inner room.*)

CHORUS. Now the representatives of Shihei
　　　　Enter the house.
　　　　Genzō and Tonami know
　　　　That the moment has come.

(MATSUŌ *and* GEMBA *sit stage-left on stools.* GENZŌ *and* TONAMI *kneel stage-right.* ONE OF THE GUARDS *places the box for the head centre stage.* THE GUARDS *squat on their heels just downstage of the platform.*)

GEMBA (*gloating*). Well, Genzō, you promised you'd behead Kan Shūsai. I've come for his head.

GENZŌ. One moment please! So great a personage as the son of Lord Sugawara cannot be beheaded without due ceremony.

MATSUŌ. Come, Genzō, do what you have promised. Don't think you can escape. The place is surrounded by men. Not even an ant can crawl out. And don't try to use a substitute! I know that face, whether in life—or in death.

CHORUS. Warned not to do
　　Just what he had planned,
　　Even the calm Genzō is disturbed.

GENZŌ. You can quiet your fears. I will behead Kan Shūsai. But I cannot hope that the eyes of a sick man will be able to recognize him.

GEMBA. Stop your talking——

MATSUŌ. ——and behead the boy!

CHORUS. And Genzō
　　Takes a deep breath
　　Rises abruptly

(GENZŌ *picks up the box for the head, goes up to the platform, turns suddenly to give* TONAMI *a warning glance. For a moment he looks down at* MATSUŌ, *then goes out centre.*)
　　Enters the room.
　　Tonami sits in trembling terror,
　　While the keen-eyed Matsuō
　　Counts the desks.

MATSUŌ. What is this? Eight children left just now, but there's an extra desk. Where is the other child?

TONAMI (*flustered*). There was a child who came today——

MATSUŌ (*violently*). What!

TONAMI. The desk—that is for Kan Shūsai.

(*A long pause, which tells on* MATSUŌ.)

MATSUŌ. We can't allow him much longer.

GEMBA. You're right.

CHORUS. Matsuō and Gemba impatiently rise,
　　When suddenly—
　　The sickening sound
　　Of steel against flesh.
　　The senses of Tonami reel.

(TONAMI *rises, as if to go within.* MATSUŌ *prevents her, striking an attitude which reveals his secret grief.*)
　　Then comes Genzō from the inner room,
　　Advances to Matsuō
　　And sets the box before him.

GENZŌ. By your order, I have beheaded Kan Shūsai. Examine the head carefully, so that you make no mistake.

CHORUS. Genzō kneels,
        Tensely,
        Hand on sword.
        If Matsuō says,
        'It is not the head of Kan Shūsai',
        Genzō's sword
        Will pierce him.

MATSUŌ. Ha! Make no mistake? This is a simple matter to decide. Guard the couple!

GUARDS. Yes, sir! Don't move!

        (THE GUARDS *surround the couple, swords raised.* MATSUŌ *kneels before the box.*)

CHORUS. Life and death
        Now wait on the words of Matsuō.
        He reaches towards the box,
        And Genzō's
        Grip
        Tightens on his sword.
        Tonami sits in prayer
        To God Almighty
        And to all the Buddhas.
        The seconds
        Crawl on,
        The very air
        Seems to wait
        As Matsuōmaru
        Looks
        At the head
        Looks
        At the head.

        (MATSUŌ *has lifted the cover of the box, his eyes closed. Then he forces himself to open his eyes and to look down. He stares, his eyes dazzle, and he replaces the cover.*)

MATSUŌ. It is the head of Kan Shūsai!

CHORUS. The words ring out like temple bells,
        Announcing a new-born child.
        Fate has given them life again!

GEMBA. Good! Good! Genzō, you've done a good job. As a reward, we'll overlook the fact that you hid the Prince. Matsuō, let's hurry and report to the honourable Shihei.

MATSUŌ (*slowly*). Yes, yes. But now that I have performed my duty,

I should like to go to my home. I am not well. (*Rises.*) Will you please report to the honourable Shihei for me?

GEMBA. If you wish it, I will. You have done your duty.

MATSUŌ. If you will excuse me——

(*He goes slowly to the gate, closes it behind him, enters the palanquin, which is carried off.* THE GUARDS *leave the house, followed by* GEMBA, *carrying the box. Outside the gate,* GEMBA *turns back to* GENZŌ.)

GEMBA. As the proverb says, necessity is a hard master. You can't remain loyal to your master when your life is in danger, can you? A lowly fellow like you, trying to imitate a loyal retainer, harbouring the son of your lord! How do you feel now, beheading your helpless master's son to save your own skin? Eh?

(*He laughs and exits triumphantly on the* hanamichi *followed by* THE GUARDS.)

CHORUS. Now the couple sigh in relief,
　　All their worry gone in a moment.
　　Then Genzō
　　Humbly gives thanks
　　To the gods in heaven
　　And the gods on earth.

GENZŌ. It must have been the Prince's exalted virtues that clouded the eyes of Matsuō. It was a miracle, and it can only mean that the Prince will live forever.

TONAMI. It was truly a miracle. Perhaps it was Lord Sugawara who clouded Matsuō's vision.

BOTH. The gods be thanked.

(CHIYO *has appeared outside the gate.*)

CHORUS. In the midst of their rejoicing
　　There is a call from outside.
　　Can it be the mother,
　　Come for her child?

CHIYO. It is I, the mother of the new pupil. I have just returned to take him home.

TONAMI. Oh, God! What shall we do? What can we say to her?

GENZŌ. Quiet! Have you forgotten what I told you? Nothing must prevent us from saving the Prince. (*Pause.*) Don't be excited!

(*He motions* TONAMI *to the centre room, and she goes. Then he moves to the gate, opens it, and* CHIYO *enters.*)

CHIYO. Oh! It is you, the honourable Genzō. I am the mother of the boy I left with you this morning. Where is he? I hope he hasn't caused you trouble.

GENZŌ. Oh! Not at all, not at all! He's inside playing with the other children. You may take him home if you like.

CHIYO. Thank you, thank you. I will.
(*She moves towards the inner room.*)

CHORUS. As the unsuspecting woman walks past him,
    Genzō draws his sword.
    But quick is the woman to sense the danger:
    With a sudden twist
    She avoids the sword.
    Genzō, in increasing fury,
    Raises the sword for a second blow.
    Quickly the woman shields herself
    With the desk of her son.

CHIYO. Wait! Wait, I tell you!

CHORUS. With a furious swing
    Genzō strikes the desk
    That shields the woman.
    Look!
    From the desk fall
    The burial clothes of a child,
    On them written
    A prayer to Buddha.
    Genzō pauses,
    Looks at the woman,
    The mother of Kotarō,
    Weeping.

CHIYO. Did you make good use of the sacrifice for Kan Shūsai? Or did you not? I am anxious to know.

GENZŌ. Ah? You sent him? To be sacrificed?

CHIYO. Yes. If not, why did I bring these burial clothes?
    (MATSUŌ *is outside the gate. He throws a small pine twig into the room, a strip of paper attached to it.* GENZŌ *picks it up.* TONAMI *enters.*)

GENZŌ (*reading*). The plum has flown to stand by me, the cherry has withered in my service. But why in this cruel world——

MATSUŌ (*entering*). ——does the pine alone stand indifferent and aloof? (*He crosses to* CHIYO.) You should rejoice, dear wife. Our son has been useful.

CHIYO (*faltering*). Yes. (*She breaks down.*)

CHORUS. The couple is amazed.
    Is it a dream
    Or is it true
    That this is Matsuō's wife?

GENZŌ. Matsuō, what does this mean? Why have you changed so completely? We thought you the deadliest of our enemies!

MATSUŌ. Genzō, I, like my brothers, am greatly indebted to Lord Sugawara. But I had to oppose him so that I might serve him better. Today Shihei commanded that he be brought the head of Kan Shūsai. I knew you would never behead the Prince. Therefore my wife and I decided to send our only son as a substitute for him. Now at last I have repaid Lord Sugawara for the suffering and torment I have caused him. (*Pause.*) Fortunate is the man who has a son——

CHIYO. And I had to scold him for running after me. It was the first and last scolding of his life.

MATSUŌ. Don't weep, my dear wife. (*Pause.*) He was so young——! Genzō, how did he die? I told him what he must do, but he was only a child. Did he try to run away?

GENZŌ. No, no! He even smiled.

MATSUŌ. My son! (*Pause.*) He smiled. He smiled. (*He cannot restrain himself.*) Genzō, forgive me! (*He weeps.*)

(KAN SHŪSAI *appears from the inner room.*)

KAN SHŪSAI. Had I known this, I would never have let it happen. There is too much sorrow.

CHORUS. At the sight of the weeping Prince
Matsuō and Chiyo are deeply moved,
And their tears of sorrow
Become tears of thanks.

MATSUŌ. And now I must present the Prince with a gift. (*He goes outside and calls.*) Bring the palanquin here.

MEN (*offstage*). Yes, sir.

CHORUS. There appears a palanquin,
The screen is lifted,
And within is Lady Sugawara.

SONŌ. Oh! Kan Shūsai!

KAN SHŪSAI. Mother! (*He runs to her.*)

MATSUŌ. Now, Chiyo, bring the body of Kotarō, and we will lay him to rest.

CHIYO. Yes.

(*She is about to go, when* TONAMI *appears from the inner room, carrying the body of* KOTARŌ *swathed in burial clothes.* MATSUŌ *takes the body.*)

GENZŌ. You have had enough pain. Let us lay your son to rest.

MATSUŌ. No, no. This is no longer our son. We now lay to rest the remains of Kan Shūsai. Let the funeral fire be lit.

(*It has grown darker and darker. They move outside the gate, where the fire begins to burn.*)

sonō. Now he will enter the school of Eternity,

matsuō. Seeking the master, Amida Buddha,

genzō. Learning from the Great Saviour of suffering souls,

tonami. Writing in the sands of the River Sai.

chiyo. What he learned in this world has all been in vain——

matsuō. Pitiful our knowledge at the gates of death.

all. Pitiful our knowledge at the gates of death.

chorus. Who will comfort the little child
   Alone
   In the darkness
   On the road of death?
   Who will comfort the parents
   Weeping
   In the darkness
   In the web of life?
   The fire
   Carries his soul to heaven,
   The fire
   Changes his body to dust.
   And all that remains
   Is the dream
   Shaped in the hearts of the parents,
   The dream of life
   They hold in their hearts.

CURTAIN

THE KABUKI

AESTHETICALLY speaking, the Kabuki was the first form of Japanese theatre to use a flesh-and-blood actor. The Nō actor, remote and hieratic, held only the most tenuous claim upon the world of reality; the actor of the doll theatre could breathe only in the hands of its animators. The Kabuki, on the contrary, from its beginnings and throughout its history, achieved its success through the almost unexplainable rapport which the gifted performer can effect with his audience. It cannot be said that the appeal of the earliest Kabuki performers, the first of whom was a renegade priestess, Okuni, resulted entirely from the audience's appreciation of high artistic endeavour. The charms of Okuni, who appeared in Kyoto in 1596, were apparently of the sort which could be displayed to better advantage on a stage than in a nunnery, and many of her imitators, who were immediate and legion, used their performances to exhibit publicly attractions which could be enjoyed for a fee privately. The performance based solely upon the physical appeal of the actor has contributed nothing to dramatic literature, but it has sometimes led to better things, has frequently kept the theatre alive in difficult times, and does not seem, fortunately, to have lost this power today. It is perhaps the lowest common denominator in securing an audience from among the masses, and such was the audience which Okuni set out to captivate. The strong impression of the times is that the commoners, after a century of civil war, were avidly seeking full-blooded and exciting entertainment, and were turning, as seems historically customary with such groups in times of social upheaval, to a more realistic theatre than they had known before. But the word realistic must be qualified, for the earliest Kabuki troupes adopted the curious practice of using women in men's roles and men in women's roles, so that the performance existed, so to speak, at one remove from actuality and on an essentially theatrical plane. Its appeal seems nonetheless to have been largely physical, and an actress determined to exploit her sexual attributes is much more likely to do so by dancing

K

than by performing in plays. Okuni danced. And in what turned out to be a characteristic pattern of the subsequent Kabuki, the materials chosen were selected in thoroughly eclectic, if not parasitic, fashion from contemporary dance forms—from the Nō theatre, from religious dances performed at shrines and temples, from folk and popular dances.

Kabuki troupes made up entirely of male performers appeared as early as 1617, and when, pointing to their immorality, the Government banished women from the stage in 1629, the remaining troupes of young men created a new dance form called *saruwaka*, which, since it involved much more literal pantomime than had been used in the women's troupes, contributed to the Government's forbidding young men's Kabuki in 1652. Only after this time, when the theatre was carried on in 'male' Kabuki, was there any significant development of plays. The dramatic element of the young men's Kabuki consisted almost entirely of short comic pieces, played between the dances, which were derived from or patterned on the comic interludes of the Nō theatre. The first work which, because it had something of a plot, can be described as a play did not appear until 1637, and a two-act play was not written until 1664. The actors were the generally anonymous playwrights, and not until 1680 did the name of an author appear on a theatre programme. The cardinal importance of the actor was thus early established, and the playwright, throughout the history of the Kabuki, was the actor's willing slave, constructing pieces suited to the talents of the actor.

When the play as such began to appear, it drew its subject matter for the most part from legend and history, both from that already used in the Nō theatre and from that which the Nō had not exploited. One rich mine of raw material was the epic works dealing with the struggle between the Minamoto and the Taira clans. The early Kabuki plays are almost entirely concerned with heroic deeds of the warrior class, with intrigue and revenge in high places, and with the amorous dalliance of samurai and elegant courtesans. When potential material was found in novels and short stories, the playwrights converted it to their needs; when the *jōruri* of the doll theatre became widely popular, the Kabuki took over the plays; when new dance forms and new tunes developed outside the theatre, the choreographers and musicians adapted them to the Kabuki. Nothing which could be utilized by the Kabuki was overlooked.

For the form of its earliest stage the Kabuki was indebted to the Nō. The stage consisted of a relatively long, narrow passageway, the bridge, used for entrances and exits, joining the rectangular stage proper at a right angle on the stage-right side. The musicians sat at the rear of the stage proper in the same area they occupied in the Nō theatre. This stage underwent no significant change for almost a century, other than that the bridge was gradually widened in the direction of the audience. When this area, which continued to be used only for entrances and exits, became as wide as the stage proper, and so no longer showed the characteristics of a passageway, this lack was remedied by constructing, some time during the years 1724–35, a narrow platform between the rear of the auditorium and the right side of the stage. The new acting area, called the *hanamichi*, was in effect a new bridge, but because it made possible the movement of the actor through the audience, it gave rise to new acting techniques. Its theatrical efficacy prompted the use, about 1772, of a similar passageway on the opposite side of the house called the temporary *hanamichi*, so that actors on the two *hanamichi* could play to each other over the heads of the audience. The temporary *hanamichi*, though rarely used today, was common until some twenty-five years ago.

The Kabuki theatre reached the characteristic architectural form it now has about 1830, but it had freed itself from the influence of the Nō stage by the early eighteenth century. The primary purposes of the physical theatre were two: to display the actor to best advantage, principally by putting him in close proximity with the audience, and to provide theatre machinery for rapid and spectacular scene changes. The earliest Kabuki scenery was merely the 'fictional things' of the Nō theatre, but after copying the scenic innovations of the doll theatre in the eighteenth century, the Kabuki not only improved upon them but also invented techniques of its own in order to cope with an ever-increasing quantity of scenic materials. Not only is there no method of scene change known to the Western theatre which does not have its parallel in the Kabuki, but the Kabuki employs various methods unknown to the West. Wagon stages were used to move small set pieces in the early 1700s. Elevator stages were introduced in 1736, and became larger and more versatile in function in the following years. The principal scene-changing machine, and the one most constantly used, was the revolving stage, appearing first in a doll theatre in 1758 and in the Kabuki in 1793. In 1827 the technical resources of the revolving stage were increased by the construction of a small revolving stage at the centre of the larger one, the inner stage moving in the opposite direction from the outer one. Elevator stages were installed within the areas of both the revolving stages. Contrary to the usual practice in the modern Western theatre, the functioning of such machines was not concealed from the spectator, and the audience was allowed to share the pleasure afforded by these mechanical delights. Huge temples rose from beneath the stage; the actor walked on the edge of the moving revolving stage as the scenery, moving in the opposite direction behind him, shifted to another locale; an interior setting was raised up from the stage floor so that the level beneath it was revealed. No Western form of theatre, including that of the Renaissance, used greater quantities of scenery or effected its scene changes with greater or more startling dispatch. The scenery was, again speaking relatively, of a realism which would have been abhorred in the Nō and undreamed of in the doll theatre.

In the midst of these lavish scenic displays it would seem likely that the actor would be totally obscured, but curiously enough such was not the case. The actor, who had dominated the physical and psychological forestage of the earliest Kabuki theatre, relinquished no part of his commanding position. With the introduction of the *hanamichi* the stage had become relatively wide and shallow, so that the actor moved in a comparatively narrow downstage plane. The installation of the elevator and revolving stages required a considerable deepening of the stage, but the actor did not move into these new areas. They had been created to provide space for scenes and machines, and the actor remained in his downstage area of prominence. The settings of the Kabuki consist, generally, of flat surfaces which oppose the body of the actor. Even with the development of plays requiring the construction of scenes set in the homes of commoners, the interiors were so arranged and the techniques of acting were so employed that the actor was not 'involved' in the setting. He achieved this effect principally by playing directly to the audience, as he had always done, and so minimized any possibility of realistically relating himself to the setting. Intimacy between actor and audience, the characteristic quality of the earliest Kabuki performances, was not diminished by the increasingly elaborate scenery. In addition, the actor had an important playing area, that of the *hanamichi*, entirely to himself, and it was here, moving through the spectators, that he brought the character into sharp and intimate focus as he moved into or away from the dramatic situation on the stage. His first and last impact on the audience, those two moments which are likely to be of greatest concern to the actor, he played alone in the midst of the spectators, claiming their entire attention. In effect, actor and setting occupied separate spheres of interest, and each was allotted its share of the undivided attention of the audience.

The direct rapport between the flesh-and-blood actor and his audience suggests that in this respect the Kabuki was aesthetically antithetical to the Nō and the doll theatres. But the immediate communication of the actor with the spectator was not based upon the audience's recognition of actuality in the actor's performance, the basis of rapport in the realistic theatre, for the Kabuki actor addressed his audience through the medium of a rigidly controlled and non-realistic vocabulary. His training in the theatre today consists in the acquisition of extensive and complex means of traditional expression. The physical images in which he communicates with his audience have their origin in actuality, but in them the casual and erratic appearances of the real world have been reduced to a rigorously designed, finely stylized pattern of physical expression which the actor, beginning his study at the age of five or six, hopes to master completely at the age of forty. The appeal of the actor's individual characteristics, the exploitation of his 'personality', which have brought both artistic havoc and audience delight to the Western theatre, appear in the Kabuki only in the performance of incompetent actors. The competent actor, imposing his laboriously achieved and finely wrought means of expression between 'himself' and the audience, reveals only the personality of the artist.

His face is not, like that of the actor in the realistic theatre, his fortune. Under heavy stylized make-up it takes on the characteristics of a mask, cancelling out the features of the person who wears it and replacing them with a face whose mobility is only slightly more facile than that of the doll. His costume similarly establishes him as the type, not the individual. As an artist, the actor chooses among the carefully defined techniques of expression which tradition has placed at his disposal and fashions the character he will play from them. And since these techniques provide all the materials necessary for the portrayal of any kind of character, the accomplished actor can play any role, except that of a child, regardless of age or sex. The absence of actresses on the stage after 1629 created no difficulties for the Kabuki, for even at that time its intrinsically non-realistic surface, which had many qualities in common with the Japanese graphic arts, had been firmly established. The Kabuki actor's most communicative moment in the performance is realized, not in an imitation of human physical expression, but in the immobile, stylized attitude called the *mie* (*mee-ay*), which visually sums up the total reaction of the character to the significant dramatic situation.

Although the actor is the centre of the performance and indeed dominates it, he is subject to the inexorable demands both of his acquired vocabulary of expression and of the strict rhythmical advance of the performance which governs him as well as the other theatre workers, not actors, who also appear on the stage. These forces control the actor as completely as the productional elements control the marionette in the doll theatre, and make him, to an almost equal degree, the instrument of a precisely determined design.

The performance is surrounded with music and grows out of complex rhythmical patterns. In the pieces which are almost completely dance, both those adapted from the Nō, played in a setting suggesting the Nō stage, and those of purely Kabuki origin, the musicians are seated on the stage, either behind or at the side of the dancing actor. The movement of the actor, in reality, conducts the orchestra, but the relation between the two is one of subtle and constant interaction rather than unilateral dominance. Actor and orchestra submit equally to the flow of changing rhythms and are borne along by it. The orchestra, which includes singers as well as instrumentalists, has as its principal instruments samisens and drums. The samisen, played with a plectrum, is sharply percussive, and this effect is both emphasized and complemented by the differing timbres of the three types of drums used. These instruments, which give the orchestra its characteristic quality, weave a tight web of intricate rhythmical design which tends to dominate the lyrical passages of the singers. When the play is one adapted from the doll theatre, the samisen is usually the only instrument used. The samisen player and the narrator-singer sit on a platform at stage-left, the position occupied by the *jōruri* performers in the doll theatre. The narrator-singer does not have the importance he enjoys in the doll theatre, for in the Kabuki the lines of the character are for the most part recited by the actor. In certain scenes, however, where the actor's movement is more important than speech, the lines are taken over by the narrator-singer. The samisen music continues throughout, giving musical definition to the actor's miming and strengthening the rhythm of the scene as it advances to a climax. Even those plays which are not dance pieces or do not derive from the doll theatre have a constant musical accompaniment provided by an orchestra and by singers in the downstage-right music room, which is a permanent architectural feature of the stage. The instruments include several which do not generally appear in the onstage orchestra. The music is on the whole less prominent than that of the onstage orchestra, but it swells to importance in climactic scenes and in those where increasingly rhythmical movement resolves into dance-scenes, for example, of conflict or murder. The sound effects of the Kabuki are also created in the music room. They are not an attempt at literal imitations of natural sounds but theatricalized versions of them, shaped by the rhythmical content of the scene. The rhythm of the actor's movement at the most important moments of his performance—in the *mie*, for instance—is given strong emphasis by beating two resonant pieces of wood on a board. The clean, penetrating sound produced (by a performer who takes a position in the extreme down-left corner of the stage) gives a sharper rhythmical impact than that of any other of the instruments used. As it approaches its high points of interest the Kabuki performance becomes increasingly rhythmical, and the rhythm reaches its most trenchant expression in the complex design of abstract, percussive sound from the wooden clappers. The rhythm of the Kabuki is not the vaguely felt and obscurely discussed productional quality of the Western realistic play but a forthright, physical statement which is as unambiguous as the rhythm felt by the dancer of the polka or the waltz.

Unlike certain forms of the Western theatre, the Kabuki rarely deals in deception or conceals from the audience the methods by which its effects are produced. It does not pretend that the stage is not a stage or that those who appear on it must be viewed as characters in the play. If musicians and singers are needed on the stage they are placed there as such and need not be explained away as actors. The man who beats the wooden clappers comes and goes as he is required, and no one in the audience questions the appropriateness of his doing so. Since the audience does not conceive the theatre as a place of illusion but one designed for the exhibition of theatrical artistry, the Kabuki has developed methods of production which are straightforward, direct, and economical. In the persons of the 'black men', who are dressed in black and wear a black cloth covering their faces, the Kabuki provides prompters and personal assistants to the actors. They help the actor with rapid changes of costume onstage, they open sliding doors so that the movement of the actor is not impeded, they place cushions on the stage floor for the actor to sit on. The 'black men' control the hand properties of the actor, giving him the necessary property at the right moment, removing it when it is no longer required, so that neither actor nor audience need be burdened or distracted by a property which is not serving an immediate dramatic purpose. This principle is extended to include large pieces of scenery. A gate, for example, which is necessary to the playing of a certain scene is removed by stagehands when it no

longer figures in the action and when the space it occupies can
be used to better advantage. The productional methods of the
Kabuki are as honestly revealed as the spectacular scene-
changes, and the purpose in doing so is invariably to facilitate
the expressiveness of the actor. The musicians and singers are
placed on stage to assure, through proximity with the actor, an
unerring rhythmical accord. The 'black men' help free the
actor from the tyranny of properties and costumes. The stage-
hands shift pieces of scenery, sometimes an entire setting, solely
to give the actor more space in which to play.

The precise form of these methods of production is not unlike
that of the Nō theatre, but since the Kabuki was innately
acquisitive, determined to seize upon everything which would
increase the range of the actor's materials and which by time-
liness and novelty would attract a large popular audience, its
plays show nothing of the extreme selectivity of those of the Nō.
The Nō carefully distinguished between serious and comic
pieces, and, since it was primarily a solemn theatre, it used
comedy only in short and inconsequential interludes between
the serious plays. Though like the Nō it was preoccupied with
weighty matters, the Kabuki did not make that formal division
but thoroughly mixed up buffoonery and seriousness in the
same play, even in the same scene, to an extent greatly surpass-
ing similar *mélanges* in Shakespeare. Certain areas of subject
matter, having neither historical nor dramatic affinity, were
combined, so that the legendary story of Okuni and her lover
was mingled with the history of the feudal house of Date, and
the unhappy existence of Sakura Sōgorō, who was crucified in
1655, was mixed with that of the elegant, royal hero of *The Tale
of Genji*, a novel written in the tenth century. In *Benten the
Thief*, as a case in point, it is impossible to determine, from
internal evidence, in what period the play takes place. In Act I
certain characters speak of the existence of a plot of Miura
Yasumura against Hōjō Tokiyori, an historical incident which
occurred in 1247. In Act II Benten quotes Ishikawa Goemon,
a thief who was executed in 1595 (or, as others have it, in 1632).
At the end of the play appears Aoto Fujitsuna, a person, perhaps
legendary, of the thirteenth century. It is difficult to explain
these and similar farragos on any rational ground, other than

that the Kabuki was concerned with striking theatrical effects to the exclusion of probability, for when events taken from actuality were used by the Kabuki they were subjected to a re-arrangement and artistic moulding as arbitrary as that imposed upon the actor's gestures. But it remains a not easily explainable characteristic of the Kabuki that its means of production should have developed with strict logic while many of its plays are so illogical that Japanese writers, seeming to throw up their hands, describe them as phantasmagoria. The plays seem to have increased in incongruity and length simultaneously; the first four-act play appeared in 1710, and fifty years later plays of twelve or more acts were not uncommon. Another irrational aspect of the plays is that certain types had to be traditionally performed at certain times of the year. The bill for January required the inclusion of a play dealing with the revenge of the Soga brothers; in the spring there must be a play set in the courtesan district; summer made necessary plays involving rain and ghosts; the autumn programme was composed largely of historical pieces. The November performance, which opened the theatrical season, necessitated a plotless scene in dumb-show introducing the principal members of the troupe. The performance of certain plays, such as the one concerning the Soga brothers, was thought to be peculiarly auspicious. An investigation of how these programmes became traditional would doubtless reveal that tradition was in most cases established by the sheerest chance; there is probably no country other than Japan in which tradition so casually, illogically, and tenaciously takes root. Apparently only a few of the playwrights felt that the theatre dealt with reality; those who wrote on the subject almost invariably declared that the theatre was not life but fiction.

The Japanese have attempted to cope with the confusing variety of the plays by classifying them according to period, subject matter, and the extent to which dance is used. The classifications are somewhat more ingenious than informative, based to a large degree upon an irrational traditionalism and admitting constant exceptions. A certain historical tendency, however, may be traced in a general way in the plays from the seventeenth century to the end of the nineteenth. The movement begins in what might be called the high heroic, the world of great warriors and epic deeds, of idealization of the military class. Towards the end of the seventeenth century, and particularly through the influence of Chikamatsu, the commoner began to play an increasing role in the 'domestic' plays, and his affairs were so lovingly dwelt upon and so glamorized that they evoked as much admiration and awe as those of the warrior class. Towards the beginning of the nineteenth century the playwrights turned more and more frequently to the depiction of licentiousness, madness, violence, and bloodshed, and in an apparent effort to shock the audience to the utmost, they wrote plays about vengeful ghosts. The nineteenth-century play was likely to draw its characters from the lowest social groups and to investigate the gruesome and morbid with bitter energy. This general development could not, however, be clearly perceived in any given Kabuki programme, for the Kabuki, never relinquishing its past successes, kept them alive in its current repertoire, playing the old pieces on the same programme with the latest novelty. Towards the end of the nineteenth century favourite plays were rarely performed in their entirety; only the most engrossing acts or scenes were played, and since entire programmes were made up of these bits and pieces, only the initiate could make much dramatic sense of them.

Even though the Kabuki never succeeded in achieving a tight dramatic structure, it created certain types of scenes for the actor which hardened into relatively strict forms, and the play came to consist of a series of these scenes. As a result, the play which when read seems structurally casual almost to the point of incomprehensibility appears in performance as a succession of rigidly patterned elements. The Kabuki audience seems always to have been quite unconcerned about extended, internally complex yet logically worked out plots. It came to the theatre to see the proficient actor exhibit his highly polished techniques, and these were shown most effectively in these traditional and basic forms, thoroughly familiar to the audience, which afforded the severest test as well as the most impressive display of the actor's ability. The performance, to draw a musical parallel, was not cast in symphonic form, but resembled a dance suite, in which the composer's treatment of such fixed forms as *bourrée*, *allemande*, and *gigue* was the concern of the listener, not intricate thematic development and continuity. Like the dances, the Kabuki forms were given names which specifically designated their qualities. It would be unprofitable to give a detailed list of these forms, but a few examples will serve to indicate their nature. A lyric passage concerning a travelling couple, usually lovers, and describing the geographical regions through which they are going is called *michiyuki*; it furnishes a quiet, poetic interlude between scenes of dramatic tension, and is therefore frequently used just before the culmination of a play of violent activity. Scenes of fighting (*tachimawari*) are based on a precise choreography in which there is no physical contact between the actors' swords or bodies; the stylization is such that conflict is expressed in non-realistic patterns of movement and defeat in somersaults. Murder scenes (*koroshiba*) are similarly designed in ballet-like fashion and generally avoid any suggestion of bloodiness. Passages in which the silent actor mimes a past event to the words of the narrator-singer and the accompaniment of the samisen are *monogatari* (tales). A frequent scene in plays having to do with historic conflicts is *kubijikken* ('head inspection'), where the correct identification of a severed but unbloody head by one who knew the person in life is of great consequence. (The last scene of *The House of Sugawara* uses this kind of scene to considerable effect.) The *yusuriba* (which occurs in *Benten the Thief*) is a scene of blackmailing, in which the interest lies in the ingenious reasons advanced by the blackmailer for his activity. *Dammari*, originally the plotless dumb-show used as a curtain-raiser at the November opening of the Kabuki season, was incorporated into longer plays; meaning 'night-fighting', this scene of conflict differs from *tachimawari* in that, although the stage is fully lighted, the actors move in slow motion as though surrounded by complete darkness, seeking each other out in silence. Of the many varieties of exits on the *hanamichi*, one of the most striking is the 'exit outside the curtain' (*maku soto no hikkomi*), for which the curtain is closed and the lone actor adds a kind of coda to the completed scene. Almost all Kabuki scenes, even the briefest, have been categorized and defined, among them, as cases in point, those in which a woman sighs and weeps as she regrets the past and those in which a young warrior reports on the progress of a battle. The strict design of these elements of the Kabuki in conjunction with the technical skill of the actor and the traditional methods of production created, despite the apparently contradictory evidence of the plays themselves, a theatre of meticulously patterned control, precision, and form. This aspect of the Kabuki is, of course, no more apparent to the uninitiated than is the mathematical clarity of the fugue.

As Japan moved towards 1868, a time of grave consequence deeply affecting its subsequent history, the Kabuki, seeming to sense that its future course would differ greatly from that of the past, produced in Kawatake Mokuami (who is always referred to by his 'given' name) one of its greatest and most prolific play-wrights. Mokuami's life, 1816–93, spanned an era of social upheaval during which the Tokugawa shogunate, the rulers of Japan since 1603, were overthrown, the Emperor was restored to a position of central importance in the State, and Japan, after centuries of carefully guarded, almost complete isolation, was exposed to the influence of the West. Fully perceptive of the atmosphere of his time, Mokuami seems to be almost the only playwright, other than Chikamatsu, whose plays were not simply ingeniously contrived theatre exercises but revelations of the attitude of the author towards the age. When Mokuami began writing plays about 1841, brutality and shock were already abroad in the Kabuki, and he augmented their dramatic effectiveness by choosing as the chief characters of his most successful pieces thieves, gamblers, and murderers. These plays, called 'living' domestic plays by the Japanese, are filled with a wry, dark pessimism found nowhere else in the Kabuki. In the late Tokugawa period an unworkable and outmoded economic system contributed to the impoverishment of many nobles of the warrior class and permitted commoners with money to buy their way into the upper class. It was a confused society which, having lost the hierarchical structure which sustained it, was directionless, frustrated, and ripe for political change. Mokuami's thieves move purposefully through this chaotic world, in which the only decisive voice is that of money talking. They live, it might almost be said, existentially, their only anchorage among the seething currents of society their abiding loyalty to their fellow thieves. The code of loyalty which shaped the lives of samurai in the historical plays is now transferred to this extra-social band, whose members often appear to be basically more honest and warm-hearted than those of the warrior class. No other existence than that of a thief is open to them in this society, and their lives are bound by despair, for their end is inevitable capture and death, with no possibility of felicity in the next incarnation. Mokuami's deep pessimism is not, however, constantly and obviously thrust on his audience, for many of his plays about thieves are filled with a humour which, however acrid and bitter, provokes laughter in the theatre.

Mokuami's unconventional concern, as a Kabuki playwright, with the shape of his times and with low-class characters make him in many ways the most realistic Kabuki writer. Unlike those who had come before him, he objected to the inconsistency and anachronism of Kabuki plays and set about to construct plays with rational subject matter and plots. At the same time he was equally the Kabuki's greatest classicist, and his plays were not technically realistic in the Western sense of the word. He made ingenious use of the spectacular and non-realistic methods of scene change, of the musical and rhythmical genesis of the performance, of the customary methods of production. He confined himself strictly to constructing his plays out of the traditional Kabuki 'forms', using them with great mastery both for serious and comic effect. His most frequent comic device was parodying the very elements out of which the Kabuki is composed. In a sense his work is a summing up and synthesis of all the techniques of production which the Kabuki had evolved, and in him the Kabuki seems to have had its last blaze of glory before setting out on the dark and uncertain path which it was to follow subsequently. Like his predecessors, Mokuami did not restrict himself to one type of play. Of his 360 works for the theatre, a third were 'living' domestic plays, but the others were cast in the traditional categories of historical plays, plays about the fall of great feudal houses, plays in the form of doll theatre *jōruri*, and pure dance pieces. Some of the latter remain the most popular in the Kabuki repertoire, among them his version of the Nō play, *The Maple Viewing*. In the traditional manner, Mokuami fashioned his pieces for particular actors, working for three of the greatest of his day, Onoe Kikugorō V, Ichikawa Kodanji I, and Ichikawa Danjūrō IX. After 1868 the actors, swept along by the fashionable intellectual currents of the time, were persuaded that it was necessary for the Kabuki to deal with contemporary life, and Mokuami was induced to write 'cropped-hair plays', so called because the male characters appearing in them, like the stylish contemporary Japanese, had forsaken the old-fashioned long hair of the Tokugawa period for the Western haircut. These plays, in whose action figured such evidences of modernity as brief-cases, steamboats, the telegraph, and foreigners, were the least successful of Mokuami's efforts, and the foredoomed attempt to combine the techniques of the Kabuki with the depiction of contemporary life was soon abandoned.

Mokuami completely dominated the Kabuki, at one time writing for each of the three important theatres in Tokyo, and some of the foremost playwrights after his death were his former pupils; but none succeeded in making any technical advance beyond Mokuami. Subsequent playwrights such as Okamoto Kidō and Fukuchi Ōchi laboured heroically for the 'reform' of the Kabuki; having become acquainted with the dramatic literature of the West, they realized that the Kabuki possessed nothing similar. Their notions of reform were based generally on the idea that the realism of the contemporary Western theatre must somehow or other be injected into the Kabuki. Since by its very nature the Kabuki was non-realistic, the effort to reform it along these lines meant an uneasy, unattractive compromise between antithetical forces.

In general, those who write for the Kabuki today do not follow this approach, but rather that advocated by Tsubouchi Shōyō (1859–1935), one of the first Japanese scholars to devote himself to a serious study of Western dramatic literature. When Tsubouchi compared the Kabuki 'historical' plays with those of Shakespeare, he found that they lacked unity and that their action did not grow out of character. Examining the plays of Chikamatsu in this light, he found them 'fantastic', and he considered the historical plays of Mokuami greatly superior.

Tsubouchi did not want a surface realism imitating mundane existence, but a psychological realism of character and situation expressed within the extant Kabuki forms. In the plays and dance pieces which Tsubouchi wrote for the Kabuki, he successfully demonstrated the validity of his theories, and most present-day writers have tended to follow his example, using the traditional Kabuki forms, writing plays set in the historic past, and introducing only minor innovations on the ground of realism. Few plays since Mokuami's seem to be assured a permanent place in the Kabuki, but the present active repertoire, consisting of some 300 plays and some 100 dance pieces, the overwhelming majority written before 1868, continues to be played to large and admiring audiences by skilful actors trained in the traditional manner.

Benten the Thief: This version omits only two passages of any length. One is a section from Act I, Scene i, in which Daihachi and Tenzō further quarrel with Shuzen and Sakon; the other occurs at the beginning of Act I, Scene iii, and involves a group of strolling musicians whom Princess Senju imagines to be figures from the underworld. Both these passages are omitted in contemporary Japanese performances. Unlike most Kabuki plays, this one is frequently played in its entirety, but two very popular parts are often played separately: Act II, Scene i, the scene in the Hamamatsu shop, and Act III, Scene i, a colourful passage of dance-like conflict. The original script is written in five acts. The stage directions are derived from Mokuami's text and from the contemporary Japanese performance.

It is perhaps gratuitous to make the point, but almost all the scenes of the play have a certain tongue-in-the-cheek quality, except, of course, the last three, in which matters come to a serious and impressive climax. For example, the scene of recognition between fathers and sons at the end of Act II is a parody of all such other scenes in the Kabuki, which are innumerable, and the audience is expected to laugh. Princess Senju is similarly made fun of as the helpless and put-upon Kabuki princess. Needless to say, these and similar matters are not played broadly and farcically, but rather in the vein of high comedy.

BENTEN THE THIEF

(Aoto Zōshi Hana no Nishikie, or Shiranami Gonin Otoko)

A Kabuki Play by

KAWATAKE MOKUAMI
(1862)

Translated by Yukuo Uyehara
English version by Earle Ernst

ACT I

SCENE I

Before the Lotus Temple, whose façade is brilliantly painted in red, gold, blue, and green. At stage-centre steps lead to a 3-foot high porch before the temple; to the right of the steps a small sign mounted on a pole informs those arriving on horseback that this is the place to dismount. The porch is surrounded by a low red-lacquered railing. There are blossoming cherry-trees on both sides of the stage, borders of cherry blossoms overhead, and painted cherry-trees on the backdrop. On stage-left is the entrance to a tea-house.

At stage-centre is an elaborate palanquin, the PRINCESS SENJU *sitting within it, her maids kneeling to either side of it, the palanquin bearers upstage. Two benches, diagonal to the footlights, are right and left of the palanquin. On the stage-left bench are seated* DAIHACHI *and* TENZŌ, *a villainous pair; left of them, in attendance, are two samurai. On the stage-right bench are* SHUZEN *and* SAKON, *honest men of the Chihara family.*

The costuming is dazzling. The PRINCESS, *like all Kabuki princesses, is dressed in red and wears an elaborate golden head-dress. Her maids are in white kimono and large pink obi. The men, each with his two swords, wear magnificent brocades.*

The curtain opens to music.

Until the argument between SHUZEN *and* DAIHACHI, *the lines are delivered in a highly formal style.*

TENZŌ. Princess Senju has come to the Lotus Temple to conduct the third anniversary memorial service for her deceased father, Koyama no Hangan.

DAIHACHI. She is also here to pray for her fiancé, Kotarō, who disappeared after the ruin of her House and is rumoured to have died in a distant province.

SHUZEN (*holding a small object wrapped in purple silk*). And here is the incense-case which the Shinoda family has sent for the occasion. It will be placed before the altar during the memorial service.

SAKON. To think that she, so young, is to perform the mass for her father and also conduct the memorial service for Kotarō, her betrothed! I sympathize with her.

MAID I. Even with such beautiful cherry blossoms all around her, Princess Senju grieves for her betrothed.

MAID II. How pitiful it is to see her so dejected!

MAID III. Like the cherry blossoms that scatter, her youth is soon gone, and she turns to Buddha.

MAID IV. A most merciful person is she, like a graceful flower.

MAID I. Yet she pines and wastes in the midst of these glorious blossoms.

MAID II. So, it is said, is the way of the world.

MAID I. Please look up, Princess Senju——

TENZŌ. ——and enjoy——

ALL. ——the cherry blossoms.

SENJU. (*She speaks from within the palanquin, and her speech is almost a parody of that of the languishing, ineffectual Kabuki princess. Her maids have spoken similarly.*) By the morrow, the petals will be scattered. Even today the branches are pained to hold them.

(*She comes out of the palanquin, and it is removed by the attendants. A stage assistant places a stool at stage-centre for her to sit on.*)

TENZŌ. You are depressed. These flowers will brighten your spirit.

SHUZEN. Please sit here and enjoy yourself.

SAKON. While the tree-tops blossom, forget your cares and enjoy the sight.

SENJU (*sitting*). I appreciate your kind thoughts. But even the cherry blossoms are meaningless to me now. If Kotarō no longer lives, I will take the vows of a nun. There are no flowers I can enjoy.

TENZŌ. Why do you speak of vows? You were not married to Kotarō. Indeed, you have never even seen him. To marry someone else would be the best thing for you now.

DAIHACHI. That is right. Kotarō disappeared without your laying eyes on him. He probably wandered about the country and died by the roadside.

SAMURAI I. Why should she remain faithful to a lordless samurai? I have heard that young Yoshimura of the powerful Miura clan is very much interested in her.

SAMURAI II. I think the best thing for her is to marry him.

TENZŌ. Princess Senju, please listen to me. Since the death of your father your House has survived only because it is under the guardianship of the Miura family. If you marry Yoshimura, the future of your House will be secure.

SHUZEN. Just a moment! I can understand your dissuading her from becoming a nun, but I do not understand your suggesting that she marry another.

DAIHACHI. Tenzō thinks of her House. Why should you oppose such a marriage?

SHUZEN. How can she marry when there is no evidence that Kotarō is dead?

DAIHACHI. Even if he lives, he is disgraced. If she should marry Kotarō, the House of Koyama will fall under suspicion.

SHUZEN. That is true. But to be unfaithful to one's betrothed is not proper for a woman.

TENZŌ. Then you do not care what happens to her House?

SHUZEN. It is not that, but——

TENZŌ. I, Satsushima Tenzō, an official of importance, will brook no meddling. Restrain yourself and be silent!

(SHUZEN *makes a gesture of chagrin.*)

SAKON. Tenzō, I disagree with you! To disobey the dead master's wishes is the greatest disloyalty.

DAIHACHI. What! A stripling like you would better be silent!

SENJU. Oh, please argue no more! I have already pledged myself to Buddha and have decided to be a nun.

MAID I. Please consider carefully, Princess Senju. There must be something we can do for you.

MAID II. Please do not take it so much to heart. Things will turn for the better.

MAID III. It will soon be time for the service.

MAID IV. Yes, we should prepare for it.

(*They all rise.*)

SHUZEN. First let us place the incense-case sent by Kotarō before the altar of the Goddess of Mercy.

SENJU. Yes, please place it there immediately.

TENZŌ. Princess Senju, please enter the temple.

SENJU. Then will all of you——

TENZŌ. But, Princess, you——

ALL. ——please lead the way.

(*Music.* SENJU *leading, they go up the steps to the temple porch and disappear stage-left.* TENZŌ, DAIHACHI, *and the* TWO SAMURAI *remain. They look about and appear exceedingly conspiratorial.*)

SAMURAI I. Tenzō!

TENZŌ. Hush!

SAMURAI I. What is the secret?

SAMURAI II. What is this about?

TENZŌ. It is this. . . . Be sure no one is listening to us.

BOTH SAMURAI. Yes, sir. (*They look around and then sit.*)

TENZŌ. Miura has decided to overthrow Hōjō Tokiyori and thus become Shogun. He has confided in me and wants me to assist him. When this is accomplished, I intend to seize the House of Koyama with your help.

DAIHACHI. If we can marry Princess Senju to the son, Yoshimura, we will be in the position of relatives to the Shogun. What

a rise in the world that would be! But the Chiharas stand in
our way.

SAMURAI I. This is the first I have heard of the great ambition of the
House of Miura. I shall serve you all the more.

SAMURAI II. There must be some way to get rid of them.

(TENZŌ *picks up a fan which* SHUZEN *has forgotten.*)

DAIHACHI. Just a moment. We could make use of that fan which
Shuzen has conveniently forgotten.

SAMURAI I. What can be done with that?

DAIHACHI. Chihara Shuzen is responsible for the custody of the
incense-case to be used before the altar. If we steal the incense-
case and leave the fan in its place we can cast suspicion on Shuzen.

TENZŌ. I am amazed at your ingenious plan.

SAMURAI I. This is a clever scheme. We will not neglect to watch
the altar.

SAMURAI II. We will steal that incense-case.

DAIHACHI. Do not fail us.

TENZŌ. Then let us go.

THE THREE. We will follow you.

(*Music. They exit stage-left, between the temple and the tea-house.*
AKAHOSHI JUSABURŌ, *wearing a costume of floral pattern, appears
on the* hanamichi, *carrying a basket of spring blossoms, and pauses
there meditatively. He is a young, melancholy, delicate aristocrat.*)

JUSABURŌ. It is springtime. And what a lively, bustling scene with
all these cheerful people! But while others sing and dance, here
am I, a penniless, masterless samurai, wandering from place to
place, ever since my lord Shinoda committed suicide and the
young master disappeared. What a shifting, evanescent world
this is! (*Pause.*) Oh, what beautiful cherry blossoms!

(*He moves to the stage. Simultaneously* AKAHOSHI TANOMŌ, *an old
man, appears from stage-left.*)

JUSABURŌ. Is this not my uncle I see?

TANOMŌ. Oh, it is Jusaburō!

JUSABURŌ. And where are you going?

TANOMŌ. Listen to me. I am at my wit's end.

JUSABURŌ. What is worrying you?

TANOMŌ. I should like to ask you a favour. But let us sit down before
I begin my story.

(*They sit on the right bench.*)

JUSABURŌ. What is it you wish to tell me?

TANOMŌ. As you know, our lord had to kill himself because of
Miura's slanders. Since then I have been trying my best to serve
our mistress. But she has fallen into a decline, and now she is not

even able to sit up in her bed. The doctor says it will take the best of medicine to cure her. But how can I buy the best of medicine when I am so poor?

JUSABURŌ. And what amount of money do you need?

TANOMŌ. One hundred *ryō*. If I don't get it, my mistress will die.

JUSABURŌ. She is my mistress as well as yours. (*Thinks.*) If I were a girl, it would be easy to do something about it. (*Turning to* TANOMŌ.) Nothing is impossible in this world. I shall do my best, and I beg you not to be concerned.

TANOMŌ. Do you mean to say you can get that sum?

JUSABURŌ (*rising*). I have something in mind. I think I can manage to get it.

TANOMŌ (*rising*). I shall be waiting impatiently to hear from you.

JUSABURŌ. I will not disappoint you.

TANOMŌ. Till then, Jusaburō!

JUSABURŌ. My uncle!

TANOMŌ. We shall see each other again.

(*He exits stage-right.*)

JUSABURŌ. Ah! No wonder he looks worn out. How can I get the enormous sum of one hundred *ryō*? In time of trouble we turn to the gods they say. If I pray to the Goddess of Mercy I may be rewarded.

(*He exits stage-left. Immediately* PRINCESS SENJU, *accompanied by* MAID I, *who carries the incense-case, appears from stage-left on the temple porch. The women hesitate and look about.*)

MAID I. Princess, I have just overheard some whispering. Tenzō is plotting with his men to steal the incense-case. Please guard it carefully.

(*She gives the incense-case to* SENJU.)

SENJU. I am glad you are so observant. This incense-case is dearer than my life.

(*They sit on the temple porch, and the other* MAIDS, *whose voices are heard offstage, join them.*)

MAID II. Ah, Princess Senju, you are here. What a beautiful view!

MAID III. Princess Senju, look there! It is the Nokendo of Kanazawa. And look at the bay! It is just like an artificial pond.

MAID IV. Look! So many people are coming this way. I want to see the handsome men. Look, look! There's a really handsome man.

MAID II. Where? Where? Oh, he *is*!

ALL. Which way is he going?

MAID II. He's coming this way. He's coming!

ALL. He's coming!

(On the hanamichi *appears* BENTEN KOZŌ *in the disguise of a warrior; he is followed by* KOMAHEI, *actually* NANGŌ RIKIMARU, *dressed as his attendant.*

They pause near the stage to look at the cherry blossoms.

BENTEN KOZŌ *looks the model of a young samurai, handsome in costume, face, voice, bearing, and sentiments.* NANGŌ *plays the role of a dignified servant with equal aplomb.)*

BENTEN. What glorious cherry blossoms! There must have been a similar sight when a poet of Cathay sang of the beautiful golden flowers that blossomed through the floating mist. This, too, is a sight to inspire poets and painters. How beautiful!

NANGŌ *(casting a lecherous eye at the women).* Sir, this is what people mean when they speak of flowers watching flowers.

(BENTEN and NANGŌ move to the stage. MAIDS I and II come down the steps. They whisper together and beckon to NANGŌ. He pretends not to notice. They go to him and pull him to stage-right. Meanwhile BENTEN sits on the bench left and takes out a white fan.)

MAID I. We have a favour to ask of you.

NANGŌ. You mean me? What is it?

MAID II. We want to know where your master comes from.

MAID I. And what——

BOTH. ——is his name?

NANGŌ *(shocked).* My master's name? That is a thing I cannot tell you.

MAID II. We, too, are in the service of a samurai family. We will never reveal his name to anyone.

BOTH. Please tell us.

NANGŌ *(reluctantly).* I will tell you, but you must keep it a secret. He is the son of Shinoda no Saemon, whose House has been destroyed. His name is Kotarō.

BOTH. Oh!

MAID I. It is he whom Princess Senju yearns for, day and night.

MAID II. He is her betrothed, Kotarō.

NANGŌ *(greatly surprised).* Is she, then, Princess Senju of the House of Koyama? Please, tell no one what I have just said.

(BENTEN raises the fan with which he has been hiding his face.)

BENTEN. Komahei, Komahei! (NANGŌ *goes to him.*) The cherry blossoms are so beautiful that I have spent an unexpectedly long time looking at them. Now I must pay my respects at the temple.

(He rises. Meanwhile SENJU, *led by* MAIDS III *and* IV, *has come down to stage-right and stands there admiring* BENTEN. *He looks at her briefly, then goes up the steps and exits left.)*

NANGŌ *(purposely pausing).* Well, I shall follow him.

(MAIDS I *and* II *move to* NANGŌ.)

MAID I. I have a little favour to ask you.

NANGŌ (*gruffly*). What! Another? I must follow my master.

MAID I. I understand. But can't you remain here a moment?

NANGŌ. Then speak quickly.

MAID II. The reason is this . . . (*Pause.*)

NANGŌ. What is it? I am impatient.

MAID II. Princess Senju is your master's betrothed. Since he disappeared, she insists she will become a nun.

MAID I. Please ask Kotarō to speak to her.

BOTH. Plead with him to do so!

NANGŌ (*horrified*). Speak to his betrothed! Oh, no! Although he is young, my master is a man of integrity. I can't suggest a thing like that!

BOTH. But couldn't you try?

NANGŌ. No, that I refuse to do.

BOTH. Won't you help us——

MAID I. ——by asking him?

BOTH. Please!

(NANGŌ *affects troubled thoughtfulness.*)

NANGŌ. Well, I shall try, although I am certain he won't agree. (*A sudden idea.*) I've got it! When I mention this to my master, he'll be sure to say no. But then Princess Senju can say that she'll kill herself. He'll be obliged to say yes to save her life!

MAID I. It is a wonderful plan.

MAID II (*moving to* SENJU). Rejoice, Princess Senju. He will speak to Kotarō.

SENJU. I shall never forget your kindness. Oh, I am so happy!

NANGŌ. It's nothing at all. But don't forget the dagger.

SENJU. The dagger? (*She isn't really very bright.*)

NANGŌ (*patiently*). Princess Senju, when the master comes I'll make the request. But if he refuses, you say (*in falsetto, imitating her manner of speech*), 'If you won't speak to me today——'

SENJU. If you won't speak to me today——

NANGŌ. It is useless for me to live any longer.

SENJU. It is useless for me to live any longer.

NANGŌ. I would rather here and now——

SENJU. I would rather here and now——

NANGŌ. End my life, (*In his normal voice*) and then pull out the dagger.

SENJU. End my life and then pull out the dagger.

NANGŌ. No! Your line stops with 'end my life'.

SENJU. It's rather difficult, isn't it?

NANGŌ (*after a look at her*). Be that as it may, try it.

(*Music.* BENTEN *appears from the left on the temple porch, and all look towards him.* SENJU *sits on the bench right.* BENTEN *comes down the steps.*)

NANGO. Oh! So you have already finished.

BENTEN. I have paid my respects. Shall we be on our way now?

NANGŌ. Please wait a while. Why don't you sit down here a moment?

(*He pushes* BENTEN *down on the bench left. Then he brings* SENJU *over and has her sit on* BENTEN's *right.*)

NANGO. I want to introduce you to this lady.

SENJU (*modestly not looking at him*). Kotarō, how have you been?

BENTEN (*showing surprise*). What! You call me Kotarō. I am not he.

SENJU. No, no! Please speak the truth. I have been told who you are.

BENTEN. What! Komahei, did you reveal my identity?

NANGŌ. Yes. . . . It was a slip of the tongue.

BENTEN. Well, if the truth is out—I am Shinoda Kotarō. But tell no one. My identity must be concealed.

(*A long pause.*)

NANGŌ. Please say something to her. It seems she is your betrothed.

BENTEN. Silence!

NANGŌ. How sweet Princess Senju is!

BENTEN. Be quiet!

NANGŌ. If you grant my request I shall appreciate it.

BENTEN (*shouting*). Why don't you shut up!

NANGŌ. Yes, sir.

(*Pause.*)

MAID I. No matter how much we plead——

MAID II. ——you will not——

ALL. ——agree?

SENJU (*weeps*). Ooooooh!

BENTEN. Yes, we are betrothed. Our engagement was concluded secretly. But if we should speak to one another now, before marriage, we would be wronging our parents.

(NANGŌ *and the* MAIDS *signal to* SENJU *to draw the dagger. She looks at them blankly, but when they have repeated the action, she gets the idea.*)

SENJU. Then, alas—— (*She takes out the dagger.*)

MAIDS. Pray wait! Wait!

BENTEN. Please do not permit her to do anything rash.

SENJU. Unless you favour me with kind words, I am prepared to die.

NANGŌ. Please, master, say something to her, otherwise she will kill herself.

BENTEN. But how can I——?

MAID II. Then you will let her die?

BENTEN. I don't want her to do that, but——

MAID III. Then you will agree to——

BENTEN. Well, but that is——

MAID IV. You will not let her die?

BENTEN. Well——

MAID I. Well——

ALL. Well, well, well?

SENJU. Please let me die!

(*She makes a show of trying to stab herself, and* BENTEN *prevents her.*)

BENTEN. Wait! I shall consent to your proposal.

WOMEN. Then you will consent to——

NANGŌ (*imitating* SENJU). Oh, I am so happy!

(MAIDS *look about cautiously.*)

MAID I. Unfortunately this is his home province. He must not be recognized here.

MAID II (*pointing to the tea-house*). Let them go in there and talk.

BENTEN (*rising*). Then, together——

WOMEN. ——let us go.

(BENTEN *leads* SENJU *into the tea-house, and* MAID II *follows them. The others remain onstage and demonstrate relief.*)

MAID I (*exhausted*). That was difficult work to be sure.

NANGŌ. I am certain he will say something to her. I will wait in the wine shop over there.

WOMEN. Then, Komahei——

NANGŌ. I shall go.

(*He exits stage-right, the* MAIDS *stage-left to the tea-house.*)

The sound of drums and the beating of wooden clappers.

JUSABURŌ *runs out from stage-right, pursued by* TENZŌ, DAI-HACHI, *and the two* SAMURAI. SAMURAI II *seizes* JUSABURŌ.)

SAMURAI I. You bastard! You look innocent, but what a thief!

SAMURAI II. You stole one hundred *ryō*—the money for masses for the dead.

JUSABURŌ. No, no! I wouldn't do such a thing!

TENZŌ. Don't think you can fool a samurai. I saw you steal it.

DAIHACHI. I'll make you confess.

(*Strikes* JUSABURŌ, *who falls.*)

TENZŌ. Daihachi, search him.

DAIHACHI. Yes, sir.

(DAIHACHI *seizes* JUSABURŌ *and reaches into his kimono.* JUSABURŌ *clutches his breast, but the money, wrapped in white paper, falls to the ground.* JUSABURŌ *hangs his head in shame.* DAIHACHI *picks up the money.*)

DAIHACHI. You wretch! Unscrupulous liar! I'll teach you a lesson! (*He beats* JUSABURŌ.)

SAMURAI I. That isn't enough! (*He kicks* JUSABURŌ.)

SAMURAI II. Take this too! (*He also kicks him.*)

JUSABURŌ (*weeping*). Wait a moment, please. It is most natural for you to be angry. I stole the money, but not for my own use. I was once a samurai myself, but now I am a masterless, poverty-stricken *rōnin*. My father has been ill for a long time, and for the past few days his condition has been critical. I tried to procure the money to buy him medicine, but I couldn't. In my extremity, I committed this disgraceful crime. Please pardon me, so that I may save my father from death.

(*They are unmoved.*)

SAMURAI I (*noticing the crest on* JUSABURŌ's *sleeve*). Look! Look at the crest he's wearing!

(*At this point* TADANOBU RIHEI *appears on the temple porch, unseen by the others, and stands watching.*)

TENZŌ. What! The snow and bamboo crest of the Shinoda family! You must be related to the Shinoda clan.

JUSABURŌ. What nonsense!

TENZŌ. Yes, you are! The House of your master was ruined because of his evil doing. Like master, like follower, eh? I'll slice you in half!

(*He seizes the hilt of his sword.* DAIHACHI *stops him.*)

DAIHACHI. To kill such a worm will pollute your sword. Let him go.

TENZŌ. This detestable beast?

DAIHACHI. It is pointless to take his life. (*To* JUSABURŌ.) I shall apologize for you. Be on your way.

JUSABURŌ. Thank you very much.

TENZŌ. No, I won't let him go. I'll kill him.

DAIHACHI. I have reasons for asking you to spare him.

(DAIHACHI *whispers to* TENZŌ. TADANOBU RIHEI *disappears stage-left.*)

TENZŌ (*to* JUSABURŌ). Since Daihachi insists, I'll let you go. But from now on you'd better behave yourself.

DAIHACHI. Let's leave this place. I have something to tell you.

TENZŌ. As you wish.

THE THREE. Then, Tenzō——

TENZŌ. Yet this cursed——

(*Again he attempts drawing his sword,* DAIHACHI *preventing him.*)
DAIHACHI. Let's get away from here.
(*Music. The four exit stage-left.* TANOMŌ *enters from stage-right. He goes quickly to* JUSABURŌ, *who is still on the ground, and beats him with a fan.*)
TANOMŌ. Jusaburō, I've heard everything! Had I known you would steal the money, I would not have asked you. What a detestable beast you are to stain my lord's name! Our relation of uncle and nephew ceases at this moment. You brazen creature!
JUSABURŌ. It is natural that you should be angry. I knew it was wrong to steal, but I couldn't bear to see you suffering. I'm greatly ashamed.
TANOMŌ. I've heard enough.
JUSABURŌ. But please understand me and—— (*He takes* TANOMŌ's *sleeve;* TANOMŌ *pulls it from him.*)
TANOMŌ. It is beneath my dignity even to talk to you.
(*Music.* TANOMŌ *goes off right.*)
JUSABURŌ. Please forgive me, uncle.
(*The temple gong sounds.* JUSABURŌ *rises, picks up his sword, looks at his crest, then moves on to the* hanamichi, *where he pauses.*)
JUSABURŌ. I realize that I am blameworthy. But the mistress is seriously ill, and if I can't get the money, I will be unable to apologize to my uncle. There is nothing left for me but to kill myself and prove my integrity. Money . . . (*The temple gong sounds and cherry blossoms fall.*) . . . is the root of all evil.
(*He exits, sadly, on the* hanamichi.
From stage-left come TENZŌ, DAIHACHI, *and the two* SAMURAI, *rapidly and purposefully.*)
DAIHACHI (*excitedly*). Princess Senju and Kotarō are in that tea-house?
SAMURAI II. That is so.
TENZŌ. No mistake about it?
SAMURAI I. None at all. The attendants may be with them, but it looks suspicious.
TENZŌ. We'll go in and see what's going on.
SAMURAI I. Certainly.
(SAMURAI I *enters the tea-house, but is thrown out immediately and rolls on the ground.* SAMURAI II *enters but immediately comes out, his arm twisted behind him by* TADANOBU RIHEI.)
DAIHACHI. Good heavens! I thought those two were in there.
TADANOBU (*a tough one*). What manners have you, entering a room wearing foot-gear? Even though masterless now, I was once a

samurai. And wherever he chooses to stop, that room is a samurai's castle. Insolent men, your lives are mine now.

ALL (*falling to the ground and bowing*). Yaaaaah!

TADANOBU. What explanation do you have?

MEN. Well, that is——

TADANOBU. What intention prompted you to——

MEN. Well, that is——

TADANOBU. Well?

MEN. Well——

ALL. Well, well, well.

TADANOBU. I'm waiting for your answer.

TENZŌ. We did not know you were an important personage. I apologize for our rude behaviour.

DAIHACHI. That is so. We would never have done such a thing had we known you were in the room.

SAMURAI II. Our impudence caused an impolite blunder.

SAMURAI I. If you would kindly grant us forgiveness——

MEN. ——we would certainly appreciate it.

TADANOBU. No, I cannot forgive you. If my friends should hear of this incident, I would be laughed at. Come, we will fight it out.

(*He puts his hand on his sword hilt, and they tremble.* TENZŌ *whispers to* DAIHACHI.)

DAIHACHI (*crawling to* TADANOBU). I really do not know how to apologize. Do forgive us! Allow me to present you with a gift as a token of our apology.

(*He slips the package of one hundred ryō into* TADANOBU'S *sleeve.* TADANOBU *moves his arm up and down slightly to estimate the quantity of money by its weight. A look of satisfaction appears on his face, but he immediately becomes stern again.*)

TADANOBU (*in great moral indignation*). What is the meaning of this? Do you think I am a dishonest, immoral samurai who accepts bribes? Take back your filthy money! (*He throws it at them.*)

SAMURAI II. We throw ourselves on your mercy. Please accept it for our sakes.

SAMURAI I. Please accept it and——

SAMURAI II. ——please grant us——

ALL. ——this favour.

(TADANOBU *permits himself to give way.*)

TADANOBU. Well, if you insist . . .

SAMURAI I. Then,—sir, you will pardon us?

TADANOBU (*sitting on bench left*). I should not forgive you, but in view of your courtesy I shall overlook this incident.

DAIHACHI. This is certainly——

MEN. ——a great favour.

SAMURAI II (*crawling to him with the money*). Then please accept this money.

TADANOBU. I should not take such money. (*Pause.*) But if I don't take it, I will be insulting your kindness.

MEN. You are right, sir.

TADANOBU. Even if I refused the money, you wouldn't take it back.

MEN. That's right, sir.

TADANOBU. Then, with reluctance, I shall accept it. (*He grabs it.*)

MEN. Thank you, sir.

TADANOBU. It is almost dusk, and I have not yet paid my respects to the Goddess of Mercy. (*He stands and looks at* TENZŌ.) You will see that these men do not speak of what has happened today.

> (*Music.* TADANOBU *walks up the steps, turns, looks at them, and they bow to the ground. He sticks his tongue out at them and exits left.*)

MEN. Tenzō!

TENZŌ (*breathless and tottery*). Heaven help us! I don't understand this.

SAMURAI II. I still think Princess Senju and Kotarō were in there.

SAMURAI I. How did all the shuffling with that brute happen?

TENZŌ. Let's have a drink at the wine shop and forget this unfortunate occurrence.

DAIHACHI. Indeed, that would be wonderful.

BOTH SAMURAI. We will gladly accompany you.

TENZŌ. Then let us go.

> (*Music. They go off right. Then from the tea-house come* BENTEN, SENJU, *and the* MAIDS.)

MAID IV. Even we girls have been blessed with your kind words.

SENJU. This must have been an act of the Goddess of Mercy. (*She takes out the incense-case.*) This is the incense-case you sent me long ago. I placed it before the altar, but being told that the evil Tenzō meant to steal it, I have kept it. Will you receive it and guard it from now on?

BENTEN (*with a touch of irony*). Yes, it will be safe in my hands.

> (*He puts it into his kimono.* NANGŌ *enters from stage-right.*)

NANGŌ. It is already dusk, and you should be on your way.

BENTEN. That is so. Princess Senju, we shall see each other again.

> (*He starts to go towards the* hanamichi, *but she clings to his sleeve.*)

SENJU. Even though we are betrothed, and it is therefore wrong to ask you, will you not please take me with you?

BENTEN (*apparently shocked*). Why, no! How could I do that?

SENJU (*weeping*). You must take me along. (*Remembering that it worked before.*) If you don't, I will kill myself!

BENTEN. This is a problem.

MAID II. Suppose something should happen to her while you're gone? Please take her with you.

BENTEN. But——

NANGŌ. I will take care of everything here.

SENJU. Then it is all right for me to go with him?

NANGŌ. Why not?

BENTEN (*with a show of reluctance*). Well, though I feel guilty about it, I shall take you to my temporary quarters.

NANGŌ. Go, before anything else happens.

SENJU (*to* MAIDS). Will you see to everything?

MAID I. We will return immediately to your castle.

BENTEN. Let us go then.

(*Music.* BENTEN *and* SENJU *exit on the* hanamichi. *The* MAIDS *exit left.*)

NANGŌ. As I watched from the shadow of the trees, I saw that *rōnin* take a hundred *ryō* away from Tenzō. There's something funny going on here. I'd like to get hold of him and find out what he's up to.

(TADANOBU *enters up-left and moves to the centre of the temple porch.*)

TADANOBU. The sun has set, and the moon has risen. The cherry blossoms are especially beautiful in the moonlight. (*He smiles.*) They say every dog has his day. That hundred *ryō* was entirely unexpected. No wonder I can't give up this lucrative business. (*He starts down the steps.*)

NANGŌ. Just a moment, if you please, sir.

TADANOBU (*on his dignity*). Are you asking me to wait?

NANGŌ. Yes, sir.

TADANOBU. What do you want of me?

NANGŌ. I am a retainer of Shinoda Kotarō whom you have just helped. I should like to thank you for that.

TADANOBU. No thanks are necessary. It is the duty of a samurai to help others at all times.

NANGŌ. In that case, I have a request to make of you. You just said that helping others is the duty of a samurai. Now the one hundred *ryō* you took away from——

TADANOBU (*reverting to type*). Ah!

NANGŌ. That money was stolen from the House of Koyama. Therefore I beg you to return it.

TADANOBU. You're asking me to give back the money?

NANGŌ. Yes, I am.

TADANOBU. Don't talk like a fool! I had a tough time getting that money. You think I'm an ordinary *rōnin*? I'll tell you who I am.

I'm a follower of the famous Nippon Daemon, the thief whose name is known all over Japan.

NANGŌ. What!

TADANOBU. I'm clever at my work. But I've had hard luck this spring, and this is the first time I've had a big haul. I'll never part with this money.

NANGŌ. I, too, am no ordinary fellow. Come on, let me have it!

TADANOBU. Why should I give it to you?

NANGŌ. If you won't, I can take it from you!

TADANOBU. Can you?

NANGŌ. It will be easy.

BOTH. You thief!

(*Music.* TADANOBU *draws his sword;* NANGŌ, *swordless, arms himself with the notice-board beside the steps; and there ensues a stylized scene of fighting. It ends in a draw and a tableau,* NANGŌ *on the steps,* TADANOBU *below him, both in static poses.*)

CURTAIN

ACT I

SCENE II

A mountain pass. Before the painted backdrop is a low platform, the width of the stage, the front of it painted with stones. On the platform at left-centre is a small, thatched, rustic shrine, with double doors at the front.

The curtain opens to gongs and drums. BENTEN, *leading* SENJU *by the hand, enters on the* hanamichi.

BENTEN. The gongs and drums must have been those of your searchers. We mustn't let them find us.

(*They move forward;* SENJU *stumbles.*)

BENTEN. I know you must be very tired, but be patient. We shall soon find a place to rest.

SENJU (*weary and almost tearful*). Yes, my dear. It is painful walking in the mountains. But when I am with you I am so happy that it isn't difficult to go on.

BENTEN (*with ill-concealed irony*). I am happy, my love, to know you think so well of me.

SENJU. Pray, always love me!

BENTEN. Why should I not? (*He looks around.*) Let us go to that wayside shrine and rest.

SENJU. Then, to the shrine.

BENTEN. Walk carefully.

(*Music. They move to the stage, and* BENTEN *sits on the platform, right of the shrine.*)

M

BENTEN. Since we have come this far, there is nothing to worry about. Have a good, long rest.

SENJU (*sitting*). I said I was not tired, but I can scarcely move.

BENTEN. You have suffered very much because of me. Please forgive me, my love.

SENJU. You are too kind. But I feel so helpless and lonely deep in these mountains. Let us go away from here quickly.

BENTEN. You need not worry when I am with you.

SENJU. But this is such a frightening place!

BENTEN (*maliciously*). That's true. I'm told that wild boars and wolves often come out of the forest and attack travellers!

SENJU. Oh my! (*She clings to* BENTEN.)

BENTEN. Why are you frightened?

SENJU. When you say things like that you make me even more afraid. Please take me to your home.

BENTEN. My home?

SENJU. Yes. Is it far from here?

BENTEN. I am a masterless samurai without a home.

SENJU. But you live somewhere, don't you?

BENTEN. Yes, and that place——

SENJU. Where is it?

(BENTEN *suddenly drops his samurai role and becomes the gangster.*)

BENTEN. ——is here! Right here!

SENJU. Oh!

BENTEN. This wayside shrine is my home.

SENJU. You are not Kotarō!

BENTEN. No! I am the thief called Benten Kozō. (*He strikes an attitude.*)

SENJU. Oh my! (*She falls to the ground.*) Then that other man was——

BENTEN. One of my gang. Nangō Rikimaru. (*Amused.*) You're scared, eh?

SENJU. I believed you were my beloved, and I was foolishly deceived. But how do you come to have the flute I sent to Kotarō at the time of our betrothal?

BENTEN. Last winter I met a pilgrim on the road, dying of cold. As I nursed this poor man, he told me his name was Kotarō. Before he died, he asked me to return the flute to the Koyama family. I buried him, and then came to Kamakura. The rest of the story you know. How strange is fate!—that I should meet the betrothed of Kotarō!

SENJU. Then Kotarō is dead! (*She weeps.*)

BENTEN. What's there to cry about? He's dead and gone. Forget about him and be my woman.

(*He seizes her hand; she shakes him off.*)

SENJU. How can I do that?

BENTEN. Then you refuse——

SENJU. Well——

BENTEN. To be my woman?

SENJU. Well——

BENTEN. Give me your answer. Be quick!

SENJU (*in despair*). I have been dishonoured. (*She rises.*) There is nothing left but——

BENTEN. Here, you!

(*A struggle. At last she frees herself from* BENTEN *and runs off right.*)

BENTEN (*looking off right, casually*). Jumped into the ravine. That's too bad. Guess I can't blame her. (*Pause.*) What I just told her was a lie. I was Kotarō's enemy. I pretended kindness, took care of him, but when I found out who he was, I strangled him and took the flute. And with the flute, I was able to get the incense-case. Not a bad job! Benten Kozō's life will be short, but his reputation will live a hundred years.

(*A door of the shrine opens, and* NIPPON DAEMON *appears. He is dressed as a travelling priest and carries a priest's staff.* BENTEN *is somewhat startled.*)

BENTEN. I must be on my way. (*He starts to move off right.*)

DAEMON (*he has a deep voice and an impressive appearance*). Young man, wait a moment!

BENTEN (*stopping, and assuming the samurai pose*). Are you speaking to me?

DAEMON (*sitting before the shrine*). I am. Please come here.

BENTEN (*goes warily to* DAEMON). You appear to be a wandering priest. Is there something you wish to say to me?

DAEMON. You will learn in time. (*Pause.*) I intended to spend the night in this shrine, but the mountain winds came whipping through the cracks, and I couldn't sleep. Then I heard a woman weeping somewhere.

BENTEN. Oh?

DAEMON. The cold is severe even for a young man like you. I'll make a fire. Stay and warm yourself.

BENTEN. I'll avail myself of your kindness.

DAEMON. Please do!

(*He collects dry leaves, takes a tinder box from his wallet, and panto-mimes lighting a fire.* BENTEN *sits near by. The two keep glancing at each other suspiciously.*)

BENTEN. I am warm now, and I am in a hurry. What have you to say to me?

(DAEMON *lights his pipe and stares at* BENTEN.)

DAEMON. You are very young, but I admire your nerve. You have a great future before you.

BENTEN. Don't talk nonsense! Tell me what you have to say.

DAEMON. I have a favour to ask of you.

BENTEN. What is it?

DAEMON (*sudden change*). I want that gold incense-case you got today!

BENTEN (*again the gangster*). You were listening?

DAEMON. Yes, I heard everything.

BENTEN. Then there's nothing to hide. But an ordinary wandering priest would ask for a few coins, and you ask for a gold incense-case. You can't be an ordinary priest.

DAEMON. I am not! Outwardly I look like a Buddhist priest. In my heart I am a fiend. I am the talked-about, the famous, the notorious thief, Nippon Daemon. (*He removes his priest's hood and strikes an attitude.*) The whole of Japan is mine, and I know every worthy thief in the land. (*He looks at* BENTEN.) You seem to be a splendid fellow. What do you call yourself?

BENTEN. As a child I was sent to the Iwamoto monastery to serve as a page. But I was more interested in stealing the collection money than in learning. When I was expelled from the temple I became a professional. I am the thief Benten Kozō. (*He strikes an attitude.*)

DAEMON. You can omit the formalities. Now, are you going to give me that incense-case?

BENTEN. No, I am not!

DAEMON. What!

BENTEN. Now that I know you are Nippon Daemon, how can I give it to you? Others will laugh at me and say I was frightened by your illustrious name. No! I won't give it up.

DAEMON. As sure as my name is Nippon Daemon, I will take it from you!

BENTEN. That is interesting. Either I'll have your head——

DAEMON. ——or I'll have the incense-case.

BENTEN. Here and now——

DAEMON. ——let's see——

BENTEN. Whether you take my head or I yours.

DAEMON. Come on, you Kozō!

BENTEN. I am ready.

(*Music.* BENTEN *draws his sword and attacks* DAEMON, *who remains seated and fights with his staff.* BENTEN *fights recklessly, without control. At last* BENTEN'S *sword is knocked from his hand, and he is pinned down by* DAEMON'S *staff.*)

DAEMON. Now, Kozō, move if you can!

BENTEN. Kill me!

DAEMON. What?

BENTEN. I said kill me. It is useless to struggle against you. Death comes sooner or later. Let me die by your sword.

DAEMON (*removes the staff*). No, I don't think I will kill you.

BENTEN. Why not?

DAEMON. I want you to be my follower.

(*Pause. Then* BENTEN *bows before* DAEMON.)

BENTEN. It will be an honour to work for the greatest thief in Japan. I will be your follower. (*He places the incense-case before* DAEMON.) As a token of our relationship, I am pleased to give you this incense-case.

DAEMON. No, if you will be my follower, that is not necessary. It is your spoil. Keep it. But you must sign this document of agreement. (*From the breast of his kimono he brings forth a scroll. Holding one end of it, he throws the scroll into the air so that it describes a graceful arc.*) Now sign your name.

BENTEN. I will.

(*He takes the end of the scroll in his hands. Music. Tableau.*)

Stage-hands come on and attach a blue-and-white 'cloud-curtain' to the bottom of the platform. The platform, being placed on a stage elevator, then rises until the 'cloud curtain' covers the entire proscenium. The curtain then falls to the stage floor, revealing

ACT I

SCENE III

The bottom of a ravine, through which flows the Inase River. This scene is indicated by a painted backdrop and cut-out wings.

PRINCESS SENJU *lies unconscious at the centre of the stage.*

The following lines, here assigned to a chorus, are a loose paraphrase of a passage done in a kind of recitative by a soloist accompanied on the samisen.

CHORUS. The moon has vanished
    Behind the mountain.
    Silent
    The song of the nightingale,
    Silent

The valley
As the Valley of the Dead.

Pitiful is the young princess!
Lured into these far mountains,
Robbed and betrayed,
Wishing to end her life,
She has thrown herself from the cliff.

Now she wakes, and looks about her.

Do I wake or dream?
Is this the Land of the Living?
Or the Land of the Dead?
Is this Earth?
Or is it Hell?

SENJU. Alas, I am a sinful woman! I must be in Hell!
CHORUS. She is deceived!
This is Earth, not Hell.
But in these evil days
The boundary between Hell and Earth
Is hard to fix:
The King of Hell has loosed his fires,
Hell stays no longer where once it did.

The fires of Hell
Devour the gates of Hell
The fires of Hell
Dissolve
The icy waters of the Styx in yellow steam
The fires of Hell
Burn
Across the Earth.

And in this hour who can say,
Here is Earth?
There is Hell?

The holy chant
Rises from the temple,
But clearer than the chant
Is the voice of a woman
Making love to a priest.

The scent of incense
Rises from the temple,
But the scent vanishes
In the stinking cloud of iniquity.

The grate of contentious voices
Drowns
The song of the bird
The voice of the lover.

The King of Hell walks among men.
His face now grown familiar
No longer frightens us,
And at his fires
Men warm their hearts.

The King of Hell
Comes not empty handed:
He brings his greatest treasure,
His greatest weapon,
Gold!
And with his coin
Corrupts
The incorruptible.

What door can be locked
When money gets the key to it?
What is honesty
When it has its price?
What is virtue
When money buys it?

All that is fragile,
Beautiful,
True,
Lies crushed
Beneath the heavy weight of money.

(*A bell sounds.* AKAHOSHI JUSABURŌ *enters on the* hanamichi,
dejected.)

CHORUS. How disappointing are the promises
Of this transitory world!
I have wandered aimlessly into these far mountains.

(*He goes to the stage.*)

JUSABURŌ. By good fortune there is a stream. I shall throw myself into it and——

SENJU. Excuse me. I should like to ask you something.

JUSABURŌ. What is this? I hear a woman's voice in the darkness.

SENJU (*approaching him*). Please tell me. In what part of the Land of the Dead am I now?

JUSABURŌ. What? The Land of the Dead? This is a road near Kamakura, on a bank of the Inase River.

SENJU. Kamakura? I thought I had killed myself. But if this is the Inase River I must have returned to life again. Ah, how cruel this world is!

JUSABURŌ. Then you, too, wanted to kill yourself.

SENJU. Do you mean that you——

JUSABURŌ. I am prepared for death.

SENJU. How strange! We meet as companions on our last journey.

JUSABURŌ. Why have you made this dreadful decision?

SENJU. I chose death because——

CHORUS. I shall never find my betrothed, Kotarō;
> Only the gods know where he has gone.
> And how cruel they are,
> Deaf to my prayers.
> Even the token of his love,
> The incense-case,
> Is lost.
> My life is meaningless,
> And I will die.

JUSABURŌ. Can you then be Kotarō's betrothed, Princess Senju?

SENJU. Yes. Who are you that knows my name?

JUSABURŌ. I was once a retainer of the Shinoda clan. My name is Akahoshi Jusaburō.

SENJU. You were a retainer of Kotarō?

JUSABURŌ. Indeed, I was.

SENJU. Why do you wish to kill yourself?

JUSABURŌ. I want to die——

CHORUS. He hesitates.
> I have done all I can
> To help the mistress of my House.
> More than this I cannot do,
> But die.
> How strange is Fate!
> Prepared for death,
> I meet the betrothed of my lord,
> Also prepared to die.

(TADANOBU RIHEI *appears up-left, stands quietly watching.*)

SENJU. Truly, this is the working of Karma! Now that we have been brought together, let us die together, Jusaburō.

JUSABURŌ. But if we die together, it will appear to be a lovers' suicide.

SENJU. Let people say what they will, Jusaburō. Kotarō was your master, my betrothed. That bond lies between us.

JUSABURŌ. Alas, you are yet a flowering young maiden.

SENJU. In the rough winds of this world the petals are soon scattered.

JUSABURŌ. The more we try to seize and fix it, the more this seems——

BOTH. ——a world of dreams.

(*They weep together. Suddenly* SENJU *rises, runs upstage, and disappears right.*)

CHORUS. She throws herself into the river
   And dies.
   The midnight winds
   Wail through the branches,
   The flowers are gone.

JUSABURŌ (*praying*). Namu Amida Butsu, Namu Amida Butsu. In the next world, even to the end of time, I will accompany her on her journey.

(*He unsheaths his dagger and is about to stab himself.* TADANOBU *comes forward and seizes* JUSABURŌ's *wrist.*)

TADANOBU. Just a moment!

JUSABURŌ. No, no, I must die! Please let go!

TADANOBU. Wait, now! Wait!

JUSABURŌ. No, no——

TADANOBU. When I say wait, wait!

(*He takes the dagger from* JUSABURŌ, *who falls to the ground disconsolately.* TADANOBU *sits near him.*)

TADANOBU. Now then! Samurai must understand and help each other. You probably have reasons for killing yourself and leaving this wonderful world. But if there's some way out, I'll do what I can to help you. Now tell me about it.

JUSABURŌ. Then listen. I was once a retainer of the Shinoda family. But my lord lost his life through slander and the House was ruined. My mistress has become gravely ill. The only thing that can ease her suffering, I am told, is an expensive medicine. So, against my will, I tried to steal one hundred *ryō*. I disgraced myself, I brought dishonour upon my lord. My only uncle severed his relationship with me. Now there is nothing left but to die.

TADANOBU. You were once a retainer of the Shinoda clan! I, too, had a close tie with that family once. What is your name?

JUSABURŌ. I am called Jusaburō, son of Akahoshi Shuzen.

TADANOBU (*surprised*). The son of Akahoshi! Please accept my deep apology for being so rude. (*He bows before* JUSABURŌ.) Now that I know who you are, I must redouble my efforts to save your life.

JUSABURŌ. I don't understand. Why should you pay such deep respect to me?

TADANOBU. I am the son of Denzō who once served your father. But then he stole two hundred *ryō* from the house.

JUSABURŌ. You are the son of that retainer Denzō?

TADANOBU. And you are the young master!

JUSABURŌ. This unexpected meeting——

TADANOBU. ——to save you from death——

JUSABURŌ. ——by parents gone to the other world——

TADANOBU. ——was planned for you!

BOTH. This blessing upon us!

JUSABURŌ. It is fortunate I have met you. Please explain to my uncle why I had to end my life.

(*He reaches for the dagger which lies between them, but* TADANOBU *grasps his wrist.*)

TADANOBU. No, Jusaburō. I cannot allow the son of my lord to kill himself.

JUSABURŌ. But unless I get one hundred *ryō*, I must die.

TADANOBU (*amused at the triviality of the problem*). Money! Don't worry about that! One hundred, two hundred, a thousand, two thousand *ryō*, I can get it for you.

JUSABURŌ. You mean you will help me?

TADANOBU (*placing a packet of money before* JUSABURŌ). Here! Please accept this one hundred *ryō* in apology for my father's disloyalty to your House.

JUSABURŌ (*taking the money joyfully*). Now through your kindness I can procure the medicine. I am greatly obliged to you.

TADANOBU. There's more to be had, so give up this idea of killing yourself.

JUSABURŌ. Oh, now that I have this money I need not die. (*Suddenly remembering.*) But I promised Princess Senju that I would go with her to the next world. I made that promise.

TADANOBU. A promise to the dead doesn't matter. Use the money and help the living. Then, if you're still in love with death, do what you wish. But don't be a fool!

JUSABURŌ. You are right, Tadanobu. I shall help the living. But I don't understand. How do you happen to have so much money?

TADANOBU (*smoothly*). Getting money is my business. Of course I seldom have a penny during the daytime, but when night comes, hundreds and hundreds of *ryō* just fall into my hands.

JUSABURŌ. And what is your means of livelihood?

TADANOBU. Livelihood? Well——

JUSABURŌ. Your occupation.

TADANOBU (*cheerfully*). I'm very sorry to tell you, but I am a thief.

JUSABURŌ. A thief?

TADANOBU (*with growing pride at his accomplishments*). I understand your surprise. But listen to me, my young lord. Inheriting my father's faults, I had light fingers even as a child. I was so thievish as an apprentice I could never last for more than half a year anywhere. Why, between the time I was ten and fourteen, I must have changed masters thirty times. Finally, even my father disowned me, and I began robbing travellers on the Tōkaidō Highway. Now I am one of the followers of the famous thief Nippon Daemon. My name is Tadanobu Rihei. (*He strikes an attitude.*)

JUSABURŌ. Then I suppose this money too was——

TADANOBU (*chuckling*). That money? I got it from the Koyama clansman Tenzō at the Lotus Temple today.

JUSABURŌ. The memorial-service money! This is what I tried to steal!

TADANOBU (*taken aback*). You do a little thieving on the side?

JUSABURŌ. I stole that money, but I was found out. Then I tried to kill myself and you stopped me. Then the money comes back to me. It's an interesting world, isn't it?

TADANOBU. It's more than interesting. It's fascinating the way money goes around so methodically. Why, it's just like a Kabuki play!

JUSABURŌ (*having made up his mind*). Tadanobu, I have an earnest request to make of you. Will you grant it?

TADANOBU. If I can, certainly.

JUSABURŌ. Will you promise, no matter what it is?

TADANOBU. How can I do otherwise?

JUSABURŌ. It is this. I ask you to let me join your company of thieves.

TADANOBU. But why?

JUSABURŌ. The only way to serve my mistress is to provide money. The only way to get money in this world is to be a thief. I made a start at the Lotus Temple. Now I'd like to become a professional.

TADANOBU. I understand, but it seems to me——

JUSABURŌ. Why hesitate, Tadanobu? Even without joining your band, I have received stolen money. That makes me a thief. (*Resolutely.*) If it is the only way to help my mistress, being a thief is the way of the samurai.

TADANOBU. If you are determined, I will grant your request.

JUSABURŌ. Then from now on, together with you, I will——

TADANOBU. ——be a follower of Nippon Daemon——

JUSABURŌ. ——and my name hereafter will be Akahoshi Jūzō!

TADANOBU. Then, my young lord——

JŪZŌ. No, don't address me that way. I am your fellow thief now.

TADANOBU. Then, Juzō!

JŪZŌ. Rihei!

TADANOBU. Let's have——

BOTH. ——a long talk.

(*The sound of a gong, then music. A scene of* dammari, *night-fighting, begins, in which the actors, though plainly seen by the audience, pantomime movement in complete darkness.*

The men look about them warily. NANGŌ RIKIMARU *comes on from stage-left and moves to the centre of the stage. The two men jump up,* JŪZŌ *putting the money into the breast of his kimono,* TADANOBU *tucking up his clothes, preparatory to fighting.* NANGŌ, *groping about, finds* JŪZŌ *and reaches into his kimono for the money.* TADANOBU *seizes* NANGŌ *around the waist. A brief struggle ensues, but the men lose contact in the darkness. They strike attitudes. Then, with slow gestures and movement, they search for each other.*

BENTEN *enters from stage-left, carrying a collapsible paper lantern, which he suddenly thrusts between* NANGŌ *and* TADANOBU. *The unexpected confrontation startles them, but then they simultaneously strike the lantern to the ground.*

There is general fighting, during the course of which, with the help of a stage assistant dressed in black, BENTEN'S *costume is instantaneously changed from that of a samurai to that of a plebeian. The money and the incense-case pass from thief to thief, and at last* JŪZŌ *has the incense-case,* BENTEN *the money.* NANGŌ *and* TADANOBU *strike attitudes at centre stage,* JŪZŌ *at stage-left,* BENTEN *at stage-right.* BENTEN *and* JŪZŌ *examine their spoils.*)

JŪZŌ (*disappointed*). What! This is the incense-case!

BENTEN (*equally so*). This is the money!

(*They strike attitudes of dissatisfaction.*)

BOTH. Oh, hell!

CURTAIN

ACT II

SCENE I

The Hamamatsu, a prosperous shop selling silks and brocades. The entrance is imagined to be about right-centre. The floor of the shop is covered with straw matting. The upstage area of the shop is a platform about 18 inches high. In the upstage wall are shelves piled with bolts of material. Up-left are sliding paper doors leading to the living-quarters behind the shop. On stage-right is a small tea-shop presided over by a young apprentice.

The curtain opens to music, revealing the clerks YOKURŌ, SAHE, TASUKE, SEIJI, *and the* APPRENTICE *very active at their work.*

NIPPON DAEMON *enters on the* hanamichi. *Handsomely dressed, wearing two swords, he is a figure of grave dignity. With him is* SAKUHE, *acting as his servant.*

DAEMON (*pausing on the* hanamichi). Sakuhe, is that shop over there the Hamamatsu?

SAKUHE. That's right. It opened only a few years ago, but it seems to be very prosperous.

DAEMON. It certainly looks that way.

SAKUHE. Do you intend to buy some gifts?

DAEMON. I was just thinking they might carry something novel there.

SAKUHE. Then let us go in.

(*They go to the entrance.*)

SAKUHE. Is anyone there?

YOKURŌ. (*Middle-aged, something of a fool. He comes running, bows low repeatedly, and is effusively polite.*) Oh, how do you do! Please come this way.

DAEMON. Allow me then.

(DAEMON *and* SAKUHE *go into the shop and sit on cushions placed for them on the floor,* DAEMON *centre,* SAKUHE *down-left.*)

YOKURŌ. Where is the tea-server?

APPRENTICE (*in the tea-shop*). Coming! (*He lengthens the word so that it doesn't end until he has placed the tea before* DAEMON *and* SAKUHE.)

YOKURŌ (*eagerly*). A beautiful day, isn't it?

DAEMON. Splendid weather. (*He takes pipe and tobacco from his sleeve and smokes.*)

YOKURŌ. Now what shall we show you, sir?

DAEMON (*impressively*). I want gifts for the House of Hōjō. Let me see some figured satin and damask.

YOKURŌ. Very well, sir! Sahe, go to the storeroom and bring out some satin and brocade.

(SAHE *goes, up-left.*)

DAEMON (*having looked around quietly but keenly*). Business is booming, isn't it?

YOKURŌ. Oh, yes, sir! We have a great many customers.

(*From the upstage-left entrance comes* KŌBĒ, *proprietor of the Hamamatsu. He is a quiet, elderly man, soberly dressed.* SAHE *follows him, carrying rolls of materials.*)

KŌBĒ (*on the platform, bowing to* DAEMON). I am glad to welcome you. I am Kōbē, the proprietor of this store.

DAEMON. So, you are the proprietor here?

KŌBĒ. We certainly appreciate your patronage. I sincerely ask for your continued favours.

YOKURŌ. Shall I show you the materials?

SAHE. Unfortunately, some of our best ones were sold this morning.

KŌBĒ. No, no. Those are common fabrics that will not please your taste. However, we have some fine materials which just arrived from Kyoto.

DAEMON. The price is of no consequence. What I want is something of good quality.

KŌBĒ. Certainly, sir. Tasuke, will you unpack the new goods from Kyoto?

TASUKE. Yes, sir.

(*He goes out up-left.*)

KŌBĒ. I am afraid it may take a little time. Please come to the inner room. This is not a proper place to receive you.

DAEMON. Don't bother. I am perfectly comfortable here.

KŌBĒ. But there's so much confusion here! Please come to the inner room.

DAEMON. Indeed, it would interfere with your business if I should remain here. I shall accept your kind offer and wait inside.

KŌBĒ. Please come this way.

(DAEMON *and* SAKUHE *exit with him, up-left.*

Music. On the hanamichi *appears* BENTEN KOZŌ *in the dress of a daughter of good family.* NANGŌ RIKIMARU, *in samurai costume, follows him.*)

BENTEN (*speaking in the manner of the* PRINCESS SENJU *and affecting the mannerisms of a high-born young lady*). Yosohachi, where is the Hamamatsu shop?

NANGŌ. That store right over there.

BENTEN (*coyly*). Don't you dare mention that I came for a trousseau!

NANGŌ. Why not?

BENTEN (*very shyly*). It embarrasses me.

NANGŌ. Well, I won't say anything about it.

(*They go to the entrance.*)

NANGŌ. Please go in.

BENTEN. No, you go in first.

NANGŌ. Then excuse me.

(*He enters,* BENTEN *standing in the imagined doorway. The clerks turn, see* BENTEN, *and are stunned by this vision of feminine beauty. Recovering their wits, they vie in politeness.*)

SAHE. How do you do?

TASUKE. Well, well! Come this way, please!

YOKURŌ (*comes between* SAHE *and* TASUKE). No, no, please come this way.

SAHE. Miss, please come this way.

YOKURŌ. Oh, no, this way, please!

TASUKE. No, no, you must come with me!

NANGŌ (*loudly*). Be quiet! You'll drive me crazy!

YOKURŌ. Yes, yes, keep still you two! Please come this way. We have lots of materials with many, many different designs. Please, this way!

THE TWO CLERKS. Please step in!

NANGŌ. Please step in, miss!

BENTEN (*prettily hesitant*). May I?

NANGŌ. Oh, yes, indeed!

(BENTEN *enters, and he and* NANGŌ *sit stage-right on cushions.*)

YOKURŌ. Where is the tea-server?

APPRENTICE. Coming! (*The word continues just as long this time.*)

YOKURŌ (*sitting near* BENTEN). Well! A beautiful day, isn't it?

(BENTEN *lowers his eyes fetchingly;* YOKURŌ *giggles.*)

YOKURŌ. Now, what shall we show you?

NANGŌ. Let's see some long-sleeve kimono material, some brocade obi material, some scarlet silk crepe dyed in Kyoto.

YOKURŌ. Yes, sir! Tasuke, go and get some long-sleeve kimono material, some brocade obi material, some scarlet silk crepe dyed in Kyoto.

TASUKE. Yes, sir.

(*He goes out up-left.*)

YOKURŌ. We will have them in a moment. (*Looking at* BENTEN, *he again dissolves in blushes and giggles. After a few moments.*) The plays seem to be very popular nowadays. Have you seen any lately?

BENTEN. Yes, I went to the theatre just recently.

YOKURŌ. Is that so? I suppose your favourite is the popular young actor Uzaemon.

BENTEN. No.

YOKURŌ. Then it must be either Gonjūrō or Kumesaburō.

BENTEN. No.

YOKURŌ. Then it must surely be (*and he uses the name of the actor playing* BENTEN).

BENTEN (*shyly*). Yes.

YOKURŌ. Well, if he's your favourite actor, you must watch out. He certainly is the ladies' man.

NANGŌ. That's a lie! I've never known such a serious actor. He doesn't drink, he doesn't run after women, he never gambles, and especially, he hates to memorize his lines.

BENTEN. Oh, don't say such a malicious thing about him!

> (BENTEN *strikes* NANGŌ *playfully with his fan.* YOKURŌ *is even more fascinated.*
>
> > TASUKE *appears with the materials and places them before* BENTEN.)

TASUKE. I'm very sorry we made you wait so long.

BENTEN. Yosohachi, which cloth shall I take?

NANGŌ. Whatever pleases your fancy, miss.

BENTEN. Then I shall take the one with the hemp-leaf pattern.

NANGŌ. For a marriage ceremony it is appropriate to have an auspicious design.

YOKURŌ. Oh, you are going to be married?

BENTEN (*with a delicate show of embarrassment*). Oh, I told you not to say anything about it!

SAHE (*aside*). Say, Yokurō, she makes my mouth water! (*His expression suddenly changes.*)

YOKURŌ. What's the matter?

SAHE. Look at that! Look what she's doing!

> (BENTEN *puts a roll of cloth into the breast of his kimono, so that his action can be clearly seen by the clerks. They are taken aback and whisper together.* BENTEN *and* NANGŌ *unconcernedly continue to look at the materials.* TASUKE *goes quickly to the inner room and returns with the head clerk,* SEIJI.)

SEIJI (*loudly*). Which one is the shoplifter?

SAHE. Sh! (*He whispers to* SEIJI.)

NANGŌ. I think we'll take two of these, the three rolls of obi brocade, and that scarlet crepe. We're going to the Hachiman Shrine now, and we'll stop in on our way back to pay for them.

YOKURŌ. Very good, sir.

NANGŌ. Now, miss, let us go to the temple before the sun sets.

BENTEN. Yes, let us do so.

NANGŌ. We're very much obliged to you!

> (*They turn to leave and find* SEIJI, SAHE, *and* TASUKE *barring their way.*)

THE THREE. Just a moment, please!

NANGŌ. What is it?

YOKURŌ. Please don't joke with us.

NANGŌ. I don't understand.

YOKURŌ. Please leave that scarlet crepe you have just stolen.

THE TWO. What? (*They look at each other in amazement.*)

SEIJI. I didn't think a pretty young lady like you would steal things.

NANGŌ. What? Are you insinuating that my mistress has stolen something?

YOKURŌ. We are in business the whole year round, and we don't make mistakes.

SAHE. If she pretends she didn't steal it, we'll undress her and prove she did.

TASUKE. Give it up before you get into trouble.

SEIJI. We won't let you go. You sit there! (*He pushes* NANGŌ *to the floor.*)

BENTEN (*about to weep*). Yosohachi, what am I to do now?

NANGŌ. Don't worry, miss! These creatures have called you a shoplifter, but I won't leave this place until they apologize.

YOKURŌ. Apologize! How dare you say such a thing?

NANGŌ. And how dare you call my mistress a shoplifter?

YOKURŌ (*goes to* BENTEN, *seizes him, and pulls out the scarlet crepe*). Look here! Where did you get this cloth from?

SEIJI. We'll give you a sound thrashing!

SAHE. That'll be fun!

TASUKE. Let's do it!

ALL. Beat them up! Beat them up!

(*Music. The clerks beat the two with sticks, and* NANGŌ *tries to protect* BENTEN. BENTEN *is struck on the forehead, cries out, falls to the floor, and remains there with his face hidden.*

From stage-right comes SŌNOSUKE, *a young man, son of* KŌBĒ.)

SŌNOSUKE. Here, here! What's going on?

YOKURŌ. Young master, these two are shoplifters.

SŌNOSUKE. Shoplifters! What have we been robbed of?

YOKURŌ. They stole a piece of scarlet crepe.

NANGŌ. You still say we stole that cloth?

YOKURŌ. Of course!

NANGŌ. I bought that cloth at the Yamagata shop. Look at the trade-mark if you don't believe me.

YOKURŌ. Oh! (*He looks at the trade-mark and is greatly surprised.*) Well now, it does have the character for mountain in a circle. That's the trade-mark of the Yamagata shop.

SAHE. Then we thought they were shoplifters——

TASUKE. ——and they're not at all!

THE CLERKS. Good heavens! (*They get down on the floor and bow.*)

NANGŌ (*taking a slip of paper from his breast*). Look at this receipt!

YOKURŌ (*abject*). Yes, sir! (*He takes it and looks at it.*)

NANGŌ. Doesn't that prove we are not shoplifters?

YOKURŌ. Well, yes, that is——

NANGŌ. Do you still call me a thief?

(*The CLERKS are speechless with embarrassment.*)

SŌNOSUKE. I am the son of the proprietor of this shop. I am embarrassed to discover that our men have wronged you. I beg a thousand pardons. (*Bowing*). Please forgive us.

CLERKS (*bowing*). We all beg of you!

NANGŌ. Now you want to apologize! Brazen creatures!

SŌNOSUKE. You are perfectly right, sir. But please be kind and forgive us.

NANGŌ. Be quiet!

SŌNOSUKE. Yes, sir.

NANGŌ. This young lady, I'll have you know, is the daughter of Hayase Mondo, retainer to Nikaidō, the lord of Shinano. She is to be married into the Akita clan very soon. You think you need merely make an apology after calling her a thief?

ALL. We are overwhelmed with shame!

NANGŌ (*sharply*). I must see the proprietor. Go and get him.

KŌBĒ (*from within*). I am coming now.

(*He appears and sits on the platform.*)

NANGŌ. You are the proprietor of this place?

KŌBĒ. Yes, sir. I have overheard everything, and I really do not know how to apologize. But please overlook the wrong done you.

NANGŌ. I cannot overlook this behaviour.

KŌBĒ. Then you will not forgive us?

NANGŌ. No, I will not! Here! Look at this!

(*He pulls up BENTEN, who is crying, and all are horrified to see a wound on BENTEN's forehead.*)

KŌBĒ. Ah! A cut on the young lady's forehead!

ALL. Oh!

NANGŌ. I can't very well return this young lady to her home with a wound on her forehead. It's unfortunate, but the only thing for me to do is cut off all your heads and then kill myself.

(*This statement creates something of a stir.*)

BENTEN. Yosohachi, is there not some way to settle this quietly?

NANGŌ. But if this incident should come to light, what explanation can I make to my master?

SEIJI. (*He has been whispering to* KŌBĒ, *and now approaches* NANGŌ.) Allow me to say something to you.

NANGŌ. What is it?

SEIJI. That young fellow made a mistake, and unfortunately we believed him. There's no sense in your cutting us to pieces. You can say the young lady slipped on the street or something of that sort. And we will give you a generous sum by way of apology.

NANGŌ (*hesitating*). What shall I do, miss?

BENTEN. Don't you think we should accept their apology?

NANGŌ (*after a pause*). Well, then, I shall do so.

SEIJI. We greatly appreciate your kindness. (*He goes to* KŌBĒ.) May I have ten *ryō*?

SŌNOSUKE. Oh! Fortunately I have the money I received today.

(SŌNOSUKE *brings forth a hundred-*ryo *package and from it takes ten* ryō, *which he wraps in paper.*)

SEIJI (*goes to* NANGŌ *and places the money before him*). Please accept this as a little token of appreciation.

NANGŌ (*unwraps the money*). Didn't you say a generous sum? This is only ten *ryō*! (*He throws it to the floor.*)

SEIJI. Isn't ten *ryō* enough?

NANGŌ. This incident may cost my life if my master hears of it!

SEIJI (*a hothead*). Well if you don't like it, don't take it!

NANGŌ. I certainly won't! I won't take less than one hundred *ryō*!

SEIJI. All right, then. We'll die at the point of your sword. Go ahead! Start with me!

NANGŌ (*reaching for his sword*). Don't worry, I will.

SŌNOSUKE. Seiji, calm yourself!

(*The* CLERKS, *greatly frightened, pull* SEIJI *to stage-left.*)

YOKURŌ. Don't start picking a fight!

SAHE. Come here, I have something to tell you.

SEIJI. No, no, let me alone, won't you?

TASUKE. Good gracious, please don't fight!

THE THREE. Now come here and be quiet! (*They all sit right.*)

NANGŌ (*in one of the higher dudgeons*). I've received humiliation after humiliation, and I won't leave until I draw blood. Prepare yourselves, every one of you!

KŌBĒ. Just a moment. I hope this will be satisfactory to you.

(*He takes out one hundred* ryō, *which* YOKURŌ *places before* NANGŌ. NANGŌ *picks up the money and smiles.*)

NANGŌ. Well, the disgrace was intolerable. But I like the way you apologized. I shall accept this one hundred *ryō*.

KŌBĒ. Then you will forgive us?

NANGŌ. Yes, I will.

KŌBĒ. Now all of us——

CLERKS. ——are quite relieved!

NANGŌ. Well, we've spent an unexpectedly long time here.

BENTEN. Since the matter has been peacefully settled——

NANGŌ. ——let us be on our way.

KŌBĒ. Then——

CLERKS. ——good-bye to you.

> (*As* NANGŌ *and* BENTEN *move to the entrance,* DAEMON *enters from the inner room.*)

DAEMON. Will you kindly wait, sir?

> (NANGŌ *and* BENTEN *stop and turn.*)

NANGŌ. Is there something you want of me?

DAEMON. Yes, there is. (*He sits on the platform.*)

NANGŌ. What is it?

DAEMON. Will you please sit down. (*They do.*) I heard all that went on here, and I am very glad you pardoned them. Tolerance is most important in human relations.

NANGŌ. It was very difficult for me to forgive them, but since this young lady is with me I——

DAEMON. That certainly was fortunate for this shop. It seems you are a member of the Nikaidō clan. Is that true?

NANGŌ. Yes indeed. This is the daughter of Hayase Mondo, retainer to Nikaidō, the lord of Shinano.

DAEMON. Are you very sure of it?

NANGŌ. I beg your pardon?

DAEMON. You're a liar!

NANGŌ. What?

DAEMON. I am Tamashima Ittō, a steward of Nikaidō, the lord of Shinano.

BENTEN *and* NANGŌ. Oh!

DAEMON. There is no one named Hayase Mondo in our clan. Furthermore, this 'young lady' is undoubtedly a man.

BENTEN (*in his natural voice*). What the—— (*Then, as the young lady.*) Dear me, why should you say that I am a man?

DAEMON. You look like a woman, but I'm sure you're not. Am I right?

BENTEN. Well——

DAEMON. Do you want me to examine you?

BENTEN. Well——

DAEMON. Or will you tell the truth?

BENTEN. Well——

DAEMON (*sharply*). You are a swindler!

(BENTEN *hesitates a moment, then becomes a man. He stands up, stretches, undoes the obi around his waist.*)

BENTEN. Well, I guess that's that!

NANGŌ. You bastard! Why didn't you wait a little?

(NANGŌ *pulls out his swords, removes his upper kimono, wraps the swords in it, and throws the bundle down.*)

BENTEN. Hell! As long as they know, why should I be uncomfortable? (*In mock seriousness to the others.*) I humbly beg your pardon!

(BENTEN *sits centre, Buddha-fashion, yanking up his kimono, and pulling the tobacco box towards him.*)

YOKURŌ. Why she's not a woman at all!

CLERKS. My, my, my!

BENTEN. That's right! I came here to swindle you. Things have been tough lately, so I decided to pick up some money by playing a woman.

YOKURŌ. What a big cheat you are! You almost fooled us.

CLERKS. A big cheat!

DAEMON. Even now that you're found out, you don't turn a hair. You must be the swindler of all swindlers.

BENTEN. You don't know who we are?

YOKURŌ. No, we don't know——

CLERKS. ——who you are!

BENTEN (*tough and bragging*). Just before he was hanged, that greatest of all thieves, Ishikawa Goemon, said, 'In time, even the sands of the beaches will disappear, but thieves will increase forever and ever.' I worked at nights on the road, I went after all sorts of petty coin, I stole mass money at the shrines and temples. Then I got smarter and went after the big things. I worked confidence games, gambling joints, clip joints, what have you. I am the young man named Benten Kozō. (*He strikes an attitude, baring his left shoulder and revealing the extensive tattooing of the professional thief.*)

NANGŌ (*just as aggressively boastful*). And I am his fellow-thief. Born into a fisherman's family, I specialized in work on the high seas. I stole from the ships. I learned courage by living on a little boat, thin pieces of board with the hell of the sea beneath them. Today I'm here, tomorrow there, moving from east to west and from west to east. Know that I am none other than Nangō Rikimaru. (*And he strikes an attitude.*)

DAEMON. So you are two of the gang known as the Five Thieves?

BENTEN. That's right! First and most important is Nippon Daemon, then comes Nangō Rikimaru, then Tadanobu Rihei, then Akahoshi Jūzō, and I am the last of the gang.

NANGŌ. Since we lost this game, here is the money we swindled from you. Take it.

(*He throws it to* KŌBĒ.)

BENTEN (*belligerently*). Go ahead and hand us over to the police.

NANGŌ. Boy, get me some tea!

APPRENTICE (*in the tea-shop*). Coming! (*Same vocal business.*)

NANGŌ (*after a sip of the tea, he makes a face*). This tea's no good!

(NANGŌ *throws the tea in the* APPRENTICE'*s face. The* APPRENTICE
raises his fist angrily, pauses, bursts into tears, and flees to the tea-
shop.*)

BENTEN. Go ahead! Turn us over to the police before it gets dark.
It's hard to say whether we'll come back to this world again. (*To*
DAEMON.) But you, kind sir, we'll be sure to call on you even after
our heads are chopped off.

DAEMON. How shameless you are! Instead of being quiet, now you
demand arrest. If it wouldn't bring trouble upon this establish-
ment I'd kill you at once, but——

BENTEN. What do I care about the reputation of this joint! Go
ahead! Kill us!

NANGŌ. That's right!

BOTH (*violently*). Go ahead and chop our heads off!

DAEMON. Since it is your wish . . .

(DAEMON *reaches for his sword and is about to stand up.* KŌBĒ *and*
SŌNOSUKE, *concerned about the shop, intervene.*)

KŌBĒ. Just a moment, sir. If you kill them, it doesn't matter about
this shop, but it will be a stain on your name.

SŌNOSUKE. I know you must be very angry, but perhaps it would be
better to let them go.

DAEMON. I've restrained myself, but now I've lost my patience.

KŌBĒ. But you are a man of importance. Please excuse them.

DAEMON (*after a moment of hesitation*). Very well, then.

KŌBĒ. You will pardon them?

CLERKS. Thank you very much.

BENTEN (*still intransigent*). Why don't you go ahead and kill us?

NANGŌ. Or else hand us over to the police?

BENTEN. It's getting late, you know.

BOTH. Get it over with.

KŌBĒ (*exasperated*). See here now! Turning you over to the authorities is my business. But rather than cause a commotion, I'll forget
about everything and you can go away.

BENTEN (*adamantly*). No! I won't go away!

KŌBĒ (*squeaking*). Why not?

BENTEN. You found out I wasn't a woman; you got back the one hundred *ryō*, you haven't lost a thing. But what about me? You called me a shoplifter and you beat me. Don't you owe me something for that?

KŌBĒ (*somewhat breathless*). Very well. I'll be glad to give you a little money. But please go away.

BENTEN. If we can come to some agreement we'll be glad to leave.

KŌBĒ. Then please accept this money.

(KŌBĒ *wraps some money in paper, gives it to* YOKURŌ, *who places it before* BENTEN.)

BENTEN (*having unwrapped the money*). What! Only ten *ryō*? If it's known that Benten and Nangō failed to swindle your shop and then came back with only five *ryō* each, what a disgrace! Take it back! (*He throws down the money.*)

KŌBĒ (*threateningly*). If that is not enough, I'll be glad to make other arrangements.

NANGŌ. Say, Benten, we might be able to squeeze twenty or thirty *ryō* out of him if we talk long enough. But that would keep us here all night. Let's take the money and get the hell out of here.

BENTEN. You crazy bastard! Leave here with only ten *ryō*?

NANGŌ. It's better than nothing. Take it! (*Ominously.*) Since the proprietor said if it wasn't enough he'd make other arrangements, we can stop in again some time.

BENTEN. All right, let's go! (*Picks up the money.*) But damn it, even in these hard times it's not enough.

KŌBĒ. Then you will accept our apology——

SŌNOSUKE. ——and go away peacefully?

BENTEN. That's right. But since we've made your acquaintance——

NANGŌ (*threateningly*). ——we'll drop in on you from time to time.

YOKURŌ. Absolutely no!

ALL. You don't need to come any more.

(*Meanwhile a stage assistant has made a bundle of the discarded clothing of* NANGŌ *and* BENTEN, *by wrapping them around* NANGŌ's *swords.*)

NANGŌ (*to* DAEMON, *ironically*). Pardon us for our rude remarks, sir.

BENTEN. Some day we'll repay you!

DAEMON. Any time you wish to.

BOTH. Be sure we will.

(BENTEN, *about to leave, suddenly realizes that he's wearing a woman's wig. He covers his head with a cotton towel, which he ties under his chin, and picks up the bundle of clothes. They go to the entrance.*)

YOKURŌ (*running over to them*). Come again the day before yesterday!

BENTEN. Shut up!

(*He strikes* YOKURŌ *on the cheek.*)

YOKURŌ. Ouch! (*Falls.*)

(BENTEN *and* NANGŌ *move out on the* hanamichi.)

BENTEN. This thing's a damn nuisance to carry. You take it.

NANGŌ. Now wait a minute. I tell you, we'll take turns. Every time a blind man passes us, it's the other one's turn.

BENTEN. All right.

(*Street musicians' music.* BENTEN *puts the bundle over his shoulder. As they begin to move, a* BLIND MASSEUR *appears at the end of the* hanamichi.)

BENTEN. There's a blind man. Now you carry it.

(*He throws the bundle at* NANGŌ.)

NANGŌ. That was quick, wasn't it?

(*The* BLIND MASSEUR, *who apparently has changed his mind, now turns and moves in the opposite direction.*)

NANGŌ. There! He's come back. It's your turn again.

(*He throws the bundle at* BENTEN.)

BENTEN. Damn it! Why doesn't he make up his mind?

(*The* BLIND MASSEUR *again changes direction and passes them, but by moving around* BENTEN, NANGŌ *prevents* BENTEN *from seeing him.*)

BLIND MASSEUR. Massage! Massage!

(BENTEN *turns and sees him.*)

BENTEN. The blind man again! You take it!

(*He throws the bundle at* NANGŌ, *almost knocking him down, and they exit on the* hanamichi, BENTEN *swaggering,* NANGŌ *sulkily.*)

DAEMON. What detestable wretches! Using such daring methods to wring money out of people!

KŌBĒ. If you had not been here they would have swindled us of one hundred *ryō*.

SŌNOSUKE. We are greatly indebted to you.

YOKURŌ. Humble as we are——

SAHE. ——we have no words to thank you.

TASUKE. Really——

ALL. We all thank you.

DAEMON (*modestly*). You embarrass me with such cordial thanks.

KŌBĒ. This is all your fault, Yokurō. It was carelessness on your part that started this trouble, and this is not the first time I've been dissatisfied with you. Therefore, as of today, you are dismissed as manager of this shop.

YOKURŌ. But—but—I haven't done anything terribly wrong.

KŌBĒ. If you can't remember your shortcomings I shall remind you when this gentleman leaves. Just wait here.

YOKURŌ. Yes, sir.

KŌBĒ (*to* DAEMON). Now, sir, would you please go to the inner room and——

DAEMON. No, thank you.

KŌBĒ. But won't you at least take some refreshment before you go?

DAEMON. No, please don't bother.

KŌBĒ. But we have some other materials to show you as well.

SAHE. We beg of you, please——

TASUKE. ——make yourself comfortable in the other room.

DAEMON. It would be very rude to refuse your kindness.

KŌBĒ. Though we can but poorly serve you——

SŌNOSUKE. ——at least have a little *sake.*

DAEMON. Then, I shall——

KŌBĒ. Please!

DAEMON. ——accept your kind invitation.

>(*Music.* DAEMON, KŌBĒ, SŌNOSUKE, *and the* CLERKS *enter the inner room.* YOKURŌ *remains, disconsolate.*)

YOKURŌ. I'm a fool! Just because the thieves came——

>(*He gets a sudden idea, looks about him, then goes furtively to the shelves, picks up the money-box, and removes the money. The* APPRENTICE, *coming from the tea-shop, catches him in the act and attacks* YOKURŌ *with a broom.*

>*Music. The* APPRENTICE *and* YOKURŌ *do a comic dance, a parody of the danced conflict at the end of the first scene of the play. The dance ends with* YOKURŌ *striking a victorious attitude, brandishing the broom, his foot on the prostrate* APPRENTICE.)

>CURTAIN

ACT II

SCENE II

The inner room of the Hamamatsu shop, the upstage wall painted on a backdrop. Trunks, and various bundles of materials.

SŌNOSUKE *is pouring sake for* DAEMON.

KŌBĒ. We have no women in the house, so I hope you will forgive my son's rude way of serving you.

DAEMON. I greatly appreciate your hospitality.

SŌNOSUKE. Please have some more.

DAEMON. Oh, no, I'm not a great drinker.

KŌBĒ. Have another one!

DAEMON. Thank you very much for your kind hospitality.

KŌBĒ (*putting a stand before* DAEMON, *on which is a package*). This is a mere trifle, but please accept it.

N

DAEMON. What is this?

KŌBĒ. A small token of our appreciation.

DAEMON. I did not help you with the intention of receiving a gift. I interfered because the name of my clan was being used by those swindlers. I can't take anything from you.

KŌBĒ. I understand. But nevertheless you saved us from losing one hundred *ryō.*

SŌNOSUKE. We thought of presenting you with whatever you like from the shop.

KŌBĒ. I'll be greatly embarrassed if you don't accept something.

DAEMON (*apologetically*). I do not wish to make you uncomfortable. In that case, I may as well ask for something I really want.

SŌNOSUKE. Please do. Anything.

DAEMON. Anything at all?

KŌBĒ. Why certainly!

SŌNOSUKE. What would you like?

DAEMON. (*Pause.*) I think I should like some money.

KŌBĒ. Of course! Sōnosuke——

SŌNOSUKE. Certainly. (*He is about to go.*)

DAEMON. Bring me all the money you have.

KŌBĒ. Hah?

DAEMON (*standing up, drawing his sword*). Give me your money or else—— (*He thrusts his sword into the stand before him and strikes an attitude.*)

> (*Music. From stage-right appear* NANGŌ, BENTEN, TADANOBU, *and* JŪZŌ, *pushing before them* SAHE, TASUKE, SEIJI, *and the* APPRENTICE, *who are tied up.*)

NANGŌ. Chief, we have done——

THE THIEVES. ——a clean job.

DAEMON. Are all the doors locked?

BENTEN. Yes. Everybody in the store is tied up too.

KŌBĒ. Then even this man——

SŌNOSUKE. ——was part of the swindlers' gang!

DAEMON. Jūzō and Rihei, keep these men tied in the kitchen and don't let them loose!

BOTH. Yes, sir!

DAEMON. But don't be too rough with them.

BOTH. Come on!

> (TADANOBU *and* JŪZŌ *herd the prisoners out.* BENTEN *and* NANGŌ *remain.*)

KŌBĒ. Then you must be that famous thief——

DAEMON. Indeed I am. Nippon Daemon. (*Strikes an attitude.*)

KŌBĒ *and* SŌNOSUKE. Oh!

DAEMON. I am the leader of the five thieves whose names are known even to children. But we are different from ordinary thieves. We don't rob the poor, but only those with thousands of *ryō*. Then we give the money to the needy. Now bring out all the money you have.

KŌBĒ. There's no help for it. I will give you everything. (*He places a one-thousand-*ryō *money-box before* DAEMON.)

DAEMON. What! Only a thousand *ryō*?

NANGŌ. You've got more than that!

BENTEN. Bring it out!

KŌBĒ. I'm not hiding anything. All our money was sent to Kyoto yesterday. This is all I have.

DAEMON. In that case, I'll kill you! (*He thrusts his sword before* KŌBĒ.)

SŌNOSUKE (*kneeling before* DAEMON). If you must kill, kill me instead of my father. Please save my father. (DAEMON *is unresponsive, and* SŌNOSUKE *goes to* NANGŌ.) Please ask your chief to grant me this favour. I beg of you! (NANGŌ *smokes his pipe, indifferent.* SŌNOSUKE *turns to* BENTEN.) Then you please ask him for me. I pray you!

BENTEN (*kicking* SŌNOSUKE). Ah, shut up!

SŌNOSUKE (*having crawled back to* DAEMON). Do not be so cruel! I cannot let my father be killed! Kill me now!

DAEMON. A courageous fellow, eh? All right! I'll kill you first. (*He takes his sword.*)

KŌBĒ. Just a moment, please. I cannot let him die in my place. You are a thief, but I have heard that you are also a man of justice. Please listen to my story. (*And they do.*) My wife and I were not blessed with a child. Every month we went to the Lotus Temple and prayed to the Goddess of Mercy. At last our prayers were granted. We were so happy that every month we visited the temple with the child to thank the Goddess. Years later, on the seventeenth of September, there was a scuffle within the temple hall, and in the confusion the child was separated from us. We saw a little child crying, and thinking he was ours, we picked him up and ran from the place. Outside, we discovered he was not our child. We tried desperately to find his parents, and to find our own child, but in vain. So we raised this boy as our own, but we never forgot that some day his parents might come for him. Now if he dies, and later his parents find their way to me, they can say that he died to save me money. We lose money today and regain it tomorrow, but life, once lost, is gone forever. I shall give you all the money I have, but please, Nippon Daemon, pity me and spare his life.

DAEMON (*something has happened to him*). Then, I shall spare his life.
NANGŌ. But in return——
BENTEN. ——give us all the money you have.
KŌBĒ. But I have only a thousand *ryō* here now. Search the house!
Then if you are not satisfied, kill me, but save the boy's life.
DAEMON (*slowly*). No, I don't want the money.
KŌBĒ. What are you saying?
DAEMON (*intensely*). Tell me! Wasn't there a crest of three tortoise
shells on the patched coat of the child you found?
KŌBĒ. Yes! A crest of three tortoise shells on the patched sleeve.
Son, show him your sleeve.
SŌNOSUKE (*doing so*). This is the family crest of my real father. I
have worn it all these years.
   (DAEMON, *quite melodramatically, holds up his sleeve, and exhibits the
   crest on it.*)
DAEMON (*choking with emotion*). Kōbē, look at this!
KŌBĒ. The family crest of Nippon Daemon!
SŌNOSUKE. The three tortoise shells!
KŌBĒ. Can it be that you are——
DAEMON (*in tears*). I . . . am his father. (*He falls to his knees.*) Not
only did I try to rob the house which reared my son, but I was
even about to kill you. I humbly beg your pardon. (*He bows to the
floor.*) I was poor then, and my wife had died. I purposely left
the child in the temple, hoping some kind person would take pity
on him. Afterwards things went worse with me, and finally I
became a thief. But for the past seventeen years, waking or sleeping, I have never forgotten my child.
SŌNOSUKE. My real father!
   (*He is about to go to* DAEMON, *but he remembers* KŌBĒ *and decides to
   bow where he is.*)
KŌBĒ. Then when you abandoned this boy, you didn't take my
child?
DAEMON. No, but to repay you for bringing up my son, I shall do my
best to find him for you. How can I identify him?
KŌBĒ. There is no way. Except that he had a red money-pouch
then, and in it was a little charm that said, 'Kōkichi, son of Kōbē,
born on April twentieth, the first year of Kambun, the year of the
hare, at the hour of the boar.'
   (BENTEN *is stricken. He reaches into his kimono and takes out a red
   money-pouch.*)
BENTEN. Could this be . . . the money-pouch?
KŌBĒ. Yes, yes, this is it!
SŌNOSUKE. Then you are——

BENTEN (*blubbering*). ——that Kōkichi! (*He falls to his knees.*)

ALL. You are?

BENTEN. And you are my father! I am ashamed!

KŌBĒ (*indignant*). Where have you been all these years?

(BENTEN, *crying, is unable to reply.*)

NANGŌ (*he's sniffling too*). Since we've been inseparable, I will tell you the story. My father, Rokuemon the fisherman, was the one who picked up Kōkichi that night at the temple. Kōkichi was brought up as though he was really my younger brother. When he was twelve years old he became a page at the Iwamoto Temple——

BENTEN. ——then everything went wrong with me. But I do not blame others. A man must take the consequences of his own deeds. I was predestined to be a thief, and so I pray that you resign yourself to it and forgive me.

KŌBĒ. Whether you are a thief or a merchant, that is the lot you are born to.

DAEMON. Oh, these past seventeen years! In this house that has been so kind——

BENTEN. ——not knowing of our relationships——

NANGŌ. ——we attempted an armed robbery——

SŌNOSUKE. ——and we almost lost our lives.

KŌBĒ. But by telling our life stories——

DAEMON. ——father and son, separated so long——

BENTEN. ——at last discover each other.

KŌBĒ. Is this not the favour of the Goddess of Mercy?

DAEMON. What a miraculous meeting——

ALL. ——this has been.

(*Tableau.*)

KŌBĒ. My son, I shall give you this one thousand *ryō*. And I beg you to give up this life and become an honest man.

DAEMON. None of us can turn back now. Even if we try to be honest men, the law will reach out for us. We must go on until our heads are hung by the roadside.

BENTEN. When that day comes, my father, will you not have a mass said for me?

(BENTEN *and* KŌBĒ *weep.*)

DAEMON (*to* SŌNOSUKE). My son, don't call me your father. Kōbē has taken care of you for the past seventeen years—he is your true father. Please perform your filial duty to him in place of Kōkichi.

SŌNOSUKE. I will be a filial son to him, but I will not forget you, even after death.

KŌBĒ (*to* BENTEN). Did you hear that, my son? You, too, should think of Daemon as your father, and behave towards him as a son.

BENTEN. I shall be a faithful son to him, even to my death.

NANGŌ (*sniffling*). I was undutiful to my parents when they were alive, and now it makes me ashamed. (*He scratches his head.*)

DAEMON. People always speak of thieves as cruel beasts——

KŌBĒ. But when I look at you now, I find that you are more honest and just than most men. You must come from a good family.

DAEMON. Indeed, my family were samurai of the province of Enshū. And you?

KŌBĒ. I belonged to the Koyama clan, but I gave up being a samurai to make my living as a merchant. Now I should like to regain my samurai status. I could again become a samurai if I could find a certain incense-case that was stolen recently. But although I have done my best to find it, I have been unsuccessful. I suppose I must die a merchant.

BENTEN. The Koyama clan! The incense-case! Not knowing anything about it——

KŌBĒ. What?

BENTEN (*dissolving in tears*). ——what have I done?
  (TADANOBU *and* JŪZŌ *rush in.*)

TADANOBU. We have to run, chief! Let's go!

DAEMON. What do you mean?

JŪZŌ. The police are on their way.

SŌNOSUKE (*recognizing* JŪZŌ). You were one of our customers. Then you are a thief too?

DAEMON (*by way of introduction*). One of my followers.

SŌNOSUKE (*to* JŪZŌ). The five silk garments you ordered are ready now. (*He takes them from one of the trunks.*)

DAEMON. Wonderful! We were looking forward to amusing ourselves with those!

NANGŌ. They were finished just in time!

JŪZŌ. Let us all together——

TADANOBU. ——in a glorious, spectacular way——

BENTEN. ——cut our swarming pursuers to pieces——

DAEMON. ——and make good our escape.
  (*The loud beating of a drum.* TASUKE, *still tied up, runs in.*)

TASUKE. Burglars!
  (NANGŌ *trips* TASUKE *and he falls.*)

KŌBĒ. Then Daemon——

DAEMON. Kōbē——

sōnosuke. May you enjoy good health!

benten. Please take care of yourself!

(*The fathers and sons, talking simultaneously, are kneeling, bowing to each other, smiling politely, as though this were a pleasant social affair. The others, though greatly concerned about leaving before the police arrive, cannot, out of politeness, interrupt the ceremony.*)

CURTAIN

ACT III

SCENE I

On the backdrop is painted a river lined with flowering cherry-trees. Downstage of it is a platform about 3 feet high, extending the width of the stage, which serves as a river-bank.

The scene is played in a formal, non-realistic, completely stylized manner.

Gongs and drums. The ten PURSUERS *run on to the platform from stage-left. They are identically costumed in black and carry short metal rods used in parrying sword thrusts.*

FIRST. We've looked for them from the Lotus Temple to the Inase River——

SECOND. ——but since they were not to be found——

THIRD. ——they may have gone through the Asahina Tunnel——

FOURTH. ——and escaped along the road to Mutsura.

FIFTH. Then let us go at once to Setobashi.

SIXTH. If they haven't got beyond that point——

SEVENTH. ——and if we stand guard there long enough——

EIGHTH. ——since there is no other way for them to go——

NINTH. ——we'll be sure to catch them. So before they slip away——

TENTH. ——under cover of darkness——

ALL. ——let's be on our way.

(*Gongs, drums, wooden clappers. The* PURSUERS *run off stage-right. To music and the striking of a temple bell, the* THIEVES *appear, one after another, on the* hanamichi, *each striking an attitude as he makes his entrance. They wear silk kimono of floral design, those mentioned at the end of Act II, and they carry paper umbrellas. They line up, equidistantly spaced, on the* hanamichi.)

BENTEN. By coming over the mountains from Yukinoshita, we have escaped our pursuers——

TADANOBU. ——but our end seems near on this spring night. Now as the bell strikes the seventh hour, let us go on to the Mutsura River.

JŪZŌ. Before the dawn comes, let us take the boat and clear the harbour——

NANGŌ. ——leave the land and take our refuge on the sea!

DAEMON. Out at sea we need not fear the eyes of men.

BENTEN. But on the way to the Mutsura River, there lies the dangerous open sea of Enshū——

TADANOBU. ——with its cunning, stormy winds. If the gale of our pursuers follows us there——

JŪZŌ. ——fate will hang on our swords alone. Until their blades are broken——

NANGŌ ——let us bravely strike down our pursuers. But not till the last bitter moment of defeat——

DAEMON. ——then and only then——

ALL. ——will we surrender to the law.

(*Music. They move to the stage. Drums and gongs. The ten* PURSUERS *appear on the platform from stage-right.*)

FIRST PURSUER. Now, Nippon Daemon, now, you five thieves——

PURSUERS. ——don't move!

DAEMON. Thus we are captured. We shall tell you who we are, and then surrender——

THIEVES. ——to receive our punishment.

FIRST PURSUER. Admirable words! And who is it——

PURSUERS. ——that steps out first?

DAEMON. I was born at Hamamatsu of Enshū. At fourteen I left my parents and made my livelihood on the high seas. I steal, but I do no cruelty to anyone. A chivalrous robber, I go from place to place, risking my life for the needy. I am that chief of thieves, notorious in every province of the country, Nippon Daemon. (*Strikes attitude.*)

BENTEN. I began my career as a page at the Iwamoto Temple on Enoshima. My favourite trick is disguising myself as a woman. Most of the time the trick has worked, but many a time it has not. I have been imprisoned in underground cells only to escape and continue robbing and more robbing. I am Benten Kozō. (*Strikes attitude.*)

TADANOBU. The next in line is a man born and bred in Edo. Light-fingered even as a child, I finally recognized my profession during a pilgrimage to the Great Shrine at Ise. I wandered over the western provinces robbing the temples and robbing the wealthy. Wherever there was big money, there was I also. My name— Tadanobu Rihei. (*Strikes attitude.*)

JŪZŌ. Next to him is one who was once a page to a samurai. But when I learned the way of the thief, I found it the only way to live. I have stolen and I have killed. But now the hour is coming when I will fade away like the stars at the coming of day. My name— Akahoshi Jūzō. (*Strikes attitude.*)

NANGŌ. Here am I, the last of the five, one who was brought up by the seashore, who broke into ships at night, who threatened with his lightning sword, who murdered many. I have no faith in prayer, but I am prepared to die. I, Nangō Rikimaru. (*Strikes attitude.*)

DAEMON. The five have flown in the pattern of the wild geese——

BENTEN. ——but now they look like a line-up of ordinary thieves.

TADANOBU. Their names resound like thunderbolts——

JŪZŌ. ——the notorious leaders of a thousand thieves.

NANGŌ. They are dauntless, afraid of nothing.

DAEMON. For the sake of your honour, go ahead——

THIEVES. ——and arrest us, if you can!

PURSUERS. Impudent thieves!

(*Drums and wooden clappers. The* PURSUERS *jump down from the platform and attack, in stylized movement, the thieves, who parry blows with their closed umbrellas.*

The dance ends with the thieves victorious, each in tableau with two conquered PURSUERS. DAEMON *is stage-centre on the platform, and others downstage.*)

DAEMON. Though we thought to give ourselves up, let us escape while we can.

TADANOBU. On then, together, to Kyoto!

DAEMON. But we must not travel together! Tadanobu and Jūzō take the Nakasendō route. Nangō and Benten take the Tōkaidō. And waste no time!

THE FOUR. And what will you do?

DAEMON. I will hide myself in Kamakura and join you later.

NANGŌ. From now on we take separate roads——

JŪZŌ. ——you to the right, we to the left——

BENTEN. ——stopping here and there on the way to steal.

TADANOBU. But in the month of May, in Kyoto——

DAEMON. ——we shall all meet again——

ALL. ——the five of us!

CURTAIN

ACT III

SCENE II

The only stage decoration is a backdrop—a plain, light-blue curtain of thin material, hung without folds.

On the hanamichi *enters* ICHIROBĒ, *carrying a bundle wrapped in cloth on his back, the ends of the cloth tied around his neck. He is followed by* YOKURŌ, *who is anxious and exhausted.*

YOKURŌ. Ichirobē, don't be so stubborn! Please wait for me!

ICHIROBĒ. Stop it! Don't follow me like a beggar!

YOKURŌ. No, no, you must listen to me.

(*They reach the stage, and* ICHIROBĒ *stops.*)

ICHIROBĒ. Yokurō! This is already the second month. How can I explain to the owner of the incense-case? I can't ask him to wait another day, not even half a day!

YOKURŌ. Yes, yes. But I must have that incense-case, and then my master will forgive me. Wait another week and I will get you the money.

ICHIROBĒ. How many times have you told me the same story? I can't wait any more.

YOKURŌ. Please wait, please!

ICHIROBĒ. When I say I can't, I can't!

(*He starts to move away, but* YOKURŌ *seizes the bundle and pulls him back.*)

ICHIROBĒ. What are you doing to me?

YOKURŌ. I'm doing this to you.

(*He pulls the cloth tight about* ICHIROBĒ'S *throat and strangles him.* ICHIROBĒ *falls to the floor.* YOKURŌ *takes the incense-case from the bundle.*)

YOKURŌ. For this rare treasure, the incense-case, the reward will be great. Oh, many thanks!

(*He raises the incense case to his forehead in the gesture of gratification.* NANGŌ *enters from stage-left, sneaks behind* YOKURŌ, *and snatches the incense-case. The men duel with their swords, and presently* YOKURŌ *falls.*)

YOKURŌ. Ah, I have seen you somewhere!

NANGŌ. I am Nangō Rikimaru, who went to swindle you at the shop.

YOKURŌ. Ah! But even if you take it away from me, you won't be able to sell it. The authorities are looking everywhere for it.

NANGŌ. I don't intend to sell it. My fellow thief, Benten Kozō, must give it to his father.

YOKURŌ. It is mine! I will get a reward for it!

NANGŌ. But it's in my hands!

YOKURŌ. Then I will fight for it!

NANGŌ. You fool!

(*They renew the fight, and in the violent struggle* NANGŌ *drops the incense-case.* YOKURŌ *picks it up and runs on to the* hanamichi. NANGŌ *chases after him and forces* YOKURŌ *back to the stage. Now* YOKURŌ *drops the incense-case, and as they attempt to pick it up, both fall. At this point,* AKUJIRŌ *runs in from stage-left, picks it up, and runs off on the* hanamichi.)

NANGŌ. Oh! The incense-case!

YOKURŌ. It's all your fault!

(YOKURŌ *pounces on* NANGŌ, *and the fight begins again.* BENTEN *enters, running, on the* hanamichi, *sword drawn. He does not go to the stage.*)

BENTEN. Nangō!

NANGŌ (*continuing to fight with* YOKURŌ). Benten! You've come just in time. Yokurō had the incense case, we were fighting for it, then suddenly Akujirō picked it up and——

BENTEN. Ran away with it?

NANGŌ. Yes! Go after him and get it!

BENTEN. Which way did he go?

NANGŌ. Straight down the road.

BENTEN. Let's go after him.

NANGŌ. Let's go!

(BENTEN *strikes an attitude, then runs from the* hanamichi. NANGŌ *runs to the* hanamichi, YOKURŌ *follows and seizes him.*)

YOKURŌ. I won't let you get it! I won't!

(NANGŌ *frees himself and wounds* YOKURŌ.)

YOKURŌ (*staggering to the stage*). Murder! Murder!

(NANGŌ *follows him to the stage, the fight continues, and at last* YOKURŌ *is killed.* NANGŌ *wipes his sword and puts it in the scabbard.*)

NANGŌ. That's the end of him. Now I must follow Benten.

(*As he moves towards the* hanamichi, *two of the* PURSUERS *enter from stage-left.*)

PURSUERS. Now we've got you!

(*They go after him, fight violently, and exit at the rear of the theatre, still fighting.*)

     Drums and wooden clappers. The blue curtain falls to the stage floor, revealing

SCENE III

Atop the Gokuraku Temple in Kyoto. The roof rises sharply at the rear. The front edge of the roof is some 3 feet above the stage floor. The area below the roof is masked by a blue-and-white 'cloud curtain', on which stylized clouds are painted.

AKUJIRŌ *runs out on to the roof,* BENTEN *follows and seizes him.*

BENTEN. Give me that incense-case!

AKUJIRŌ. Let me go, you fool!

BENTEN. You can't go anywhere but to your death. You can't climb any higher, and down there lies the hell of the Nameri River. Give me the treasure!

AKUJIRŌ. It's mine, I tell you!

BENTEN. Idiot!

(*They draw their swords and fight, and* AKUJIRŌ *is soon defeated.* BENTEN *takes the incense-case from* AKUJIRŌ'S *kimono.*)

BENTEN. This is it! This is the incense-case!

AKUJIRŌ. Give it back to me!

(*He tries to take it, but* BENTEN *prevents him.*)

BENTEN. Many thanks!

(*He holds it to his forehead.* AKUJIRŌ *takes a small object from the breast of his kimono and throws it down behind the 'cloud curtain', shouting as he does so. There is a distant explosion, then the sound of a drum from the rear of the* hanamichi. BENTEN *strikes a tense attitude.*)

BENTEN. What did you do?

AKUJIRŌ. That was the signal for your arrest!

BENTEN. What!

AKUJIRŌ. You fell for it! The incense-case was just the bait to get you up here. Now you can't escape!

BENTEN. I'm going to kill you!

(*And, after a little sword fighting, he does, and* AKUJIRŌ *falls from the roof, behind the 'cloud curtain'.* BENTEN *strikes an attitude, holding his sword in his mouth, then puts the incense-case into the breast of his kimono.*

Drumming, and the PURSUERS *appear on the roof.*

A ballet-like scene of fighting begins. At the start and the end of it BENTEN *fights all the* PURSUERS, *but of the six other 'scenes' all but one are pas de deux and pas de trois, with variations in the weapons used—swords, ladders, bamboo spears. At the end the tempo increases, and during this sequence* BENTEN *drops the incense-case. One of the* PURSUERS *gets it, and when* BENTEN *is about to wrest it from him, he throws it from the roof.*)

BENTEN. My precious treasure!

ALL. What!

(BENTEN *fights violently and, one by one, drives the* PURSUERS *over the edge of the roof. Then he strikes an attitude.*)

BENTEN. This is the end of Benten the thief. I strangled Kotarō, I drove Princess Senju to her death. And all the while, I did not know that Kotarō's father was my father's lord. In truth, I am the murderer of my own master. The treasure of his House has fallen into the torrent, it has disappeared in the whirling waters. My body, too, will plunge into the waves of hell. My pursuers, look upon the death of Benten Kozō!

(*He holds his sword before him, drives it into his belly, and falls to the roof.*

The entire roof then lifts upstage, moving like the cover of a book, until the underside of the roof, painted with a landscape of cherry-trees, is perpendicular to the stage floor. The 'cloud curtain' is dropped to the stage floor and pulled offstage by stage-hands.

Simultaneously, through a trapdoor, rises the top storey of a Buddhist temple, on the porch of which sits NIPPON DAEMON.)

DAEMON. In the spring we dream a dream that knows no dawn. Even the mountains slumber in the hazy, misty moonlight, dreaming that the cherry blossoms are clouds of snow. But I am awakened from my dream by the beating of a drum. As I look down, I see hundreds of lights, like flickering stars. But these are not stars—they are the lanterns of my pursuers.

(*From behind the temple, right and left, appear two subordinates,* SANJI *and* GOSUKE.)

THE TWO (*bowing before him*). Our chief!

DAEMON. So you have remained here!

SANJI. They have pulled down the ladders and surrounded us. Unless we have wings——

GOSUKE. ——we can never escape. Let us fight gloriously to the end.

SANJI. Benten Kozō has already journeyed to the Land of the Dead. On the ridge of the roof——

GOSUKE. ——he has killed himself.

DAEMON. (*Pause.*) Benten is dead! The beauty of the cherry blossoms lasts but a few days, and the petals are scattered. Seventeen short years! Scarcely grown to manhood, Benten has fallen in the flower of his youth. It is a great pity! (*He is moved to tears.*)

(*The subordinates exchange a glance.*)

SANJI. Daemon!

BOTH. Are you ready?

(*They seize him by the arms.*)

DAEMON. You have betrayed me!

SANJI. Life is dear to us, and we have told the authorities where you are.

GOSUKE. Nippon Daemon, since there is no escape——

BOTH. ——let us have the honour of capturing you.

DAEMON (*laughs*). Snivelling traitors! A man must be a hero to understand a hero! But you shall serve as a blood offering. I will send you two to Hell before me!

BOTH. We'll see about that!

(*They fight briefly, and* DAEMON, *without rising, kills them.
       The temple bell sounds, and cherry blossoms fall.* DAEMON *looks below.*)

DAEMON. There in the moonlight is the Nameri River, and hundreds of men search along its banks by torch light. What a beautiful sight this is! (*He strikes an attitude, thrusting out his sword, and putting a foot on the railing.*)

(*Music. The temple ascends until the bottom storey is revealed. Simultaneously, a downstage trapdoor opens, and through it rises a garden bridge, on the bridge three handsomely costumed men:* AOTO FUJITSUNA, *a high official noted for his righteousness, holding a fan;* SŌNOSUKE, *with the incense-case; and* SAKON.)

FUJITSUNA. Under the glorious, virtuous authority of our ruler, the whole country would be at peace but for the unrest caused by Nippon Daemon. On our way to apprehend him, one of our men dropped a ten-sen coin.

SŌNOSUKE. To recover a ten-sen coin and not waste even the smallest part of the national wealth——

SAKON. ——we are searching for it, burning fifty-sen torch lights and hiring hundreds of men.

DAEMON. Ah, then this is Fujitsuna, a man of great wisdom!

FUJITSUNA. Looking for the ten-sen coin, we accidentally found this incense-case—the treasure of the House of Shinoda.

DAEMON. The incense-case Benten sought!

FUJITSUNA. Are you, then, that Nippon Daemon?

SŌNOSUKE. Already three of the five thieves have been captured— Nangō Rikimaru, Akahoshi Jūzō, and Tadanobu Rihei.

SAKON. And Benten Kozō has killed himself on the temple roof. The only one left is Nippon Daemon.

DAEMON. I hid myself here at the Gokurakuji Temple to escape the watchful eyes of the demons that pursue me. But now that the wise and just Fujitsuna comes for me, I will no longer resist. I give myself up.

SŌNOSUKE. These are admirable words, Daemon!

SAKON *and* SŌNOSUKE. We will come and bind you!

FUJITSUNA. Do not be hasty! Even the huntsman does not kill the bird flown into his bosom for refuge. In the fourth month we will celebrate a high mass for our late lord. Until after the day of that memorial service, let Daemon go free.

DAEMON. Why will you let me go?

FUJITSUNA. Because you are a chivalrous thief!

DAEMON. Though you are a kind, a forgiving man, Fujitsuna, I must bow to the will of Heaven. Come and seize me!

FUJITSUNA. Then it is Daemon's wish to be taken?

DAEMON. I wait impatiently for punishment and death!

FUJITSUNA. Here is a man extreme in evil and extreme in good.

SŌNOSUKE. The great and worthy——

ALL. Nippon Daemon!

DAEMON. Come! Come! Seize and bind me!

    (*Tableau, with gongs and drums.*)

CURTAIN